A Better Pencil

■ ■ ■

A Better Pencil

■ ■ ■

Readers, Writers, and the Digital Revolution

DENNIS BARON

OXFORD
UNIVERSITY PRESS
2009

OXFORD
UNIVERSITY PRESS

Oxford University Press, Inc., publishes works that further
Oxford University's objective of excellence
in research, scholarship, and education.

Oxford   New York
Auckland   Cape Town   Dar es Salaam   Hong Kong   Karachi
Kuala Lumpur   Madrid   Melbourne   Mexico City   Nairobi
New Delhi   Shanghai   Taipei   Toronto

With offices in
Argentina   Austria   Brazil   Chile   Czech Republic   France   Greece
Guatemala   Hungary   Italy   Japan   Poland   Portugal   Singapore
South Korea   Switzerland   Thailand   Turkey   Ukraine   Vietnam

Copyright © 2009 by Oxford University Press, Inc.

Published by Oxford University Press, Inc.
198 Madison Avenue, New York, NY 10016

www.oup.com

Oxford is a registered trademark of Oxford University Press

Library of Congress Cataloging-in-Publication Data
Baron, Dennis E.
A better pencil : readers, writers, and the digital revolution / Dennis Baron.
p.   cm.
ISBN 978-0-19-538844-2
1. Writing—Materials and instruments—History.
2. Written communication—Technological innovations.   I. Title.
Z45.B37 2009
302.2'244—dc22
2008055214

3   5   7   9   8   6   4   2

Printed in the United States of America
on acid-free paper

for Iryce, Rachel, and Jonathon,
to whom all my work is dedicated

■ ■ ■ Contents

■ ■ ■ Preface: Technologies of the Word

In the past twenty years, our attitude toward computers and the internet has moved from suspicion or curiosity to dependency. When the World Wide Web was young, people used to find something online and ask, "How do I know if it's any good?" Now we think, "If it's not online, it's probably not worth looking for."

In what seems from a historical perspective like the blink of an eye, we've shifted our focus from distrusting the internet to embracing it. Computer technology has taken control over our words in ways and at a speed that no previous technology of literacy ever did before. Some of us approached the computer revolution with optimism, others with suspicion, and many with caution. But most of the people reading this book by now own a PC, or use one regularly at work, at school, or in a public library. In the decades between the 1980s and the present, the personal computer has gone from an expensive and forbidding, and far from personal, curiosity to a near necessity. The 2000 census reported that more than half of America's 105 million households had a computer. That percentage is a lot higher today.

Not everyone celebrates our increasing dependence on digitized words, and a few staunch critics see the computer destroying life as we know it. But for most Americans, and for more and more people elsewhere in the world, the computer is becoming the tool of choice for writing, whether for work, for school, or for what we do when we're not working or studying, and while not too many people are reading electronic books yet, more and more of us are gradually shifting the rest of our reading from the page to the screen.

Computer users regularly shop online, bank online, meet online, read online, and write online, not just in America, but elsewhere in the world as well. Even so, there are always trust issues with text, and even the most wired users have some internet activity that they shun: they may choose to have their paycheck deposited electronically, but they won't pay bills online; they may embrace virtual shopping but draw the line at online dating services; they may have found their soul mate on JDate but balk at the idea of citing Wikipedia in a research paper.

Worse yet, there's a lot of dark matter in cyberspace: fraud, hate, and exploitation abound online, not to mention inconsistency and inaccuracy and a whole lot of cyberjunk. We're still in the process of sorting the good from the bad online, the useful from the spam. We're still in the process of figuring out just what to use the internet for. And we're still learning to trust the web, even as we become ever more dependent on it for the things that we need to do every day.

▪ ▪ ▪ READ ME

A Better Pencil puts our complex and still-evolving hate-love relationship with computers and the internet into perspective. It's a book about how the digital revolution is impacting our reading and writing practices, and how the latest technologies of the word differ from what came before. It looks at our use of computers as writing tools in light of the history of communication technology, a history of how we love, fear, and actually use our writing machines—not just computers, but also typewriters, pencils, and clay tablets; how we deploy these technologies to replicate the old ways of doing things while actively generating new modes of expression; how we learn to trust a new technology and the new and strange sorts of texts that it produces; how we expand the notion of who can write and who can't; and how we free our readers and writers while at the same time trying to regulate their activities.

The World Wide Web wasn't the first innovation in communication to draw some initial skepticism. Writing itself was the target of one early critic. Plato warned that writing would weaken memory, but he was more concerned that written words—mere shadows of speech—couldn't adequately represent meaning. His objections paled as more and more people began to structure their lives around handwritten documents. Centuries later, the innovative output of Gutenberg's printing press was faulted for disrupting the natural, almost spiritual connection between the writer and the page. Eventually we got used to printing, but Henry David Thoreau scorned the telegraph when it was invented in the 1840s because this technology for quickly transporting words across vast distances was useless for people who had nothing to say to one another. The typewriter wasn't universally embraced as a writing tool when it appeared in the 1870s because its texts were impersonal, it weakened handwriting skills, and it made too much noise. And computers, now the writer's tool of choice, are still blamed by skeptics for a variety of ills, including destroying the English language, slowing down the writing process, speeding writing up to the point of recklessness, complicating it, trivializing it, and encouraging people to write who may, as Thoreau might put it, have nothing to say.

Despite Plato's warning, we have come to value writing, sometimes even more than speech. But at the dawn of letters, few people could read, and fewer still could write. People greeted the first written texts with distrust: "How do I know that Philoflatus really wrote this?" they'd ask suspiciously when they received a letter, or, looking at a deed, a royal decree, or a set of directions for turning lead into gold, they'd wonder, "How do I know it's not all a pack of lies?" Before writing became an ordinary activity, any words not delivered in person, directly from the horse's mouth, not only lacked the personal touch; they could also be some kind of trick.

▪ ▪ ▪ BECOMING USER FRIENDLY

Not all writing technologies begin with communication in mind. Writing, the first and most basic communication technology, was conceived initially as more of a memory device than a medium for transmitting words across time and space. Archaeological evidence suggests that it arose in the ancient Mediterranean to track inventory, not to record speech. Had writing remained just a storage device, we probably wouldn't be considering how computers shape reading and writing today.

Like writing, the pencil is a repurposed technology. Graphite chunks may have initially been used to mark sheep. Carpenters later attached handles to the graphite and used their new "pencils" to mark where to cut their wood. But when wordsmiths and artists got hold of the invention, its success was assured. At first the computer, as its name suggests, had nothing to do with writing. It was invented to simplify long, tedious arithmetic calculations and was meant to replace the adding machine, not the typewriter. But while we still use calculators—pocket-sized digital adding machines—typewriters are long gone from our desks.

Other successful communication technologies have the transmission of words as their primary goal: the printing press, the typewriter, the telegraph, and the telephone were designed to facilitate reading, writing, and speaking.

But all of these technologies, from writing itself to the digital computer, were difficult to learn and far from user friendly. The materials required to put them into play were expensive, hard to find, and labor intensive to prepare. In the early days of writing, it took dedication to be a writer. Not too many people thought that carving marks into wood, clay, or stone was worth the effort, nor were they keen on preparing their own pens and inks, drying animal skins, or pulping plant matter and weaving it into a suitable writing surface.

At the other end of the timeline, thousands of years after the earliest writing appeared, telegraphy was an option confined to those willing to learn Morse code. Until recently, even "wireless" radio operators couldn't be licensed without first demonstrating their proficiency in sending and receiving the dots and dashes that had been invented for the first wired telegraphy. The earliest computers weren't writer friendly either, and not even computer programmers used them to write their programs. Plus, few of the writers who were actually willing to tackle the complexities of writing with digital machines could actually afford to buy time on a mainframe. Nor could they justify spending $6,000 on a PC in 1983, for that was the cost of the new machine that could do less than a good electric typewriter or a much cheaper No. 2 pencil.

To really achieve broad adoption, all of our word technologies had first to overcome the initial barriers of a steep learning curve and sticker shock, becoming both simple enough to learn and cheap enough to acquire. The task of writing down a list of facts should be at least as quick and easy as memorizing them, and while writing can never be as cheap as memorizing, it should be affordable. In the same way, there must be an obvious advantage to typing a letter before people are willing to give up writing it by hand. Keyboarding a text must prove itself better than typing it, and economical to boot. And looking information up online should be quicker, and at least as reliable, as looking it up in the library.

As the recently literate try their hand at the new technology, they recreate the old ways, the ones they're comfortable with, using new methods. But they also develop new ways to communicate, and new kinds of texts emerge. Writing itself, initially an aid to memory, began to be used for business, for religion, for art, for education, for just plain entertainment. The printing press reproduced well-known texts previously only available in manuscript form: Bibles, prayer books, the works of a few classical authors. But soon presses began rolling out newspapers and novels, preprinted forms and instruction manuals, postcards, stamps, and the money to pay for them. Some of these genres of writing could have come about without printing, but none could have attained the level of use they have today if they had to be written by hand.

And as the mysteries of communication technologies give way and the technologies become accessible, new readers and writers are tempted to give them a whirl. More people learn to read, and some of them even join the authors club, the group for whom writing—the creation of text, not just its copying—is a profession, or at least an everyday phenomenon. Growing numbers of readers in the nineteenth century created a demand for more text and a corresponding increase in the numbers of journalists, poets, novelists, and business and technical writers. Computers have had an even greater impact on the authors club than any previous technology: given something to write with and a broadband connection, more and more of us are finding the right words and an online audience eager to read them.

In addition to changing who could read and write, and what got written and read, the print revolution created new standards and procedures for publication, and new ways of storing, sorting, and retrieving the information that had become available through print. Printing revolutionized literacy in exciting as well as dangerous ways, creating new problems as it addressed old ones. But in many ways the printing press did for literacy what earlier manuscript revolutions had also done: it created new means and opportunities for textual transmission; it both reinforced and threatened established ways of meaning; and it stimulated disruptions in the social, political, educational, and economic realms.

Computers too achieved their initial impact by allowing writers to produce familiar documents, but they also claim our attention, and a place in our reading and writing, by disrupting the older ways of doing things textually. Computers have allowed us to create new genres—internet chat, email, the web page and the blog—that cannot exist outside the virtual world.

In addition, computer technology radically reshapes how and what we say, breaking the rules of spelling, usage, and the formatting of discourse to a degree that some critics find alarming. But there is an opposing force for correctness and conventionality at work in the world of digital writing as well, one that counters the frontier spirit we associate with computers, that reins in the linguistic freewheeling of virtual text. As discourse communities form themselves in cyberspace, we see a clear, self-regulating pressure to establish standards for virtual writing and to police and correct those who violate the emerging norms. It turns out that spelling counts online, just as it counts on the page.

The post-Gutenberg explosion of print also brought censorship to the fore: increasing the amount of information available to readers was useful, empowering, and liberating, but because it could also be dangerous, subversive, and corrupting, secular and religious authorities stepped in to control access to the printed word. Again, today, the "authorities," be they parents, teachers, employers, or governments, face the same issues of regulating computer texts: how to keep children away from pornography or predators; how to keep students from downloading assignments instead of doing their own work; how to keep employees focused on work instead of digital games, e-shopping, or personal email; how to keep the faithful safe from heresy and insulate the citizen from politically dangerous ideas.

New communication technologies also spread literacy. They open up the means of communication to more and more people in more and more situations. This process proceeds slowly. It took not just centuries, but millennia for literacy rates to climb above 50 percent in parts of the world that already had highly literate cultures. The industrial revolution and the spread of universal education created more readers and writers, but the digital revolution of the past twenty years has produced a genuine explosion in the number of writers.

Whether we regard the changes accompanying computer textuality as radical or incremental, there is a paradoxical effect that accompanies the shift in literacy from conventional to digital technologies: On one hand, the new literacy is expansive, allowing more and more people to read and write. On the other hand, it remains expensive and not always accessible. That makes digital technology exclusive, with the clear potential to widen the literacy gap in society, closing doors for some, even as it is opening them for others, fencing off the new ways of reading and writing from all of those who are without computer access and a reliable source of electricity—and creating what we commonly call a *digital divide*.

It is still not clear whether computers will increase or limit literacy, or whether computer-mediated literacy is an improvement over what came before it. If the computer revolution parallels previous shifts in the technology of literacy, it is likely that both technology and literacy will continue to spread. But the computer won't necessarily cause us to learn more, to learn better, or to learn faster. The computer won't in and of itself improve the content we create online or our understanding of the content uploaded by others.

Like the computer, earlier technologies came with the promise of better learning. The telephone would bring lessons to the masses; so would film and, later, radio. I still remember the weekly radio hour that our third-grade class enjoyed in 1952, though I don't remember any of the programs we heard: while an educational program poured out of a giant FM radio receiver that was wheeled into our classroom each Friday morning, our teacher read quietly at her desk and the rest of us escaped into the land of daydream. Educational television came and went as well. Of course we still use radio, television, and the phone. All three are vital to our communication practices, and they occasionally play a limited classroom role as well. We just don't use them to replace teachers.

Computers have been embraced as the newest best hope for schools, but while they represent significant upgrades to the older blackboards and overhead projectors, and they help instructors find materials and communicate with students outside of class, my guess is that computers won't take the place of conventional, face-to-face lessons in American schools any more than earlier technologies did.

And speaking of earlier technologies, sometimes fears that new technologies will drive out old ones are justified, sometimes not: We still buy pencils but we don't buy typewriters. Clay is for sculpture or for play, not for writing, and while papyrus continues to be made in Egypt, it's mostly sold to tourists as a souvenir.

Finally, each new communication technology remixes our notions of public and private, bringing the public world into previously private space and exposing the private to public scrutiny. Books transport the world outside to our desks and armchairs; and they expose the writer's private thoughts for all to read. The blog transforms the personal diary into a billboard, and habitués of social networking sites parade their secrets for all to see, while at the same time we struggle to keep our e-communications safe from hackers and complain when someone unexpected visits our "private" Facebook or MySpace page.

But all this, the journey from pencils to pixels, is just a start. Computers and the internet are neither the best developments in the history of writing nor the worst. They are simply the latest in a series of innovations in how we do things with words.

▪ ▪ ▪ SYSTEM REQUIREMENTS

The first chapter of *A Better Pencil* explores how we moved from treating writing as a malevolent distortion of speech or, at best, a novelty, as Plato did, to a position where writing is often considered more valid, more authoritative, more authentic than the spoken word. Chapter 2 confronts the fears that accompany new communication technologies, fears that sometimes lead to physical as well as verbal violence. The next three chapters look at precomputer writing. Chapter 3 discusses the pencil as a paradigm of writing technology. Initially created by woodworkers *for* woodworkers, pencils quickly achieved widespread popularity among writers and artists, particularly as pencil technology improved. More pencils continue to be made and sold today than any other writing implement, and even though the computer has become the instrument of choice for the vast number of writers who have access to digital technology, pencils retain an important place in every writer's toolbox.

Chapter 4 treats another writing technology that isn't usually considered to be technological: handwriting. Before the printing press, all writing was done by hand, and even after the press achieved widespread success, handwriting remained the vehicle for recording business transactions until the typewriter and adding machines began to take over these functions in the early twentieth century. Both friends and foes of the technology see in the success of the computer the eventual death of handwriting, and it's undeniable that writers who use computers write less and less with pen or pencil.

Chapter 5 considers what happens when a twenty-first-century writer tries out a writing technology that actually has become obsolete—writing on clay. It turns out that writing in an antique and unfamiliar medium forces us to pay attention to aspects of writing that we take for granted when we use more familiar writing tools. This in turn leads us to consider what writers do when they use a new technology like the computer to do their writing.

My students insist that, for them, writing on a computer is simpler than writing on clay; most prefer computers to paper and pencil as well. The next two chapters trace the movement of the computer from a forbidding machine that was poorly adapted to writers' needs, to one that for all intents and purposes works as simply as a ballpoint pen: take it out of the box, click it on, start writing. While my students don't need a user's manual to get started, chapter 6 reminds us that the first mainframe computers and the personal computers that followed them in the 1980s were far from plug 'n' play. It took some time before people actually learned to trust this new and often recalcitrant technology, or the text that it produced. Chapter 7 traces how we are learning to trust the output of new writing technologies, showing that just as we developed ways to evaluate the handwritten and the printed text, we are developing means to test the authority of computer-generated documents.

Chapters 8 through 10 examine the new genres that the computer has enabled: email, the instant message, the web page, the blog, social networking pages such as MySpace and Facebook, and communally generated wikis like Wikipedia and the Urban Dictionary. And in chapter 11 we consider some of the darker sides of the web, looking specifically at hate groups and at the struggle between the free flow of information and concerns about regulating the newest of our writing spaces. The chapter summarizes as well the impact of our latest digital technologies on our communication practices; discusses how we deal with information overload; explores the paradox whereby companies such as Google and Microsoft argue strongly for the free and open exchange of information on the internet by means of closely guarded, top-secret formulas and data storage facilities; and examines the attempts by internet marketers to harvest information about us in order to predict our behavior.

Chapter 12 ends the book with another look back, this time at an experiment designed to demonstrate the effectiveness of typewriters in improving the learning of elementary school students. Typewriters promised to do for education everything that educators now claim computers will do. But it never happened. While the typewriter was the most important new writing instrument of its day, typing never made its way into schools the way computers have, so the impact of that analog machine on learning was never put to the test.

It turns out that the digital revolution is playing out as all communication revolutions do. Computers don't live up to the grandiose promises of their biggest fans. Nor do they sabotage our words, as critics loudly warn that they will. Instead, as we learned to do with earlier writing technologies, once we adopt the computer, we adapt it to our needs, and along the way we find new and unexpected ways of changing what we do with words, and how we do it.

▪ ▪ ▪ ACKNOWLEDGMENTS

I received support for this project in the form of generous amounts of time for research and writing funded by the University of Illinois Center for the Study of Cultural Values and Ethics, the university's research board, and its College of Liberal Arts and Sciences. Many colleagues and students listened patiently to my ideas as I developed them or read one of the many drafts and iterations of this manuscript, giving me leads to pursue as well as valuable and occasionally sobering advice. Even though the computer landscape changes so quickly that much of what I write here may be obsolete by the time you read this, I suppose I should also thank the computer: word processors make revision so easy that I would have finished this book much sooner had I just been typing it on my old Selectric, though the resulting text would be even more imperfect than what I've managed to come up with in the pages that follow.

I particularly want to thank Peter Ohlin and Brian Hurley, my editors at Oxford, for their astute comments and suggestions for improving the text and their skill at helping me nail down permissions for the many illustrations in this book.

▪ ▪ ▪ END-USER AGREEMENT

END-USER AGREEMENT

ENGLISH

HARDCOPY END-USER AGREEMENT FOR *A BETTER PENCIL*

PLEASE READ THIS END-USER AGREEMENT ("END-USER") BEFORE ACCESSING HARDCOPY. BY USING THE HARDCOPY, YOU ARE AGREEING TO BE BOUND BY THE TERMS OF THIS LICENSE. IF YOU DO NOT AGREE TO THE TERMS OF THIS LICENSE, DO NOT READ THE HARDCOPY. IF YOU DO NOT AGREE TO THE TERMS OF THIS LICENSE, YOU MAY RETURN THE HARDCOPY TO THE PLACE WHERE YOU OBTAINED IT FOR A REFUND OR A STORE CREDIT. IF THE HARDCOPY WAS ACCESSED ELECTRONICALLY, CLICK "DISAGREE." IF YOU OBTAINED THE HARDCOPY FROM A LIBRARY OR OTHER THIRD-PARTY HARDCOPY DISTRIBUTOR, YOU MAY RETURN IT WITHOUT PENALTY IF SUCH RETURN IS MADE BEFORE THE DUE DATE ("DUE DATE") STAMPED ON THE HARDCOPY CASE OR ENCLOSURE.

IMPORTANT NOTE: This hardcopy may be used to create or reproduce ideas. It is licensed to you only for creation of ideas which you have thought up yourself, or reproduction of ideas which you have permission or authority to reproduce. This hardcopy may also be used for remote access to previously stored ideas, whether for ideas stored in your own personal wetware, or for ideas stored in other hardcopy. Remote access of ideas ("homage") is only provided for lawful personal use or as otherwise legally permitted. If you are uncertain about your right to copy or access any idea you should contact your legal advisor.

1. General. This hardcopy, documentation, and any words and images accompanying this License whether in hardcopy, on disk, in read only memory, or any other media or in any form (collectively, the "Hardcopy") are licensed to you for use under the terms of this License. Any subsequent upgrades are covered by the terms of this License unless such upgrades are accompanied by a separate license in which case the terms of that license will govern.

(Disagree)   (Agree)

Users don't typically read software license agreements before clicking on "agree." Fortunately, books ("hardcopy") still don't require readers to sign a license like the one above before reading.

A Better Pencil

■ ■ ■

1

■ ■ ■ Writing It Down

■ ■ ■ WRITING TO REMEMBER

In Plato's *Phaedrus*, the earliest and best-known critique of writing, Socrates warns his companion Phaedrus that writing will only make human memory weaker:

> This invention will produce forgetfulness in the minds of those who
> learn to use it, because they will not practice their memory. Their trust in
> writing, produced by external characters which are no part of themselves,
> will discourage the use of their own memory within them. (Plato 1925,
> 274e–275a)

We remember this, of course, because Plato wrote it down. Plato's problem with letters goes beyond the worry that the new technology of writing will sap our ability to recall. The philosopher, keen to distinguish between reality and its shadow, saw the written word as only a representation of the spoken: for him, writing can never be as *real* as speech.

In the *Phaedrus*, a dialogue between Socrates and Phaedrus that is written as if it were a transcript of an actual spoken conversation, though in Platonic terms it's not a faithful recreation but a mere shadow of such an interaction, Socrates recounts the story of Theuth, the Egyptian god who invented letters. Reporting on the strength of his invention to Thamus, the chief of all the gods, Theuth claims that writing "will make the Egyptians wiser and improve their memories; for it is an elixir of memory and wisdom that I have discovered" (274e).

But Thamus doesn't think that writing makes good medicine at all. Instead, he objects that writing aids not memory, but mere reminiscence. Listeners like Phaedrus and Theuth have the opportunity to hear wisdom firsthand. In contrast, readers will display merely "the appearance of wisdom, not true wisdom," because they have had no face-to-face instruction, no encounter with actual words, but only with symbols standing in for spoken words (275a).

Worse still, for Socrates, writing is ambiguous, if not downright deceitful. He cautions Phaedrus that written words don't mean what they say: "He who receives [them] in the belief that anything in writing will be clear and certain, would be an utterly simple person." Instead, all that writing is good for is jogging the memory: "Written words are of [no] use except to remind him who knows the matter about which they are written" (275c–d).

In addition, because writing is a one-way communication, not an interactive one, it has the same relationship to truth that painting has to life:

> [F]or the creatures of painting stand like living beings, but if one asks
> them a question, they preserve a solemn silence. And so it is with written
> words; you might think they spoke as if they had intelligence, but if you
> question them, wishing to know about their sayings, they always say only
> one and the same thing. (275d–e)

For Socrates, as for other critics of the written word, writing is defective and untrustworthy because symbols on a page can't respond to questions. The problem with writing, in this view, is that it's little more than a set of things that one already knows and needs to remember, the ancient equivalent of the shopping list.

For Plato, only speech, not writing, can produce the kind of back-and-forth—the dialogue—that's needed to get at the truth. And just as we may have trouble interpreting another person's shopping list today (yes, it says "bread," but what kind?), not to mention figuring out what Hamlet really meant when he asked, "To be or not to be?" the written word is always subject to the potentially whimsical interpretation of the all-too-often unreliable reader. To Plato, the text, orphaned by its author once it's on the page, cannot defend itself against misreading, and readers can never really know if they've got it right. That's why he has Socrates say,

> And every word, when once it is written, is bandied about, alike among
> those who understand and those who have no interest in it, and it knows
> not to whom to speak or not to speak; when ill-treated or unjustly reviled
> it always needs its father to help it; for it has no power to protect or help
> itself. (275d–e)

These are strong arguments, but even in Plato's day they had been rendered moot by the success of the written word. Although the literacy rate in classical Greece was well below 10 percent, writing had become an important feature of the culture (Harris 1989). People had learned to trust and use certain kinds of writing—legal texts, public inscriptions, business documents, personal letters, and even literature—and as they did so, they realized that writing, on closer examination, turned out to be neither more nor less reliable or ambiguous than the spoken word, and it was just as real. Even Plato, as he recorded the dialogues of Socrates for us to remember, must have been well aware that writing could do much more than simply remind his fellow Athenians what to buy when they went to the agora.

▪ ▪ ▪ I WANT THAT IN WRITING

It turns out that Socrates was wrong: "I want that in writing" is a common reply that most of us have made to some statement likely to be forgotten, denied, or retracted. When the stakes are high, or we're dealing with someone who may not be on the up-and-up—a landlord, or a car dealer, or a stranger on a train—we greet a spoken promise with skepticism and a written one with trust.

That was not always the case. When writing was a new and uncommon practice, it was letters on a page, not face-to-face speech, that sparked distrust. When few people could read, and fewer still could write, trusting writing—if trust came at all—required an enormous leap of faith. Plato's objections aside, writing was still an unproven gimmick, and people might have reasoned that at least with the spoken word, they knew who they were talking to, friend, foe, or total stranger. Friends could be trusted. With enemies, you knew where you stood. Strangers had to prove themselves. But words scrawled on a piece of paper, or a sheepskin, or a lump of clay, those were always strangers, always worthy of suspicion.

Things have changed. Over time, writing and its many technologies became more familiar. They're now easier to learn, easier to use, and, in part because writing is all around us, they've become easier to trust. As a result, more often than not the balance between speech and writing has shifted toward writing. Our sacred texts are books; our laws are written down; our bets are guaranteed by IOUs; our purchases, both big ticket items and sticks of gum, are all receipted. Still, as we will see, from the first days of writing to the present, each time a new communication technology appeared, people had to learn all over again how to use it, how to respond to it, how to trust the documents it produced. "I want that in writing" is still the goal, but sometimes that demand is qualified: I want it typed, not handwritten; signed and witnessed;

Writing in stone is no guarantee of permanence, as we see in Rembrandt's well-known representation of Moses smashing the Ten Commandments, painted in 1659. University of Leipzig; used by permission.

in ink, not pencil; a printout, not a digital file. Better still, carve it in stone, Ten-Commandments-style. Of course, just as digital files can vanish into thin air, stone tablets can be smashed or eroded by the elements.

In many parts of the world today, literacy rates are high and writing is everywhere: not just on stone or in books, letters, and newspapers, but on signs, on television, on t-shirts. Ordinary objects are covered with text. Although

Ice-thaw cycles and acid rain have worn away some of the writing on the gravestone of Thankful Higins, d. 1712. From capecodgravestones.com; used by permission.

few people besides collectors and counterfeiters pay attention to them, there are eighty-one words and twenty-three numbers, including MDCCLXXVI, engraved on a dollar bill. The soft drink can on my desk is covered with more than 120 words and 20 numbers, many of them in very small print. While the text on our cereal boxes may preoccupy us early in the morning when we're not yet awake enough to confront the day, we don't usually read our money or our beverage containers. We don't normally think of them as something to read. And yet, in a world where writing creates familiarity and constitutes proof, these objects promise everything from economic value to good taste to zero calories by means of the written word.

We've come to expect writing on many things that aren't primarily documents, and if everyday items such as paper money, soda cans, and cereal boxes were suddenly stripped of their words, we'd notice the glaring absence of text, and we might even question their contents and worth.

Although there are millions of people around the globe who cannot read, there's no doubt that the world is filled with print. Certainly in the United

States, driving a car presents us with a plethora of signs and placards telling us where we are, where we're heading, how fast we should go, and what we should buy when we get there. Not content with the reading matter beyond the windshield, some drivers even read while driving, their book or magazine nestled in the steering wheel. And more drivers are not just talking on their phones while operating a motor vehicle, they're actively texting, tapping the keys as they steer. Seeing another driver under the influence of text may be a signal to pull over and walk. But walking down the street presents even more opportunities to read the signage on buildings and sidewalks, or on the cars, buses, and trucks going by, and reading while walking can also lead to collisions with lampposts, hydrants, and parking meters, or with other pedestrians similarly distracted by environmental text.

Surrounded as we are by the written word, we have come to treat writing as both normal and reliable, permanent and unchanging. Sometimes it's even legally binding. As for speech, well, people lie, or forget, or they change their minds. Better to get it in writing.

Writing entertains and informs, but it also remembers. In fact, because we often forget what we think, or dream, or say, as Socrates predicted, writing has become a major tool of memory. The humorist Robert Benchley complained that surefire ideas for new stories often woke him up at night, but by morning they'd be gone. A friend advised him to place a pad and pencil on his nightstand, and to say the words "Write it down" several times before retiring. Benchley tried that. After setting a paper and pencil by the bed, he dutifully repeated his mantra, "Write it down," over and over as he fell asleep. In the middle of the night Benchley woke with another brilliant idea, scribbled on the pad, and went back to sleep, content that he had preserved his fleeting thoughts on paper. He awoke the next morning having forgotten the idea, as usual, and when he consulted the pad, he found that what he had written was

> write it down

Benchley probably made up that anecdote, but the written word routinely documents our lives, reinforcing or supplanting memory to provide the official version of what happened. It turns out that the permanent record—that written transcript of grades, honors, and misdemeanors that haunted us through our school days—now follows everything we do, both large and small. It's not just births and deaths, marriages and divorces, awards and diplomas that are routinely inscribed, many of them on certificates suitable for framing. We can also reconstruct our more mundane routine by means of the receipts we collect for each doughnut and candy bar, for each meal or trip to the store, each movie or game of miniature golf. Our commutes are recorded electronically on MetroCards stashed in our wallets or FasPasses stuck to our windshields, and on receipts for gas churned out at the pump each time we fill up. Credit card records track our vacations more accurately than any travel journal, though they lack the sentimental value of our snapshots. And web browsers dutifully record our keystrokes as we surf the internet so that advertisers can offer to sell us products related to the sites we visit. For the French novelist Marcel Proust, the fresh-baked aroma of a madeleine brought back enough childhood recollections to trigger a three-thousand-page series of novels. Were he alive today, Proust wouldn't have to worry about remembering things past: he could reconstruct his life from the crumpled bits of paper he had pulled out of his pockets each day and stored in a shoebox. And if that written record proved deficient, with just a few clicks he could summon up an image of a madeleine from the World Wide Web, together with this food-network.com recipe:

8 tablespoons unsalted butter, divided
4 eggs
1/2 cup plus 2 tablespoons granulated sugar
2 tablespoons light brown sugar
1/8 teaspoon salt
2 1/2 teaspoons baking powder
1 1/2 cups cake flour
1/4 teaspoon pure vanilla extract
1 tablespoon honey
(Gand 2004)

And those virtual documents might in turn trigger a memory not of childhood, but of the dangers of cholesterol, which he could then write about on his never-ending blog.

So thoroughly has writing taken over our lives that we have all become Prousts, externalizing our thoughts, once our most private activities, as we keyboard our way through work and study and what little free time may remain in a ceaseless stream of emails, MySpace posts, instant messages, and Twitters collected, backed up, and stored for eternity in computer memory banks all over the world.

But it's not novelists, historians, or diarists, not government spies or private snoops, not sociologists or visiting space aliens who use this ever-growing

Madeleines. Photograph by the author.

mountain of digital data to recover our memories or reconstruct the details of our existence. It's the data-mining market researchers, the statisticians, the experts on consumer behavior who are tracking the electronic trail we leave as we work, study, and play our way through the day, all so that they can better figure out what they can get us to buy next. They are using the latest writing technology, the computer, to turn us—by means of a few simple keystrokes—into a vast test market.

▪ ▪ ▪

We don't save our grocery lists, because not all writing is memorable, even if its immediate purpose is to aid our memory. Nor is it all trustworthy. Despite the faith we place in it, there is nothing about writing that makes it inherently less fraudulent or more accurate than speech. Certainly writers lie and cheat at least as much as nonwriters: some students fudge assignments; some best-selling authors plagiarize their prose; some contracts are only as good as the paper they're printed on; and some paper money is counterfeit. In addition, the technologies of writing permit objectivity, or at least its illusion, since the text exists independently of both writer and reader. But our world is full of lawyers and clerics, of movie reviewers and literary critics, of political commentators and satirists, whose very existence confirms Plato's suspicion that written texts can be interpreted in multiple ways, though each of the legal, religious, and political experts insists that his or hers is the most correct reading of all.

The meaning of laws and sacred texts often provokes controversies, many of which are resolved by imposing one party's interpretation, sometimes in court, occasionally through violence, rather than through Socratic dialogue or consensual reading. That in itself is just another way of saying that writing is subjective, that its meaning exists only in the eye, and sometimes the sword, of the beholder. Writing also allows authors to cloak themselves in anonymity or to create false identities for themselves. We as readers know this, and as part of learning to trust the text, we've developed ways of assessing and authenticating writing, just as we've developed means to test whether the speakers whom we encounter face to face are telling us the truth.

▪ ▪ ▪ WRITING IS A TECHNOLOGY

Writing is a technology, and a fairly recent one at that. Human speech is probably as old as *homo sapiens sapiens*, which means that people began talking anywhere from one hundred thousand to two hundred thousand years ago, and it's possible that an older variety of *homo sapiens*, which has been around for about half a million years, talked even earlier than that. Writing is much newer, a mere six thousand years old, give or take. In that sliver of geological time, we have gone from thinking of writing as a novelty, or something to be regarded with suspicion, to valuing it in many cases more than speech.

While a few enthusiasts and visionaries surely saw the potential of a technology like writing when it consisted of just a few symbols scratched into clay or painted on a wall, it's equally likely that some people feared and rejected this new form of communication. But most everybody else probably viewed writing as unnecessarily complicated or too obscure.

When the uses of writing became more obvious, when writing became cheaper and easier to learn and deploy, people took to writing in ever-greater numbers. More people became writers, and still more became readers. Each new development in writing technology—the move from clay to pencils, from manuscript to printed page, from notebook to typewriter, from pencils to pixels—led to the expansion of the authors club, not just those who copy texts, but those who create them.

But even today, with computers turning people into writers at a record pace, critics still attack the newest technologies of writing not simply as deceptive, but also as impersonal, mechanical, intellectually destructive, and socially disruptive. Such attacks on new technologies of literacy always come too late: digital writing is quickly replacing the older ways, just as print replaced script, and while pencils and traditional books still fly off the shelves, both writers and readers are shifting more and more of their literacy practice from the page to the screen.

▪ ▪ ▪ INVENTING THE WHEEL

Most technologies that we now take for granted didn't become popular overnight. The first writing seems to have been used not for transcribing human language, but as an accounting tool for tracking inventory (Schmandt-Besserat 1996). Only when writers saw that the new technology could also record speech did it become attractive to people who weren't simply engaged in bean counting. And even then it took centuries, if not millennia, for writing to outrank speech in our esteem. Other communication technologies that we can't imagine doing without today, like printing, took a while to catch on as well. Centuries after the printing press had become the primary means of duplicating texts in Europe, writers were still composing their books, letters, diaries, and office documents with pencils and pens. The typewriter, and more recently the computer, eventually changed all that.

New inventions are often expensive or tricky to use, both obstacles to their widespread adoption. But the shock of the new often brings out critics eager to warn us away. We don't know how the wheel was received when it first came on the scene, but we can assume that the early supporters of the wheel saw it as the best thing since sliced bread—or they would have seen it that way had anybody at the time known what sliced bread was.

But it's also reasonable to assume that the wheel, like all new technologies, had its detractors. The antiwheelers probably argued that the old ways of locomotion—walking, running, skipping, crawling, riding on the backs of unfriendly animals—were better; that the wheel sped up the pace of modern life way too much; that round technologies would place mankind on a slippery slope leading precipitously downward to the end of civilization as they knew it.

In response to the wildly optimistic promises and dire warnings about the wheel, the average person probably took a sensible, wait-and-see approach to the new technology. As it turned out, while antediluvian Luddites may have gone around smashing wheels the same way that nineteenth-century Luddites smashed looms or twentieth-century ones attacked computers, it eventually became apparent that the wheel was not going to go away, and today the wheel ranks alongside writing and the silicon chip as one of the most important human achievements of all time.

As it was with the wheel, once writing came on the scene, there was no turning back. Trust in writing grew slowly, as people gradually saw how reducing

The oldest known wooden wheel, discovered in the Ljubljana Marshes of Slovenia in 2002, was built more than 5,100 years ago out of two radial boards of ash wood, 72 cm. in diameter, and was attached to an oak axle that turned along with the wheel. Photograph courtesy of Dr. Katarina Čufar and Dr. Anton Velušček, University of Ljubljana.

words to symbols on a page could help them remember or transmit information. But in order for writing to really catch on, not only did it have to become easier to learn and to do, but the cost of writing technologies, whether they were clay tablets, quill pens, or laser printers, also had to come down. Furthermore, the new technologies required cheap and ready sources of parchment, ink, and paper. Even though paper is common enough to be a throwaway item today, the first dot matrix printers required special tractor feed paper, sold only in large quantities, that was both expensive and hard to find. Today twenty-four-hour grocery stores sell reams of computer paper. Staples and Office Depot didn't create the computer revolution in America, but they certainly facilitated its spread by setting up a reliable supply infrastructure.

But even after people accepted the basic assumption that the written word could be useful and reliable, they greeted each new writing technology with renewed suspicion. At the outset, the majority of readers and writers typically thought that the old ways were better, preferring handwriting to typewriters, or mechanical typewriters to electric ones, or pencils to computers, which even now are always breaking down, and initially they saw no need to learn yet another difficult and expensive way to process their words.

Once people finally accepted the usefulness and authenticity of handwritten texts, or of words carved in stone, they balked at the new technology of printing, which threatened both to democratize reading and to depersonalize it. A few hundred years later, the typewriter upset our literacy practices once again. It was bad enough that the clacking typewriter joined the equally noisy adding machine in the increasing mechanization that was permeating and, in the eyes of many, dehumanizing the modern office of the early twentieth century. Typewriters also threatened to render handwriting obsolete. These new writing machines produced reasonably clear, consistent letters with each keystroke, which meant it was no longer necessary for writers to keep up a uniform and legible penmanship. Typing threatened to supplant with cold, unfeeling uniformity not just routine business correspondence, but also the thoughtful individuality of the handwritten note as a vehicle for polite as well as intimate personal interaction, and, what was even worse, because typing resembled printed texts, critics groused that typewriters gave too many would-be writers access to authorship.

Despite such complaints, the typewriter proved as unstoppable as the printing press in taking over major writing functions both on the job and off. But after a century in which they progressed from an oddity manufactured as a sideline by rifle and sewing machine makers to a fixture on every desk in the American office or home, typewriters have gone the way of the dinosaur. According to the latest generation of critics and naysayers, today it is computers that are producing texts whose value and credibility we question; computers that are giving too many people control over the creation and publication of text; computers that are wreaking havoc with our handwriting. And to top it off, digitally enabled writing such as email, instant messaging, and texting are now causing us to rethink the differences between speech and writing while at the same time redefining the boundaries between public and private communication.

▪ ▪ ▪

Whether we embrace them or fear them, the technologies that we use to compose, disseminate, and archive our words—the machinery that ranges from pencils to pixels, from clay tablets to optical disks—not only make reading and writing possible, they also have affected our reading and writing practices. The technologies of our literacy—what we write with and what we write on—help to determine what we write and what we can't write. But the technology works two ways: it channels what we do, but it also changes to meet the needs of writers and readers, who play a role in modifying the direction that writing technology takes.

■ ■ ■ VISIT US ON THE WEB

Right now that technology is taking us to the World Wide Web, where more and more Americans are reading and writing, and more and more people around the world are following suit, communicating online. Today's computer screen looks like a page but functions like a portal, leading the reader into a multidimensional as well as a multimedia space. That can be very exciting, offering writers new ways of composing and readers new ways of reading. Or it can be threatening. It turns out that Marshall McLuhan was only partly right when he said that the medium was the message. Wrapping texts in the exciting layers of a new technology, moving us from one link to the next, may be fun at first. But when the newness of the latest writing upgrade wears off, the content, as always, will have to make it on its own. The digital word can be as important or as trivial, as effective or as meaningless, as the analog variety. Sometimes, it turns out, a great American novel is great, no matter what its format, while a sales pitch is just a sales pitch, whether it jumps off the page or off the screen.

Here's an illustration of such a sales pitch: About ten years ago, after coming home from a routine trip to the grocery store, my family began to unpack and sort our purchases at the kitchen table. Examining the fine print on a box of detergent, perhaps because she found the words so compelling, or just to get out of having to put things away, my daughter suddenly cried out, "Look! Tide has a website."

Sure enough, there on the carton was an invitation that read something like, "Visit us on the World Wide Web at www.tide.com." It was already common for everyday products such as shampoo to list 800-numbers on their labels so consumers could call up and get more information. I myself have never had any shampoo-related questions—what more is there to know after, "lather, rinse, repeat"? But I assume that the existence of shampoo customer support meets a significant consumer need. What I couldn't fathom at the time was why a laundry soap would need a website.

Rushing to the computer, we dialed up (this was long before broadband) and logged on to discover that Tide had indeed mounted a website. There, for customers who needed more to read after they were done reading the Tide box, we found screen after screen detailing the many uses of Tide. For example, it can be used to wash dirty clothes. We found information on how to get out all sorts of pesky stains on our clothes (predictably, we were told to pretreat stains with Tide before washing them in yet more Tide).

Perhaps conventional print media could have conveyed the same message: buy our product, use as much of it as you can, then go out and buy some more. But the Tide website offered both an amount of text and a level of interactivity that magazine ads or soap boxes couldn't begin to equal.

With a few simple clicks of a mouse we could buy Tide online (shipping and handling charges rendered this an option only for the very rich). Or we could get free Tide. Website visitors were invited to submit essays about interesting ways they had used the product to clean their dirty clothes, and any essay picked for publication on the web won the writer a year's supply of the detergent. I admit that as a writer who has also dealt with dirty clothes, I was tempted to try my hand at a twenty-five-words-or-less laundry op-ed, but when I actually sat down to count the ways I had cleaned things, I couldn't come up with anything more original than "lather, rinse, repeat."

Finally, the Tide website offered t-shirts and caps with the logo of the Tide racing team, which visitors could buy online (hint to fans of Team Tide: don't clean those gasoline- and oil-soaked rags in the same machine you use for your fine washables, and by all means keep them away from a hot dryer). That Tide had a racing team was as much news to me as the fact that Tide had a website.

A good ten years on, the Tide website is still going strong, and it still offers the same sorts of articles on fabric care. Readers can now sign up for an e-newsletter offering even more ways to use Tide to get clothes clean, and the graphics today seem more sophisticated: on my initial visit I recall moving through links on the site by clicking a series of pastel t-shirts waving in jerky animation on a clothesline. Clearly, enough people who have questions about washing, or who simply have nothing else to do, are visiting Tide dot com to make it worthwhile for the company to maintain and expand its web offerings.

Nowadays every self-respecting business has a website. Many individuals have one too, but not as many as one might have predicted from the headlong rush to get on the web. A few years ago I began asking my students whether any of them kept a web page. Initially only two said yes—one did it for a class assignment, the other just for fun. Students never really joined the personal website craze, which today remains the preserve of businesses and organizations. Individuals surf those sites routinely, finding them a major source—if not their primary source—of news and information, as well as a major marketplace. But students in particular have found a more attractive alternative to having their own URL: today it's the rare young American who doesn't have a personal page—what I will refer to as space pages—on Facebook or MySpace.

It's common for the more highbrow among us to sniff at vanity publishing—the practice of writers paying to put their own work between covers rather than going through the conventional process of submitting work to a publisher who accepts or rejects it on its merits and salability. Though there are occasional exceptions, conventionally printed self-published writing

Screenshot of the current Tide home page. From www.tide.com.

doesn't typically draw many readers. In contrast, self-published websites, and, more recently, highly personal blogs and space pages, seem not to go unread. Website visits don't necessarily translate into soap sales, but at least critics who worry that computers are ruining our literacy should be reassured by indications that the people who visit Tide on the web, or the growing number of blogs and Facebook entries, are actually reading what they find there, and many leave comments as well. In fact, the web has become so compelling that one enterprising manufacturer of high-end appliances actually put a web-browsing computer into a refrigerator, right next to the ice dispenser.

Computers are everywhere these days: they sit on our desktops, on our laps, in our palms, pockets, and purses. Computers are shrinking to fit our cell phones, bringing the World Wide Web to the palm of our hand, and soon we may even find them on our wristwatches. But with LG's computer on ice, we can also get connected by means of a large kitchen appliance. According to the full-page *New York Times* ad for this fashion-forward appliance, the future is now, in the form of a refrigerator able to compete with the cereal box for our early-morning attention. The twenty-six cubic foot model—recently discontinued—let consumers keep abreast of terrorism, check their stocks, update their Facebook pages, IM with relatives, and buy tchotchkes on eBay, all for a retail price of about $8,000. And, because LG had the foresight not to include a webcam in its digi-fridge, they could do all this while standing barefoot and unkempt in their kitchens at 6:30 in the morning, clutching mugs of coffee, staring glumly at the screen.

LG extolled its product's ability to interact with the homeowner: the refrigerator's computer could let owners know when the light bulb in the freezer needed changing or when the icemaker was due for service. And it could show videos or display a slide show of the owners' digital photos or their children's artwork.

That's all well and good, but besides the prohibitive price and the need to install a cable jack behind the refrigerator, what might have kept people from buying the web-enabled fridge was its lack of a keyboard or mouse. There was no direct way to upload videos or graphics to the LG's computer, and to input text, which seems to be what most people want to do with their computers these days, users had to stand in front of the refrigerator, stooping awkwardly if they're average-sized or taller adults, to tap out an instant message or key in a URL on the touch-sensitive screen.

Although writing it down on the digital refrigerator may be almost as hard as writing on the first computer mainframes, the internet refrigerator doesn't simply allow interaction, it can actually initiate that interactivity, emailing its owner if it needs service. And since LG makes cell phones too, it might have been possible to program the fridge to text you when it ran out of milk. Imagine this scenario: you're in the middle of an important meeting when suddenly, *ring ring*…"Uh, excuse me, I have to take this. It's my refrigerator calling."

2

■ ■ ■   TeknoFear

Even though the public isn't scooping up the computer-in-a-refrigerator, people aren't about to give up their computers (emphasis on the plural) any time soon. But not everyone is enthusiastic about these cranky, high-tech typewriters. Computers make enemies as well as friends: not just those who disparage computers because they think that the machines are too hard to figure out, but true enemies who fear that computer technologies will destroy life as we know it. These computerphobes are convinced that the machines will corrupt our writers, turn books into endangered species, and litter the landscape with self-publishing authors. In addition, computers will rot our brains, destroy family life, put an end to polite conversation, wreak havoc with the English language, invade our privacy, steal our identity, and expose us to predators waiting to pervert us or to sell us things that we don't need.

One enemy of computers, John Zerzan (1994), writing long before the age of the digital refrigerator, warns that the computerized office is no better than a sweatshop. And the environmentalist writer Kirkpatrick Sale, who agrees with Zerzan that computers mechanize and dehumanize production, once expressed his personal contempt for computers by destroying one during a lecture on the evils of the "technosphere."

Sale explained in a 1995 *Wired* magazine interview the joy of his computer-smashing experience:

> It was astonishing how good it made me feel! I cannot explain it to you.
> I was on the stage of New York City's Town Hall with an audience of
> 1,500 people. I was behind a lectern, and in front of the lectern was this
> computer. And I gave a very short, minute-and-a-half description of what
> was wrong with the technosphere, how it was destroying the biosphere.
> And then I walked over and I got this very powerful sledgehammer
> and smashed the screen with one blow and smashed the keyboard with

FBI sketch of the Unabomber, later identified as Ted Kaczynski. From wikimedia.org.

another blow. It felt wonderful. The sound it made, the spewing of the undoubtedly poisonous insides into the spotlight, the dust that hung in the air...some in the audience applauded. I bowed and returned to my chair. (Kelly 1995)

Sale's concern about the biosphere didn't stop him from exposing the Town Hall audience to the computer's "poisonous insides," but perhaps the most extreme reaction against computers has been that of Theodore Kaczynski. Over a period of eighteen years beginning in 1978, Kaczynski went after, not the offending machines themselves, but the people he held responsible for them, computer scientists and executives of the technology industry. Kaczynski mailed or planted sixteen bombs in his effort to turn the world away from technology, killing three people and injuring more than twenty others with his homemade devices. He was dubbed the Unabomber by the FBI because many of his victims were associated with universities and airlines, but for most of his teknofear campaign no one knew for sure what his motives were. Finally, in 1995, the Unabomber wrote a letter to the *New York Times* demanding the immediate publication of a thirty-five-thousand-word manifesto outlining his complaints against the technological world. He threatened to step up his killing spree if the newspapers didn't comply. Kaczynski explained, in an aside, that although universities were among his targets for their complicity in developing technology, not all academics were worth killing:

> We have nothing against universities or scholars as such. All the university people whom we have attacked have been specialists in technical fields.... We would not want anyone to think that we have any desire to hurt professors who study archaeology, history, literature or harmless stuff like that. [From the Unabomber's ransom letter to the *New York Times*, reprinted in the *San Francisco Examiner*, April 26, 1995, and retrieved from that newspaper's website. Kaczynski writes in the plural to give the impression that he is not a lone gunman, but is instead part of a larger movement mobilizing against technology.]

Archeologists and historians may have been grateful that they weren't in the Unabomber's sights, but Ted Kaczynski was wrong in his assessment of humanists on two counts. Humanists can be harmful, and, more to the point, humanists are heavily involved in technology, particularly the writing technologies that the computer has enabled. But since the Unabomber seemed ready to kill anyone, technocrat or not, just to make his point, I for one was afraid to speak out, at least until a plausible suspect was in custody.

It was the *Washington Post* that published the Unabomber Manifesto. That newspaper was technologically better prepared to do so than the *New York Times*, and that was not a problem for the Unabomber, who proclaimed in his manifesto that revolutionaries could use modern technology—for example, the mass media—so long as they did so to attack the technological system (Kaczynski 1995).

The manifesto's publication eventually led to the Unabomber's identification and capture. When David Kaczynski read the manifesto, he was reminded of the ranting letters he had received from his brother Ted, who lived in an isolated cabin in Montana. After some soul-searching, David Kaczynski alerted the FBI, and his brother was finally captured a year after the manifesto's publication, in April 1996. The Unabomber pleaded guilty to avoid the death penalty, and he is presently serving four life sentences in a maximum security federal prison in Colorado, without possibility of parole.

So now it can be said: the humanities—and the arts—can be just as dangerous as cloning sheep or genetically altering corn. Books are technology, after all, and sending them through the mail may not have the direct impact of sending bombs, but the written word has always had the power to anger people to the point where they act irrationally, even violently, banning or burning books, destroying entire libraries (the word for this, reflected in the title of a new book on the subject, is *libricide*), and physically attacking authors and readers.

The computer is not the first writing technology to be censored, controlled, or sabotaged. Whether it's *Ulysses* or *The Merchant of Venice*, *Huckleberry Finn* or *Harry Potter*, *Catcher in the Rye* or *Soul on Ice*, literature is often too radical, too sexual, too threatening to the status quo for it to sit quietly on the shelf. Sacred literature can be especially controversial: there's a fine line between exegesis and heresy. One person's scripture is another's blasphemy, and the devout don't always suffer blasphemers quietly. In pre-Reformation England translating the Bible into English was a capital crime. (In 1536 William Tyndale was strangled, then burned at the stake for his English version of the Bible.) Mixing the secular with the sacred may prove even more explosive. Salman Rushdie is but one prominent example of an author who had to go into hiding—in his case from religious fanatics who feared and hated, but hadn't even read, the portrayal of Islam in his novels.

In extreme cases, books contribute to wars and political upheavals. Certainly the goal of manifestos like those of Karl Marx or Ted Kaczynski is to overthrow the state, and revolutions of any magnitude are more likely to be bloody than bloodless. On a much narrower scale, in the Unabomber's case, it was the act of publication of his manifesto by a computer-savvy newspaper that led to Kaczynski's capture and incarceration. As Hamlet might have put it, Ted Kaczynski was hoist by his own petard, which translated into modern English means that the bomb maker was blown up by his own bomb.

Fortunately, most books and their authors abide by the same rule that guides physicians: first, do no harm. That goes for archeologists, historians, and students of literature and harmless things like that. They mean to do the right thing; but the Ted Kaczynskis of this world should not underestimate their impact.

■ ■ ■ THE POWER OF THE PRESS

Humanists have dangerous minds, and they are also as heavily involved in technology as scientists and engineers and even mathematicians like the Unabomber himself. That's because writing is technology.

The texts that writers write are the products of machinery: pencils, pens, typewriters, and now computers. And it is not just the writing of these books, but also the technology of their dissemination that can spark trouble. The machinery of publishing includes writing on clay, carving in stone, and copying manuscripts by hand onto paper, parchment, vellum, papyrus, bamboo, or silk. In the age of mechanical reproduction, the printing press, the typewriter, and the mimeograph reproduced reading matter in quantities that scribes could never match, and now, in the digital age, computers serve to compose and disseminate both wired and wireless text in ways that are revising the definitions of *reader* and *writer*.

These technologies of the word are never neutral. At the very least they limit who in a given society gets to write and read. The technologies are always exclusive at the outset, because they are both expensive to acquire and difficult to use. They may facilitate the mass production of text, but they don't always put that text in the hands of the masses.

At their most powerful, the technologies of literacy control not just who can read and write, but also what can and can't be said. Civil and religious authorities alike insist on their imprimatur—literally, their permission to print—to license and censor writing, to direct it toward politically or spiritually desirable ends.

Today it's a given in American society that literacy is a universal good, that reading and writing are essential for good citizenship, not to mention economic success, and in many parts of the world literacy has come to separate the haves from the have-nots as effectively as money or land does. Whether it's an opposition between those who can read the stone tablets and those who have to have the inscriptions read to them, or between those who write letters and those who must pay someone else to write for them, access to the mysteries of the written word is reserved for people who can manipulate its technologies—wielding the pen, reading the scroll, keyboarding and uploading the prose.

The literacy divide between those who possess the written word and those who don't is minimized as literacy levels rise, but oddly enough some present-day opponents of technology object to reading and writing, which most people are inclined to think of as essential skills, because these activities require technology.

Kirkpatrick Sale, the self-righteous smasher of computers, is no friend of the printing press either. Calling literacy a tool of industrialism, Sale blames the printing press for the destruction of the European forests as the West became ever hungrier for paper. Asked in a face-to-face interview whether the alternative—less paper and less to read—would really have been preferable, Sale, a contributing editor to the *Nation* and the author of a dozen books of nonfiction and poetry, responded without a single beat of ironic self-reflection that literacy, a product of the industrial revolution, led to the destruction of oral culture and there isn't much worth reading in any case (Kelly 1995).

As Sale's extreme position indicates, the machines and materials of literacy can inspire suspicion as well as veneration. In its day the printing press was a development that some people feared, as well as one that promised to edify an ever-growing readership. As an instrument of enlightenment, printing brought relatively cheap texts to increasingly literate populations. But book learning can also threaten the status quo, and political systems, whether ancient or modern, don't necessarily want their citizens educated beyond what the established authorities deem good for them. Alexander Pope may have warned, "A little learning is a dang'rous thing," but in some cases, a lot of knowledge—if it's not the authorized version—can prove more dangerous still.

The printing press offered writers a chance to reach a larger public at the same time that it provided governments with a means to control public access to information and to limit the spread of dangerous ideas. But controlling the printed word is always difficult. It doesn't take long for unlicensed books to evade the censor and get published, and fatwas against authors invariably backfire by increasing readership. As a result, authorities bent on controlling access to ideas may go beyond banning books and seek to punish the readers who read them. This is not a phenomenon restricted to autocratic regimes in the developing world. So prevalent are calls for removing books from libraries and classrooms in the United States that every year since 1982 the American Library Association, together with other library, journalism, and publishing groups, has cosponsored "Banned Book Week" during the last week in September—a chilling reminder that even in a democracy, the right to write and read requires constant vigilance.

▪ ▪ ▪ THE NEWEST AGENT OF CHANGE

Elizabeth Eisenstein (1980) called the printing press an agent of change, but Ted Kaczynski was thinking about the computer, not the printing press, when he picked the targets for his teknofear campaign; for the computer has become the new agent of change in the world, the source of the technological revolution that so troubled the Unabomber. The computer can reach further than the printing press, vastly increasing readership while sidestepping the controls of conventional publication: text can be uploaded to the internet without government licensing and oversight (in most parts of the world), bypassing editorial judgment, peer review, or fact-checking, even avoiding so basic a publishing process as copyediting. The internet is a true electronic frontier where everyone is on his or her own: all manuscripts are accepted for publication, they remain in virtual print forever, and no one can tell writers what to do.

Governments seek to regulate access to the internet and to control its content, which can be on one hand educational, enlivening, and enlightening, and on the other hand politically, morally, and economically destabilizing. But controlling so unwieldy a phenomenon as the World Wide Web isn't easy to do. As a result, computers have the potential to create exactly the kind of anarchy that Kaczynski calls for in his Unabomber Manifesto, but because the internet is technology based, and technology is by Kaczynski's definition an instrument of mind control, it's an anarchy that the Unabomber cannot approve of. It is ironic, then, that his manifesto is widely available online, where he himself has become something of a populist, antiestablishment icon. In cyberspace, Kaczynski's ideas can reach readers who find them sympathetic, as well as those who see them as evil or simply crackpot. Kaczynski fascinates those neo-Luddites who have carved out a space of their own within the technology they oppose.

▪ ▪ ▪ RAGE AGAINST THE MACHINE

The intense rejection of technology by the likes of Zerzan, Sale, and Kaczynski is certainly not a new phenomenon, and the fear of mechanization prompts both actual and mythical rage against machinery. For the Unabomber, and perhaps for others as well, the target of that rage is sometimes the people who are seen as technologically complicit. At the start of the industrial revolution, bands of European workers rose up to protest working conditions, and in some cases they apparently wrecked the machines that they feared would throw them out of their jobs. In England these technology foes were called Luddites, after the weaver Ned Ludd, who may or may not have actually existed, and who may or may not have actually destroyed a loom.

Ned Ludd, sometimes called Captain, General, or even King Ludd (or Lud), is supposed to have taken a sledgehammer to his loom sometime in the 1790s. He did this because he found the increasing mechanization of the art of weaving alienating, or possibly because the machine threatened his livelihood. One version of the story has it that Ludd broke his loom in a fit of pique because it wasn't doing what he wanted it to do—a response with which those of us who have dealt with recalcitrant computers might sympathize.

Stories have Ludd doing either more or less mechanical damage, at a variety of times or locations in the English midlands. But whatever Ludd may have done grew in the retelling until it reached the stature of a heroic act of worker resistance. One man's destruction of machinery that was perceived as displacing workers came to be celebrated in ballads, stories, and poems, and twenty years after Ludd's name first began to garner fame, the Luddites took up their namesake's rage against the automated loom. Like Ludd, they were weavers in and around Nottinghamshire, and they feared that the increasing mechanization of the textile industry was costing them not so much their artistry as their jobs. From 1811 to 1813, these workers sporadically attacked the new textile mills, wrecking some of the stocking frames and mechanical looms that were replacing hand weaving.

The Luddite rebellions were disorganized, unfocused, and ultimately ineffective, but they produced a strong response from the British government. In 1812 a group of Luddites was shot down by government forces, and the following year there was a widely publicized trial after which many Luddites were either hanged or transported. The Luddite rebellions fizzled out as the British economy improved and jobs became more plentiful, but Luddism—never a coherent doctrine but rather an agglomeration of objections to technologically mediated economic change—came to be romanticized as a grassroots, anarchic resistance to modernization, a last-ditch defense of handicraft against mechanical production. The name Luddite came to signal stubborn resistance to inexorable progress.

In nineteenth-century France the technology fighters—many of them also weavers—became saboteurs, a name that suggests its origin in the wooden shoes, or sabots, worn by the working classes. One story has it that in 1831, rioting silk workers in Lyon threw their sabots into the mechanized looms to shut them down. Although the Lyon silk revolt resulted in more than 160 deaths among workers, and the militia was called in to restore order, the sabot story is not confirmed in the more detailed histories of the rebellion. A competing account, and perhaps a more accurate one, has disgruntled French railway strikers in 1910 cutting the sabots, shoelike clamps holding the tracks in place, and the *Oxford English Dictionary* locates the first English use of *sabotage* in that year, in reference to these same strikes. The website of Book It, the Pizza Hut literacy program popular with American school children because they earn free pizzas for reading books, conflates the English and French sabotage myths, reporting them not as mythic milestones in the development of technology or the first rumblings of worker resistance, but as a "fun fact about clothing and accessories" that the English Luddites wrecked looms with their wooden shoes (www.bookitprogram.com). Not everything on the web or on the page is necessarily accurate.

Whatever its origins, sabotage in response to economic or technological development remains rare but prominent today: environmental activists in the American Southwest burn down new housing developments and attack SUV dealerships; animal rights supporters trash research laboratories; and opponents of globalism disrupt economic summits. By the 1990s, the neo-Luddite target had become computers, not mechanized looms, although most modern followers of Ludd or Kaczynski are less demonstrative, wrecking neither machinery nor lives, but contenting themselves instead with complaints about the impact that computers have on contemporary life, or simply unplugging their machines.

▪ ▪ ▪ DON'T TRY THIS AT HOME

Using the technology of the mass media helped Ted Kaczynski get his words before the public, and it helped catch him as well. But the Unabomber could not have carried out his antitechnology campaign without the technology of bomb making. True, his devices were homemade, the product of an individual craftsman, not a munitions factory. But all nonmilitary bombs are either homemade or stolen, and it would be difficult to argue that one goal of the do-it-yourself bomber is to restore craft, artistry, and human dignity to the manufacture of explosives.

The Unabomber took home bomb making to the extreme, preferring to fashion his own components out of scraps of metal and wire rather than using easy-to-find, mass-produced, and untraceable parts from hardware or electronics stores. Kaczynski encased his bomb components in wooden boxes whose parts he cut, sanded, and fit together. His sense that handmade is better than store-bought is common among those who are suspicious of technologies. Kaczynski ignored the fact that *manufactured* literally means *handmade*, but more important, he forgot that handmade is also technological, that explosive devices, no matter how lovingly crafted, are machines for blowing up people. .

Although Ned Ludd's loom breaking was well-publicized, we don't know if he was actually much of a weaver. It is also fair to argue, despite the objections of the first Luddites, that mechanized looms produced better stockings, not just cheaper ones. As far as the quality of the Unabomber's work goes, we know that it was uneven. Some of his early bombs misfired because, though he had a Ph.D. in mathematics, he was an indifferent engineer. One expert who examined the completed device and the many bomb parts found in Kaczynski's shack when he was arrested reported that Kaczynski's craftsmanship was not of the highest quality either:

He polished and sometimes varnished his wood pieces, but it was clear, from the skewed corners and amateurish joints, that he was not a trained woodworker. "He's not a craftsman," Don Davis, a top postal inspector in San Francisco, said months ago. "His cuts aren't straight. They don't make right angles. He spends a lot of time; he does a lot of polishing and sanding to make it feel nice; but they don't look really craftsmanlike." (Gibbs 1996)

Both the dwelling that he built for himself and Kaczynski's handmade wooden bomb-casings left a lot to be desired. Although wood had come to symbolize for Kaczynski the superiority of natural materials worked by hand (he once targeted a victim named Wood to push home this point), even worse for his reputation as a back-to-basics, throw-away-your-power-tools kind of guy, the Unabomber's joinery was actually pretty sloppy stuff.

Not that it's any consolation for his victims or their families, but Ted Kaczynski's woodworking couldn't have been much worse than his prose. The Unabomber's writing style is wooden, plaintive, droning, and clumsy, and his argumentation is unfocused, repetitive, and not particularly sophisticated. To put it mildly, despite the fact that Kaczynski had among his possessions a copy of Strunk and White's *Elements of Style*, which stresses the need for brevity and clarity, his manifesto is not a page-turner (Perrone 2005). Here's one example: with regard to the overzealous, technophilic belief that science will cure all the ills of the world, Kaczynski can only manage the schoolyard retort, "Yeah, sure" (par. 170). Concisely put, to be sure, but this is not Tom Paine, not Karl Marx. Ted Kaczynski—a.k.a. the Unabomber—may have proclaimed himself a terrorist in the war against technology, but the man proved more dangerous than his words, and his is not the manifesto on which to build a revolution.

▪ ▪ ▪ REVERSING THE DIGITAL WAVE

As part of the plea agreement with the federal government, the evidence against the Unabomber, including his journals, was suppressed. Those journals might shed more light on the reasons why Kaczynski hated technology so passionately. Despite its length, his manifesto is fairly unhelpful on that subject, not going much beyond blanket claims that technology is incompatible with freedom, that good technologies don't offset bad technologies, and that, in a sort of Zen of bombing, only by completely disrupting the industrial-technological complex can balance be restored to the world. In his manifesto,

Kaczynski equates technology with mind control, accuses scientists and computer engineers of belonging to the power elite, and predicts that the government will soon start regulating the genetic constitution of children.

In his letter to the *Times*, the Unabomber would have the public believe that his attacks were indeed selective, that he specifically targeted computer scientists and behavioral psychologists for elimination. But if machines were a disaster in Kaczynski's eyes, life for him was cheap. He claimed that the killing of a business professor with one of the bombs had been a mistake—though Kaczynski insisted that it was a mistake worth making for the good of the larger cause. It was only by killing people, Kaczynski explained in his manifesto, that he was able to attract enough attention to get his anticomputer message before the public.

And yet, despite his monstrous acts and patent insanity, there are Kaczynski fans out there in cyberspace who come back time and again to the fact that he made his own bombs and wrote his own manifesto, as if these feats of self-sufficiency put him in a league with Henry David Thoreau, who also adopted an antiestablishment pose and did time both in a homemade cabin in the woods and in jail (in a well-known act of civil disobedience, Thoreau briefly went to jail for refusing to pay taxes to support what he considered the unjust Mexican War).

Do-it-yourself may be a challenging, more satisfying, possibly less alienating method of getting the goods than off-the-shelf, if it goes right. That explains why Home Depot is always so crowded. But in the end, as many bombers whose products detonate prematurely find out, not all wheels are worth reinventing, and not all DIY projects are worth doing yourself.

■ ■ ■ LUDDITES ON LINE

The opening message on the Luddites on Line website (the URL of the now defunct site was www.luddites.com) once read, "Welcome to the only place in cyberspace devoted exclusively to Luddites, technophobes and other refugees from the Information Revolution." In a twist that seems not to have been fully appreciated by the Luddites on Line webmaster, the site boasted that on May Day, 1996—the day celebrating the revolution of the working classes worldwide—luddites.com was selected by Yahoo or some other search engine as an internet "Cool Site of the Day." But while the internet continues to thrive, Luddites on Line has vanished.

Most of the neo-Luddite sites that do survive are content to launch sarcastic attacks against computers, or to yearn for the good old days when the pencil was king. The Unabomber went beyond this brand of cultural criticism, signaling a return to the anarchic violence of the early Luddites, and although today Ted Kaczynski might well have chosen the blog rather than the bomb as a way of promoting his ideas, his acts of terrorism did get our attention; and his letter, his manifesto, and his story found homes both in print outlets and in cyberspace.

Unfortunately, many technologically savvy people downplay his criminal behavior, or explain it away as the product of a troubled childhood or bad experiences at Harvard, only to focus sympathetically on his claim that technology and industrialism are inimical to human freedom. A lot of the internet chatter about Kaczynski's writing takes the position, "Hey, the guy's got a point; our lives are run by machines." According to the online Luddite Kirkpatrick Sale (1995), the Unabomber's assessment of the industrial-technological complex as disastrous should become a national priority. While Sale acknowledges that killing is not a good thing, he nonetheless condones violence when it is directed not at people but at things—hence his own gratuitous Town Hall display of computer smashing.

But murder is even more inimical to human freedom than machinery is. Opponents of technology rarely mention the true impact of Kaczynski's teknofear: the killing, the hands and eyes blown away, the terror that people may still feel—even people in no way connected to the Unabomber's attacks—when unmarked packages show up in the mail. The unstoppable Frankenstein or Terminator notwithstanding, we will always have more to fear from the all-too-real, all-too-crazed kitchen bomb makers than from the imaginary cyborgs whose deadliness is the product of Hollywood dream factory computers.

However, none of this explains why some people see technology as the beginning of the end and decide that they must take strong measures to oppose it. It is clear that technology has negative as well as positive impact, some of it planned and much of it inadvertent. Just about all of human activity has unintended consequences, and it takes a great deal of vigilance, planning, and sometimes legal or even extralegal action to clean up the messes we insist on making—the bans on DDT and asbestos are two examples; nuclear weapons treaties and massive BSE testing to eliminate mad cow are two others.

These "Silent Spring" disasters waiting to happen have spurred some of us to imagine that scientific nightmares are lurking everywhere, that every lab and every computer sits poised to push us toward the abyss. But genetic engineering has not produced what its opponents call Frankenfood—at least not yet. And more to the point, although Mary Shelley wrote *Frankenstein* by hand, and Ted Kaczynski wrote his ramblings by hand as well, the impact of these two undeniably technological artifacts has been different. *Frankenstein* became a cultural emblem while "Industrial Society and Its Future," the actual title of the Unabomber Manifesto, is destined to be little more than a footnote in Kaczynski's brief reign of terror. And despite the fact that computers and other new communication technologies are dramatically changing the ways we do things with words, from the early experiments in computer-generated poetry to the emails, blogs, and instant messages that pervade our personal and professional lives, digital machines have not yet produced anything that remotely resembles Frankentext. Still, nostalgia for the old ways won't go away, and, as the next chapter shows, voices continue to proclaim the superiority of the pencil to the pixel.

3

■ ■ ■ Thoreau's Pencil

One defender of the pencil against the encroaching computer is Bill Henderson. Henderson is no countercultural terrorist hermit like Ted Kaczynski. He is a mainstream literary figure, director of the Pushcart Press, which showcases some of the best American contemporary short stories, essays, and poems. Yet Henderson has a problem with technology: he doesn't like computers. In 1993 Henderson founded the Lead Pencil Club, a place where like-minded people could express their dislike of the new technology and celebrate the good old ways of writing.

Looking for literary precedents to support his anticomputer stand, Henderson applauds the fact that in the very first chapter of *Walden*, Henry David Thoreau disparaged the information superhighway of his day, a telegraph line connecting Maine to Texas. As Thoreau put it, "Maine and Texas, it may be, have nothing important to communicate" (1849). To top it off, Henderson boasts, Thoreau wrote his antitechnology remarks with a pencil that he made himself (Henderson 1994).

Most people don't want to smash computers. And they don't go to the other extreme of putting them on refrigerators. They simply accept computers for what they can do, which is a lot, and grumble or panic when they break down, which is often. Others, like Henderson, wax nostalgic for pencils, or see romance in the quill pen. Not too many people miss writing on clay tablets. Not all the old ways are good ways.

The pencil may be old—the first pencils appeared in Europe in the sixteenth century—but like the computer today and the telegraph in 1849, the pencil is a communication technology. Bill Henderson concedes as much when he adds that Thoreau's father founded "the first quality pencil [factory] in America."

Samuel F. B. Morse, the developer of the telegraph, was lucky that Thoreau was no Ted Kaczynski. The only letter bombs Thoreau sent from his cabin on Walden Pond were literary ones. Kaczynski built his cabin in Montana to get as far away from neighbors as possible. But Thoreau's Walden getaway was just a stone's throw from his home in Concord, and he left his cabin frequently to dine with the Emersons nearby. Nor was Thoreau the complete Luddite that Bill Henderson would have us believe. He was, instead, an engineer, and although Thoreau went to the woods to get back to the simple life, while he was there he behaved like an engineer as well as a philosopher, surveying, mapping, and sounding Walden Pond by day, exposing human folly and speculating on the meaning of life at night.

Moreover, Thoreau didn't make pencils because he considered them simpler than telegraphs, or because he was old-fashioned. Rather, Thoreau designed pencils for a living: when he wasn't vacationing at Walden, pencils were his day job, one he took seriously. Instead of waxing nostalgic about a golden age when pencils consisted of little more than a lump of graphite on a stick, Thoreau sought to improve the wood-cased pencil of his own day by developing a cutting-edge manufacturing technology. And he did so because he needed the money.

In Thoreau's America, a good pencil was hard to find, and until Thoreau's father and uncle began making pencils in the New World, the best ones were imported from Europe, where their manufacture was a proprietary secret as closely guarded as any Microsoft computer code. The Thoreau family money came from the earnings of their pencil company, and Henry Thoreau not only supported his trip to the Maine woods and his sojourn at Walden Pond with pencil sales, he himself perfected some of the techniques of pencil making that made Thoreau pencils profitable best sellers.

The wood pencil may seem a simple device in contrast to the computer, but although it doesn't use electricity and has no moving parts, it too is an advanced technology. The common No. 2 pencil represents a subtle complexity dressed in apparent simplicity. According to Henry Petroski (1990), an engineer who has written the definitive history of pencil making, the wood-cased pencil is a paradigm of the engineering process. Petroski writes that a pencil builder needs to solve two essential problems: blending graphite and clay so that the "lead" is neither too soft nor too brittle, and getting that lead into the wood case so that it doesn't break when a writer sharpens the point or presses down on paper to write with it.

As Petroski explains, pencil technologies involve advanced design and manufacturing techniques: powdering the graphite, mixing it with various clays, baking and curing the mixture, extruding it to form the "lead," and preparing and finishing the wood casings. To do this requires a knowledge of dyes, shellacs, resins, clamps, solvents, paints, woods, rubber, glue, ink, waxes, lacquer, cotton, drying equipment, high-temperature furnaces, abrasives, and mixing (Petroski 1990, 12). These are not simple matters. A pencil enthusiast can't just go out to the garage workshop—or a cabin in the woods—and make a pencil.

Frank Remington (1957) reports that to produce the modern wood pencil requires 40 different materials and 125 different production steps. Remington estimated that it would cost a 1950s do-it-yourselfer more than $50 to craft that pencil. That's $447.30 in 2008 dollars (minneapolisfed.org/index.cfm). Not only that, but Thoreau's pencils weren't exactly cheap. Pencils were more expensive commodities in the 1840s than they are now, and Thoreau pencils, among the most expensive at the time, went for 75 cents a dozen, or 6.25 cents apiece. That comes to $2 a pop in 2008 dollars. In Thoreau's day, a single Thoreau No. 2 could go for as much as 25 cents, a price that Ralph Waldo Emerson found high (it's about $8 today), though he still endorsed his friend's product. A recent online price check showed Staples selling No. 2 wood pencils for as little as 3.9 cents each, proof, if we need it, that pencils, like computers, get cheaper over time.

▪ ▪ ▪ THOREAU AND PENCIL TECHNOLOGY

It is true that Thoreau, who was a philosopher as well as an engineer and businessman, rejected modern improvements like the telegraph as worthless illusions. In *Walden* he calls them "pretty toys," merely "improved means to an unimproved end" (Thoreau 1849). But as Petroski points out, Thoreau didn't have much to say about pencils. He even omitted them from the list of items that he took into the Maine woods, though Emerson remarks that Thoreau never went anywhere without notebook and pencil, so it's likely that Thoreau carried a pencil on his twelve-day excursion in order to record his thoughts (Petroski 1990, 4). Despite his own silence on the subject of pencils, Thoreau devoted ten years of his life to improving pencil technology at his family's pencil factory.

In one of his most famous essays, Emerson argued for self-reliance. Thoreau practiced self-reliance not just by building a cabin at Walden Pond, but also by building a better pencil. As Petroski tells it, the pencil industry in the nineteenth century was buffeted by such vagaries as the unpredictable supply of graphite, dwindling cedar forests (cedar proved the best wood for pencil casings), protective tariffs, and, for much of its history, an international consumer preference for British-made pencils. All of this affected John Thoreau and Co., manufacturers of pencils. Until the nineteenth century, the best pencil graphite (called plumbago, from the Latin, "to act like lead") came from

Borrowdale, in the Cumberland Valley in England. There were other graphite deposits around the world, but no other ore was as pure as Borrowdale's. Impure graphite crumbled or produced a scratchy line. In the later eighteenth century, the Borrowdale graphite deposits began to run low, and exports were curtailed. After the French Revolution, with his supply of English graphite embargoed, the French pencil maker Nicholas-Jacques Conté learned to produce a workable writing medium by grinding domestic graphite, mixing it with clay and water, and forcing the mixture into wooden casings which were then baked to harden the lead (this account of pencil history draws largely on Petroski 1990).

This process allowed the French to produce their own pencils instead of importing them, and it also permitted manufacturers to control the hardness of the lead, which in turn controlled the darkness of the mark made by the pencil. The more clay, the harder the lead, and the lighter and crisper the mark; less clay in the mix produces a softer lead, which in turn gives a darker, grainier line. So successful was Conté's process that the name Conté became synonymous with pencil, and Conté crayons are still valued by artists. In Nuremberg, Staedtler mixed ground graphite with sulfur. He and rival pencil maker Faber eventually experimented with more effective clay and graphite mixtures, as Conté had, and like Conté, their names are still found on pencils made today.

The superiority of Borrowdale graphite was evident to American consumers, who regularly preferred the English imports that used pieces of pure plumbago to domestic brands, whose low-quality graphite had to be ground and mixed with bayberry wax, glue, or other binders. In 1821 Charles Dunbar discovered a deposit of reasonably good plumbago in Bristol, New Hampshire, and he and his brother-in-law, John Thoreau, went into the pencil business in Concord, Massachusetts. By 1824 Thoreau pencils were winning recognition. Their graphite, while better than most of the local ore, was not as pure as Borrowdale, and since the Conté process was unknown in the United States, American pencils, though cheaper than imports, remained inferior (Petroski 1990, 108–9).

Henry Thoreau set about to remedy this deficiency, to put American pencils first in the hearts of American consumers. Thoreau began his research in the Harvard Library, but then, as now, there was little written on pencil manufacture. William Munroe also made pencils in Concord, and Thoreau knew the importance of keeping industrial secrets from the competition. So while he described in minute detail how much he spent to outfit his Walden cabin, Thoreau never revealed what he learned from his reading about pencil making, or what he figured out through trial and error and his own intuition (Petroski 1990, 111–13).

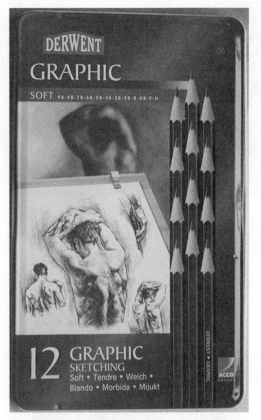

Although the original Borrowdale mine closed in
1890, the British art supply company Derwent
still makes a high-end line of art pencils using
Cumberland Valley graphite. An ad for the pencils
reads, "Experience the exquisitely smooth flow
of fine graphite from the Cumberland Valley in
England. Derwent's Graphic Pencils are made
from the finest quality graphite and purest clays
for a smooth line. They are ideal for crisp, detailed
illustrations or tone drawings." Derwent also
sells chunks of natural graphite for sketching.
Photograph by the author.

We do know some of the changes Thoreau introduced. He designed a
grinder that used puffs of air to separate out the finest graphite powder (Petroski 1990, 114). He then mixed this pure graphite not with wax but with
clay, like Conté. Thoreau also experimented with pencil casings, though this
endeavor was less successful. Most pencil makers still use a traditional two-
piece wood casing. They place the extruded lead between two grooved cedar

Top of a box of John Thoreau & Co. drawing pencils. From
the Walter Harding Collection (Thoreau Society Collections),
courtesy of the Thoreau Society and the Thoreau Institute at
Walden Woods.

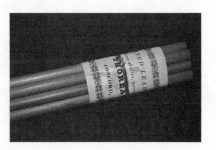

A packet of Thoreau pencils. From
the Walden Woods Project Collection,
courtesy of the Thoreau Institute at
Walden Woods.

strips and glue the halves together. There is a story that Thoreau invented
a long, thin drill so that the hardened graphite and clay mixture could be
inserted directly into one-piece wood casings, but it's not clear that the Tho-
reaus switched to this difficult method of getting the lead into the wood.
In any case, Thoreau's improvements, combined with the high import duty
that America imposed on British pencils after the War of 1812, led to great
demand for Thoreau-brand pencils.

Nostalgists frequently claim that the old ways were better because they
were more natural. While the members of the Lead Pencil Club fetishize the
pencil as "responding directly to the mind" (Henderson 1997), Thoreau did
not ascribe transcendent value to pencils. As Petroski sees it, Thoreau's goal

was simply to make money. Once he developed the best pencil of his day, Thoreau actually claimed that he saw no sense in trying to improve on his design (Petroski 1990, 122).

It is easy for us to think of Thoreau only as a romantic who lived deliberately, disobeyed civil authority when he thought it wrong, and single-handedly turned Walden Pond into a national historic site (it's actually a Massachusetts state reservation). But Thoreau underwrote these activities by deploying his expertise as an engineer and marketing expert. Even though his pencils were the best, Thoreau acknowledged that he couldn't compete with new German imports from Faber, who made reasonably good pencils for a lot less money. As pencil competition grew, shaving his profit margin, Thoreau stopped pushing pencils and began selling his graphite wholesale to electrotypers because this proved more lucrative. But he also kept making small quantities of pencils just to hide from his competitors the fact that the main focus of his business had shifted (Petroski 1990, 122).

A cynic might say that Thoreau, despite his own technological expertise, belittled Morse's telegraph because he thought that it would threaten the family business. It is more likely, though, from the absence of references to pencil making in any of his writings, that Thoreau honestly thought pencils were better for writing than electrical impulses, and he simply kept his business life and his literary life in separate compartments. In any case, Thoreau's resistance to the telegraph didn't stop that project. Nor have the new developments in communication—the telegraph, the telephone, the typewriter, and the computer—dampened the demand for pencils. Faber-Castell, the largest of the world's major pencil producers, makes more than two billion pencils a year (www.faber-castell.de/17199/The-Company/The-Company-of-today/Facts-and-Figures/index_ebene3.aspx). That should be good news for the Lead Pencil Club.

▪ ▪ ▪ THE FIRST LAPTOP

One story surrounding the development of pencil technology asserts that the first use of graphite, or wad, as it was called in the Borrowdale area of Cumberland where it was first discovered in the mid-sixteenth century, was to mark sheep. Even if this is true, the earliest commercial use of graphite was not for writing, but for cannon ball molds. Even so, it was also immediately apparent that graphite was good for making marks that were both highly visible and easily erased. It was probably woodworkers and not shepherds or armorers who were the first to put graphite into holders for easier use. For one thing, woodworkers had the know-how and the tools to create these early pencils (see, for example, Petroski 1990, 60). They also had an incentive: the pencil made it much easier to mark wood for cutting, drilling, and joining. Before the pencil, cabinet makers scratched cut marks into wood with an awl or knife. But these techniques, which some still use today, leave an indentation in the wood that has to be removed from finished surfaces. Pencil marks don't mar the wood, and they are easily erased with rubbing or light sanding (sanding is preferable since erasers tend to smear the mark, which is why carpenter's pencils don't come with erasers).

Even if cabinet makers did develop pencils primarily for their own use, it was obvious that the pencil was an important writing tool, and it quickly became the first laptop. This portable, self-contained writing instrument let writers get up from their desks and work anywhere without having to carry messy ink bottles, which were always prone to spilling or drying out, and a supply of goose feathers. Travelers didn't have to take cumbersome travel desks with them if they wanted to write on a hillside or at an inn. Artists— who were still mixing their own pigments—could leave their bulky paint boxes, their brushes, and their turpentine in the studio and still be able to sketch wherever they happened to be. And pencils quickly found a home in classrooms as well.

The Borrowdale graphite discovery probably occurred sometime between 1550 and 1560, and in just a few years, naturalists and artists were using pencils in the field. As Petroski reports, the first picture of a modern pencil appears in a book on fossils, gems, and a whole lot else, written by the encyclopedist Konrad Gesner (1565). The graphite holder in the illustration has a knob at one end, allowing it to be tied to a notebook, a further convenience for the pencil's "end users."

The enthusiastic reception that the first pencils enjoyed in turn prompted pencil makers to find better ways of packaging graphite to meet the demand for more and better pencils. Placing the graphite into a wood case seemed the best way to go for several centuries: when this was done well—and it was often a technological challenge—the wood kept the brittle graphite from shattering or breaking off and minimized graphite stains on writers' fingers or clothes.

Shaving the wood to expose the graphite and sharpen its point was not a big obstacle for writers already used to pointing their quills with pen knives (the steel pen did not come into wide use until 1830, when mass production of steel nibs began in England). And while the pen had to be dipped into ink every few words, slowing down the writer and interrupting the flow of ideas, a pencil could run for pages on a single pointing. Not only were pencils more convenient than pens, they also made writing faster.

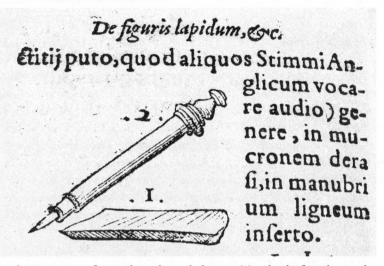

De figuris lapidum, &c.

&titij puto, quod aliquos Stimmi Anglicum voca-
re audio) ge-
nere, in mu-
cronem dera
fi, in manubri
um ligneum
inferto.

First known picture of a wood-cased pencil, showing (1) a chunk of graphite, and (2) a complete pencil consisting of pointed graphite inserted into the wooden handle or holder. Gesner writes, "Stylus inferius depictus, ad scribendum factus est, plumbi cuiusdam (factitii puto, quod aliquos Stimmi Anglicum vocare audio) genere in mucronem derasi, in manubrium ligneum inserto" [The stylus depicted below is made for writing, out of some kind of lead (which I have heard some call English antinomy), shaved to a point, inserted in a wooden handle] (Gesner 1565). Photograph by the author and used courtesy of the Rare Books and Special Collections Library, University of Illinois at Urbana-Champaign Library.

Computers are often credited with speeding up writing as well, to the point where critics actually fault the computer for making writing too easy. Seduced by speed, these critics warn, writers may pay less attention to what they are doing, and writing quality deteriorates. Perhaps early adherents of the older ways of penmanship complained that the newfangled pencil made writing too fast and was leading to a similar decline in prose, but if they did, none of those complaints has managed to survive. In fact, the pencil may be the one writing technology that has never been openly attacked by advocates of the good old ways.

In the twentieth century, pencil makers, seeking to distinguish their pencils as better than competing brands, not to mention other popular writing instruments such as fountain pens and ballpoints, boasted of their product's word-processing capacity. Eagle's Mirado pencil could write a line thirty-five miles long (Petroski 1990, 310; presumably individual mileage may vary). This sounds impressive but is hard to visualize, so Faber framed its claim in the more familiar terms of unit cost: their Mongol pencil was good for 2,162 words per penny (Petroski 1990, 304).

The pencil is even faring well in the age of the computer. It is true that the computer is establishing a strong presence in test taking, long the home of the ubiquitous No. 2 pencil, and even though the GRE, GMAT, Praxis, TOEFL, and other common standardized tests are abandoning pencils for computers, according to pencil maker Dixon Ticonderoga, pencil sales are up. While the company won't disclose exact figures—secrecy is still the rule in the pencil industry—they claim to make "nearly half a billion [Ticonderoga] pencils a year" (http://dixonusa.com/index.cfm/fuseaction=Ticonderoga.home). Not shy about product placement, the company boasts that the artist Norman Rockwell sketched with Dixon pencils (omitting the salient fact that Dixon commissioned Rockwell to paint pictures for the company) and that George Lucas drafted the first episode of *Star Wars* with a classic yellow Dixon Ticonderoga No. 2 (Obejas 1999).

Joseph Dixon, the company's founder, made his first pencil in 1829 in Salem, Massachusetts. Petroski (1990, 107) notes that Dixon may have taught Thoreau's father the pencil-making craft. But Dixon focused his business not on pencils but on other graphite products, and the company didn't really become a player on the American pencil scene until after the Civil War. Today Dixon's mission statement, which could double as a motto for the Lead Pencil Club, implies that its pencils, pens, markers, and crayons are superior to computers because they are a natural, effective, even transcendental means of expression:

> More than a writing and art products company, Dixon Ticonderoga
> is a company that empowers people to take conscious and subliminal
> thoughts—facts, ideas and dreams—and preserve them using tools
> that are simply extensions of themselves. (dixonusa.com/index.cfm/
> fuseaction=about.home)

▪ ▪ ▪ ERASERHEAD

The computer has changed drastically in the past twenty years. Computers from the 1980s, like the IBM 8088 that I started with, are now museum pieces. Even if they still work, they're useless for today's storage- and speed-hungry applications. Pencils have changed too, though much more slowly. The pencil assumed its modern form in the eighteenth century: a rod of graphite encased in wood. Since then, technological changes to the pencil have been important but subtle. Better compounds ensured better lead consistency, fewer broken points, and more uniform grading of pencils from hard to soft. Improvements in preparing and gluing woods made pencils easier to sharpen. Finishing techniques created brand identity through distinctive colors and markings. As we learned from Thoreau's experience, branding is important to pencil manufacturers, though aside from Norman Rockwell and George Lucas most writers probably don't notice what kind of pencil they pick up. But there was one major change to the modern wood pencil that everybody noticed. In the mid-nineteenth century, American manufacturers learned to attach the eraser to one end of the pencil using a brass ferrule or socket (officemuseum.com/pencil_history.htm).

One of the advantages that pencils had over pens was that pencil marks could be erased. Erasers became popular in the late eighteenth century as West Indian gum elastic, or India rubber, reached Europe. In fact that substance, actually the resin of ficus or hevea plants, was called "rubber" because of its ability to rub out pencil marks. Erasers were sold as separate cubes, and people carried them along with their pencils. The one-piece American pencil, with point on one end and eraser on the other, was initially greeted with suspicion, in part because only low-quality pencils first sported built-in erasers, but also because critics charged that erasers would adversely affect the quality of writing.

Plato warned his fellow Athenians 2,500 years ago that the new technology of writing would weaken human memory. But after millennia spent writing things down, people still keep vast quantities of information in their heads, not just the data, formulas, and procedures they need for work and school, but also song lyrics, sports statistics, jokes, phone numbers, family stories, and assorted strings of trivia.

Nonetheless, we still fear that new communication technologies will sap our intellectual strength. Just a few years ago, math teachers complained that if students were allowed to use calculators, they'd never learn to add and subtract without resorting to technological help. The first calculators (expensive items, to be sure) were banned from classrooms. But now calculators are inexpensive—some are almost as cheap as mechanical pencils—and they do much more. Many math teachers now require them, and they've become must-use tools on standardized tests such as the SAT and ACT.

About the same time that schools began encouraging the purchase of the calculators they had once prohibited, my university introduced computers into writing classes. At the time, instructors hotly debated whether to tell students about the spell-check programs on their word processors. The fear was that if students knew about spell-checkers, they would become dependent on the technology and forget how to spell. The teachers decided to hide the spell-checker, but on the first day of the semester, the hackers in the class found the spell-checkers anyway, and the rest is history. Now writing teachers expect their students to spell-check before they turn in their papers.

Even the deceptively untechnological pencil became a victim of the wrath of educators who feared the impact of new technologies. For much of their history, American schools allowed no crossing out. Once students put pen or pencil to paper, there was no turning back. What pupils wrote was not just indelible, it was what they were graded on. The educational philosophy was "think before you write," an ideal that few students, or their teachers, ever achieved.

When the pencil with its own built-in eraser came on the scene, some teachers wanted to ban it from the classroom, arguing that students would do better, more premeditated writing if they didn't have the option of erasing and revising. The anti-eraser group argued that if the technology makes error correction easy, students will make more errors. Other teachers feared the impact of erasers not just on student cognition, but on student health as well: children might chew on the ends of the new eraser-equipped pencils even more than they already chewed on their all-wood pencils (Petroski 1990, 178–79).

Just as students won the battle of the calculator and the spell-checker, they won the short-lived school eraser wars. Nowadays it's hard to find a pencil without an eraser, particularly in the United States. Artists prefer eraserless pencils because they use many different grades of pencils and several different types of erasers in their work. Golfers also use pencils without erasers. There may be an issue of trust there. The only other place where crossing out, or at least self-correction, is not permitted today is the spelling bee, which is in itself a throwback to the good old days of American education: once a speller says a letter, it can't be taken back. Everywhere else, students, and writers in general, in fact just about everyone but golfers and spelling bee champs, are expected to erase, cross out, delete, and do their words over till they get them right.

In fact, writers depend so much on their erasers that they frequently throw away their pencils when the eraser wears down, long before they run out of graphite, for without an eraser, the pencil's usefulness seems gone. Writers have warmed to the computer as a composing tool because it permits infinite revision; digitized erasing doesn't wear out the paper or smudge the text, and no matter how many changes one makes, the revised text always looks like a finished product. Of course these advantages can also be drawbacks: with computers it's harder to compare multiple versions of the text, and clean copy may look like professional writing without actually being professional in its content.

Although the history of the pencil is a history of popular and technological successes (cheap pencils mean cheap access to writing tools) and the anticomputer crowd champions the pencil without considering its actual complexity, there is also a strong prejudice against pencils and pencil writing. For one thing, because they're inexpensive and ubiquitous, pencils are often overlooked and undervalued as cultural artifacts. Petroski observes that old tools, clothes, furniture, pots and pans, and other scraps of everyday life are often written about, preserved in museums or sold in antique shops. But old wood pencils are not. Even on eBay, where just about everything is on offer, a search for antique pencils comes up empty. In addition, because pencil marks are erasable, the myth has grown up that writing in pencil is like writing with vanishing ink. As a result, many people assume that pencils are only good for first drafts of documents, not final copies.

It's a common but mistaken assumption as well that checks, contracts, and other legal or official documents aren't valid if they're signed in pencil. Many pencil manufacturers stress that pencil documents and signatures are legal everywhere unless specifically prohibited, but despite these disclaimers on pencil makers' web pages, the universal preference for ink as a vehicle for "important" texts doesn't change. Even so, this antigraphite prejudice hasn't put a dent in pencil sales: more than 5 billion wood-cased, mechanical, and colored pencils were sold in the United States in 2007 (www.wima.org/industry/index.htm), and about 14 billion pencils are manufactured annually worldwide (www.readersdigest.com.au/discovery-channel-mag/history-of-the-pencil/article109024-1.html).

▪ ▪ ▪

Thoreau's complaint about the telegraph shows that even engineers can be suspicious of new technologies, and no one can safely predict the directions that technology will take. As Thoreau feared, the telegraph eventually did permit people in Maine and Texas and just about everywhere else to say nothing to one another, as well as to convey important information. In turn, Samuel F. B. Morse, who patented the telegraph and invented its code, saw no use for an even newer device, Alexander Graham Bell's telephone. Morse refused Bell's offer to sell him the rights to the telephone patent because he was convinced that no one would want an invention that was unable to provide any permanent record of a conversation. As these minutes from a Western Union meeting where investing in telephony was discussed make clear, others agreed that this was a problem:

> Bell's instrument uses nothing but the voice, which cannot be captured
> in concrete form. . . . We leave it to you to judge whether any sensible
> man would transact his affairs by such a means of communications. In
> conclusion the committee feels that it must advise against any investment
> whatever in Bell's scheme. (Minutes of a Western Union meeting, circa
> 1880, russell.whitworth.com/quotes.htm)

Many telegraphers were skeptical of the new voice competition, but their comments also reveal a deeply ingrained cultural bias that sees writing as more significant than speech. One of Thomas Edison's motivations for inventing the phonograph was to remedy this deficiency in the telephone, though sound recording succeeded not because it could preserve phone calls for posterity, but because of its potential for entertainment. As it turned out, despite the hesitation of some investors, the telephone was an almost instant success, in large part because it mimicked conversation, a communication form we use comfortably every day without written backup.

Whether computers will one day be as ubiquitous and as invisible as pencils, and as taken for granted, is an intriguing question. They are certainly becoming more important in offices than telephones, and the cell phone, the technology phenom of the 1990s, is trying to capture an even bigger share of the high-tech market by becoming more computer-like, letting callers surf the web and send written messages across the ether.

▪ ▪ ▪ WHAT WOULD THOREAU DO?

Ask most people what they mean by *technology* today and they are likely to reply that it has something to do with computers. Some may also complain that computers have taken over the workplace and the home. It's impossible to represent a contemporary office in film or on television without showing a computer on a desk. Computers are becoming common furniture in the home as well, to the point where their absence may already be more noticeable than their presence.

We have a way of getting so used to the technologies of writing that we come to think of them as natural rather than technological. We assume that pencils are a natural way to write because they are so old—even though they're actually newer than pens—because we have come to think of them as being old. We form Lead Pencil Clubs to revive the old ways, and we romanticize do-it-yourselfers who make their own writing equipment, and even their own paper, because, the Unabomber notwithstanding, *homemade* has come to mean "better than store-bought." And some of us believe manufacturers' claims that the pencil is an extension of the body and a gateway to the mind, though many of today's students, the first all-computer generation in the United States to reach college, actually think the keyboard, not pens or pencils, offers a hard-wired connection to their inner thoughts.

Despite the common tendency to romanticize the good old ways, Bill Henderson was wrong to place Thoreau among the antiquarians and nostalgics.

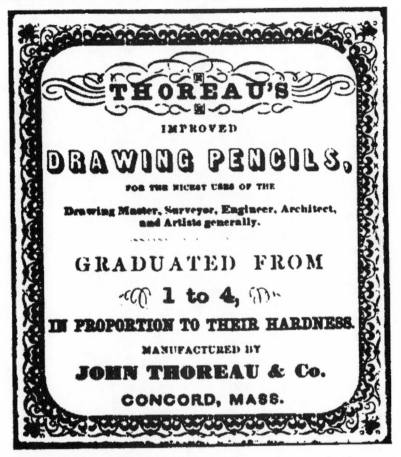

Thoreau, the great American idealist and iconoclast, was as concerned with branding, marketing, and the bottom line as any robber baron, captain of industry, or present-day Microsoft executive. From www.psymon.com; used by permission.

Considering his engineering know-how and his penchant for social criticism, I'm sure that were Thoreau alive today, he would not be writing to the *Times* with a pencil of his own manufacture. He had better business sense than that. More likely, he would be keyboarding his complaints about the information superhighway on a personal computer that he assembled from spare parts in his garage.

4

■ ■ ■   National Handwriting Day

Those who embrace new technologies of communication may do so gladly and never look back. But for many of today's writers, digital technologies exist alongside the older pencil and paper varieties. Even so, the importance of handwriting, the product of pen and pencil, seems to have declined significantly, to the point where schools debate whether to take children straight to keyboarding once they learn to print their letters and skip those tedious penmanship lessons of the past. But handwriting hasn't yet become a lost art, and it still inspires some reverence in our culture. The pencil and pen industry would like to capitalize on that by setting aside a special day to celebrate the art of handwriting.

January 23 is National Handwriting Day. Robert B. Waller, Jr., director of WIMA, the Writing Instrument Manufacturers Association, which has sponsored the event since the 1970s, urges writers to celebrate the occasion by taking a break from "the rigorous world of electronic communication" and writing "a good old-fashioned letter, complete with your penned signature." Waller is no Luddite—he made these remarks, after all, on WIMA's website, wima.org. But in reminding us that handwriting has a place in our communication practice, Waller echoes Bill Henderson's fear that new technologies like the computer tend to drive out older ones, like the pens and pencils made by writing instrument manufacturers. WIMA links National Handwriting Day with John Hancock's birthday (although Hancock was actually born on January 12, not the 23rd) since Hancock penned one of the most famous signatures ever on the Declaration of Independence.

According to Waller, handwriting is creative, artistic, and personal. Electronic communication, he implies, is just the opposite: "Nothing will ever replace the sincerity and individualism expressed through the handwritten word." The WIMA website tells us, "There's something poetic about grasping a writing instrument and feeling it hit the paper as your thoughts flow through your fingers and pour into words" (wima.org).

John Hancock's signature, detail from a facsimile of the
Declaration of Independence.

Sales figures for pens and pencils show that the old writing technologies
are thriving in the digital age, but as we pour more and more of our thoughts
into words, handwriting has fallen on hard times—and it's not just because no
one celebrates National Handwriting Day.

Waller is correct in supposing that computers have displaced other writing technologies for many people, not just those who visit WIMA on the
internet. But the frequently voiced fear that digital word machines have
eclipsed the good old days of handwriting obscures the fact that typewriters had already "signed" the death warrant of handwriting, particularly as
a business skill, early in the twentieth century. Those who want to revive
penmanship romanticize handwriting as more immediate and visceral than
keyboards. But such a view makes it easy for us to forget that pens, pencils,
and even handwriting itself are technologies too. If people actually used
pens and pencils only on special holidays or only to create writing that is
also fine art, then the writing instrument business would really be in serious
trouble. Instead, we're finding that writing by hand, the oldest of writing
technologies, retains an important if somewhat diminished place in the
digital age.

▪ ▪ ▪ ROMANCING THE QUILL

It used to be doctors who had bad handwriting, or at least that was the ste-
reotype. But now, if the increasingly common complaints are to be believed,
no one writes legibly anymore, and it's all the computer's fault. Even though
pencil and pen sales are on the rise, keyboards have become the preferred
mode of writing both in and out of the office, the classroom, and the home for
Americans, who are well on their way to forgetting how to write in longhand.
And that may not be a bad thing.

Illegibility is not the only problem with handwriting. WIMA's Waller expresses a common belief that handwriting offers a direct, almost physiological connection between the brain and the word, a connection which computers are accused of disrupting. Capitalizing on this assumption, manufacturers market pens and pencils as powerful, bold, passionate, and highly personal, despite the fact that they are mass produced and about as individually made-to-order as a Big Mac, and the writing instrument industry could well boast "billions sold," just like McDonald's.

Writers do take their writing personally, many developing strong preferences when it comes to the tools they use, preferences they don't always bring with them to the computer. A writer who insists on a Montblanc Meisterstück, a blue fine-point roller ball, a lilac gel pen, or a chisel tip black calligraphic marker to draft something as trivial as a shopping list may be content to pick up whatever keyboard the computer comes with to create everything from a memo to a best seller. This passion for nonelectric writing tools reinforces the perception that the hands-on nature of manuscript creation puts a bit of the writer on paper, along with the graphite or ink, while the computer filters out personality from the words on the screen or page.

Theodore Roszak, a self-proclaimed neo-Luddite in the tradition of Kirkpatrick Sale and John Zerzan, warns against the growing use of computers in schools because, in his eyes, they interrupt the natural flow of ideas from writer to paper: "Even user-friendly machines are a barrier that need not be there between the kid and the idea." For Roszak, the old ways of pencil and crayon are best, a feeling he sums up with the mantra, "A child with a pencil in hand is ready to write. A child with a crayon in hand is ready to draw" (Roszak 1999).

To illustrate his point about the immediacy of pencil and crayon, Roszak fondly recalls the writing scenes in the movie *Shakespeare in Love*, where the young bard uses a goose quill and an inkpot to pen the masterpiece whose working title is *Romeo and Ethel, the Pirate's Daughter*. Although no autograph manuscripts of Shakespeare's plays survive, the movie presents a likely depiction of what writing was like for the penmen of his day: Shakespeare continually fiddles with his quill, preparing the point, sharpening it repeatedly, dipping it in the inkwell every couple of words, then discarding the quill and breaking in a new one when the point wears out after a few pages. The resulting manuscripts are full of smears and spills, with words and passages crossed out or added in the margins or between the lines. According to Roszak, that's the way to create great literature. Using only a simple quill pen, *Hamlet* and *King Lear* "were laboriously scribbled into existence by an inspired poet who cared above all for the depth, eloquence and intellectual force of his work and got right down to it."

The key word in Roszak's description of the Shakespearean writing process is "laboriously." It's likely that Shakespeare only got right down to writing after a lot of prep work. Like Roszak's computers, Elizabethan writing tools were not exactly plug 'n' play. Writers of Shakespeare's day maintained their own quills, mixed their own ink, and sprinkled each sheet of paper with a powder called pounce to prevent the ink from being absorbed in an illegible blot.

This fiddling and adjusting is a technological barrier between writer and page, equivalent in its own way to booting up a computer, clicking an icon, or refilling a paper tray. But Roszak feels that because the quill pen worked for Shakespeare it must be better than the computer. He says, "I'd like my students to ponder the fact that by the time they have located their style sheets and selected their fonts, Shakespeare was probably well into Act One, Scene One." But it is equally likely that by the time today's students have completed their assigned computer exercise, checked their Facebook page, downloaded some MP3 files, and moved on to an intense chat session, the Bard was still chasing geese around the yard to get his first quill of the day.

Of course Roszak is right that computers are more complex than pencils. It doesn't take much experience with computers, which require constant technical adjustments, for writers to realize that the machines speed up some writing tasks, but they also offer frustrating ways to slow writing down. And Roszak is also right that pencils and crayons need no booting up. But like goose quills and computers, pencils and crayons require frequent maintenance. Crayons stay sharp until the first time they are used, and all too soon they develop a dull, rounded point that renders them unfit for drawing. As for pencils, their points break under the best of circumstances, and a trip to the sharpener at the back of the classroom has always been a good excuse for a child with a pencil in hand who was not particularly ready to write.

Maintenance and motivation issues aside, it's not clear that today's teachers want their students to be more like Shakespeare. No manuscripts survive that Shakespeare drafted himself, but if, as Roszak suggests, he produced pages with ink blots, crossed-out passages, and marginal insertions, then he would not have fared well with the many teachers who demand neat work, not caring if it is Shakespearean in quality.

Just writing, without interruptions from others or pauses for mechanical adjustments, is not something most writers get to experience. Technical interruptions can cause any writer to lose the thread. On the other hand, a forced pause can actually provide a welcome distraction from the stresses of composition, permitting writers to reflect and refocus and come back to the task with renewed energy.

▪ ▪ ▪ MACHINING THE WORD

The computer was not the first writing technology to be accused of disrupting the flow of words from brain to page. When the typewriter initially swept across America's offices, it too threatened traditional literacies by skewing writing practices. Typewriters appeared in the 1880s, and by the 1920s it was clear that they were not only changing the way office writing got done, they were also affecting personal writing.

An early ad for the Remington "type-writer" (see figure on next page) touts the machine as superceding the pen and calls it "an ornament to an office, study, or sitting-room." The ad further suggests that the typewriter is easy to use: "It is worked by keys, similar to a piano, and writes from thirty to sixty words per minute—more than twice as fast as the pen.... Anyone who can spell can begin to write with it, and, after two weeks' training, can write faster than with the pen." The Remington typewriter makes a "beautiful Christmas present for a boy or girl," and it's a boon to women: "No invention has opened to women so broad and easy an avenue to profitable and suitable employment as the Type-Writer" (Remington 1875).

Although it bills the typewriter as an improvement over the pen, the Remington ad assumes that the typewriter was invented to facilitate the work of copyists and clerks, not authors. Writing in the *Atlantic Monthly* in 1895, Lucy Bull complains that this business machine doesn't really meet the needs of the serious writers who are also adopting it, and she wonders what a typewriter designed for the authors, philosophers, and scientists might look like:

> Undoubtedly, its efficiency in affairs has been the immediate cause of its popularity; but, unfortunately, business has too largely dictated its construction, and given it the character of a mere time-saver and makeshift. In literature its use is even now hardly more than an afterthought, and its structure is essentially different from what it would have been had literature first discovered its merits.
>
> Is it not a little curious, when we reflect upon it, that a machine which is beginning to supplement the labors of clergymen, lecturers, and contributors to the magazines should continue to be constructed almost entirely in accordance with the demands of business? Does it seem reasonable that the number of characters, the marks of punctuation, the entire typographical capacity of that piece of mechanism to which, directly or indirectly, the man of science confides his conclusions, should be prescribed by the flour merchant and the dealer in all kinds of property except manuscripts? (Bull 1895, 822)

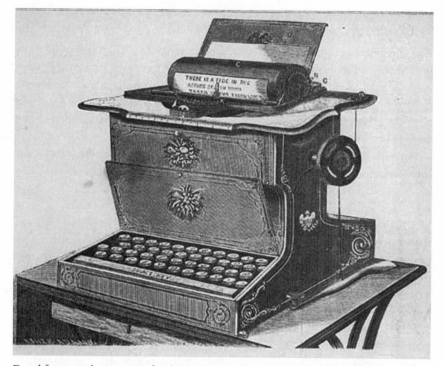

Detail from an advertisement for the Remington Type-Writer. The text being typed is Shakespeare's "There is a tide in the affairs of man which, when taken at the flood..." but it is clear from the ad that the machine is intended for copiers, not creators, of text. From *The Nation*, no. 346 (Dec. 16, 1875), p. xviii.

In 1938 the *New York Times* thought the problem of typing had become serious enough to editorialize against the machine that had usurped the place of "writing with one's own hand," warning that "the universal typewriter may swallow all" as if the typical memo, report, or invoice needed the personal touch that only longhand could provide ("Of Lead Pencils" 1938). While the *Times* editor may have scrawled this lament about the increased mechanization of writing on a pad of narrow-lined, yellow paper, reporters in the newsroom were most likely clacking away at their typewriters, pouring their souls into their words, trying to meet their deadlines. Any metro editor suggesting that their work would be more honest and direct if it was handwritten would be facing a revolt.

Complaints that writing machines bring impersonality, killing off both handwriting and the soul, are just one more way of saying that the old ways were better. But that hasn't stopped writers from switching to the keyboard, and even Theodore Roszak, who wrote his praise of the quill pen using a computer, admits that he himself dreaded handwriting class:

> The steel-nib pen may have been a breakthrough in the history of the written word, but it was a torment for me. Every careless upstroke left the newsprint paper my school supplied shredded and smeared....Everything I wrote with pen and ink was an eyesore. (Roszak 1999)

Roszak is not the only writer to complain that penmanship in school was torture. Even though the writing instruments industry may market pens and pencils as vehicles that make visible a writer's inner self, the schools have never favored a cult of personality when it comes to handwriting. Their goal was always to produce a uniform script, not an individualized one, a script that would prepare students for the world of work.

▪ ▪ ▪ A BIG ROUND HAND

In the pretypewriter age, office work required uniform, legible handwriting, nothing idiosyncratic or personalized. In *H.M.S. Pinafore*, Gilbert and Sullivan satirize the role that a plain vanilla handwriting played in elevating Sir Joseph Porter, K. C. B., First Lord of the Admiralty, from office class to officer class:

> As office boy I made such a mark
> That they gave me the post of a junior clerk.
> I served the writs with a smile so bland,
> And I copied all the letters in a big round hand—
> I copied all the letters in a hand so free,
> That now I am the Ruler of the Queen's Navee!
>
> "When I Was a Lad," *H.M.S. Pinafore*, Act 1

Sir Joseph's "big round hand"—often called English round hand because of its regular, rounded letters—was a style of writing that every office clerk needed to master in Gilbert and Sullivan's day. Even though by the seventeenth century books had begun to replace manuscripts as vehicles for literary and scientific thought, government and business depended on handwritten documents until well into the twentieth century, when office machinery severely narrowed the scope of penmanship. School-based writing, always behind the times when it comes to technology, relied on pen and pencil even longer. Despite an ambitious experiment claiming to prove the superiority of typing for all aspects of learning—one we'll look at more closely at the very end of this book—with the exception of a few typing classes for future secretaries, schools ignored the typing revolution in favor of continued handwriting instruction. It's only in the past few years that American schools have acknowledged the fact that many children have already made the switch from pencil and paper to writing online.

Before the typewriter and the adding machine, offices couldn't function without writing in pen and pencil, and as it had in the days of the medieval manuscript, a uniform handwriting system ensured that any reader could read any document. Clerks who had to draft or copy an office document had to have perfect penmanship—Sir Joseph was a copier of letters, not an author creating prose from scratch—and the schools aspiring to produce students ready to enter the office workforce created a curriculum of office-preparatory skills, including cursive writing, spelling, and alphabetizing.

Initially, handwriting was taught through the copying of models (Thornton 1996, 17). Essentially an act of tracing or imitating letters created by a writing master, there was no room in the methodology for injecting the writer's personality into the script. The teaching of writing, or composition, was also rote: students copied model essays as well as model invoices so that they would internalize the structures used by successful clerks and authors.

Nineteenth-century instructional methods sought to make writing even more exact by developing assembly-line models that broke letters down into their constituent parts, slants, ovals, curves, and lines, whose lengths and angles had to be memorized and recited. As Tamara Thornton recounts, Platt Rogers Spencer, the most influential writing master of the century, broke away from this mechanical model to some extent by arguing that the constituent forms of letters were ones to be found in nature, and by focusing on the ennobling aesthetics of his subject. But perhaps because contemplating the ideal and natural forms of letters didn't improve students' abilities to reproduce those forms, writing instruction quickly shifted its focus from the abstractions of moral improvement to a more utilitarian emphasis on physical conditioning and rote repetition.

As Thornton notes, instructional manuals specified in great detail the correct sitting posture that writers needed to adopt and gave minute instructions for positioning fingers, hand, and arms in order to produce each letter correctly. They even instructed writers where to place their feet. For writers who couldn't follow instruction, there was the talantograph, a kind of harness for the wrist and fingers, which forced the hand into the correct position for writing. Instructions explained without irony that this binding would guide the writer to free and natural penmanship (Thornton 1996, 53–55).

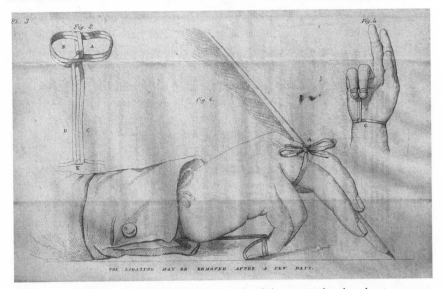

Benjamin Franklin Foster designed this harness to bind the writer's hand so that it assumes the correct position for writing. He suggests that the ligature may be removed after a few days. From Foster 1832, plate 3, graphic by the author.

Sir Joseph Porter's "big round hand" probably looked like this sample from George Bickham's *Universal Penman*. Bickham writes, "As a legible and free Running hand is indispensibly Necessary in all Manner of Business, I thought proper to introduce these Examples for the practise of Youth, and their more speedy Improvement." From Bickham 1743, 163.

The Spencerian hand popular in the nineteenth century abounded in detail, flourish, and general artistry. In the Palmer method, the even more "natural" handwriting methodology that supplanted Spencer and dominated twentieth-century instruction, writers were urged to do calisthenic warm-ups to produce a quick, legible, utilitarian handwriting even better suited to office work (Thornton 1996, 68). Practice for the Palmer method began with extended drills, with students producing page after page of ovals, and slants called push-pulls, before they were allowed to advance to forming letters and, after that, whole words.

What both the Spencer and Palmer methods offered was a factory-like system of letter production. Carefully scripted physical movements produced a hand that was not just legible, but also was as interchangeable as a machine part and as unremarkable as an ambitious law clerk's bland smile. It was, in effect, a writing technology designed to meet the needs of a mass of readers, and, like all such technologies, it worked to some extent, and sometimes it failed miserably.

■ ■ ■ BREAKING THE MOLD

Theodore Roszak's problem with neat handwriting places him within a grand tradition of resistance to uniform penmanship. In contrast to the infinitely reproducible and interchangeable big round hand, an illegible scrawl has always marked those who either thought themselves too important for routine office work or who could never aspire to anything so grand. Roszak would be happy with Thornton's observation that even the Prince of Denmark sought to unlearn the clerkly handwriting he had acquired in his youth (Thornton 1996, 13). In Shakespeare's play, Hamlet tells Horatio,

> I once did hold it, as our statists do,
> A baseness to write fair, and labored much
> How to forget that learning.

> —*Hamlet*, act 5, scene 2

Apparently Hamlet, still in his teens, discovered that good penmanship didn't go along with the brooding, world-weary, college dropout pose he had adopted. Perhaps Shakespeare shared his protagonist's sentiments on penmanship. In any case, the play's denouement depends in part on Hamlet's ability to fake the secretary-style handwriting that he had earlier labored to forget. When King Claudius sends a secret letter to the English King asking that Hamlet be put to death, the young prince intercepts the message and, using the "fair" hand in which that letter had been drafted, he revises the message, requesting that the bearers of the letter, his false friends Rosencrantz and Guildenstern, be put to death instead. But Shakespearean tragedies turn on fate, not penmanship, and in the end it was neither the prince's poor handwriting, nor his ability to forge documents convincingly in a big round hand, that kept him from avenging his father's death and replacing his uncle Claudius as king.

A century after Shakespeare penned *Hamlet* in a handwriting that Roszak assumes was reasonably sloppy, French aristocrats, like their earlier Danish counterparts, also scorned the uniform script that had by that time become a marker of the bourgeoisie (Thornton 1996, 13). Perhaps they consoled themselves with their bad handwriting as they were marched off to the guillotine. But it wasn't until the later nineteenth century that some intellectual support finally arose for those who for whatever reason could not get with the handwriting program. Toward the end of the Victorian period, the idea that handwriting reflected individual character gradually joined physiognomy (reading human traits through facial features) and phrenology (reading it through bumps on the head) as popular, if unreliable, attempts to show how external human features reflected internal talents and personality, and the pseudoscience of graphology was born.

Graphologists claim that signatures or short handwriting samples reveal personality. A glance at someone's script allows these adepts to identify untrustworthy individuals and to finger criminals; to vet potential mates or employees; to advise the troubled; and to correct negative behaviors. In graphology, nonconforming script is classified as pathological, though in some cases it may also reveal genius or other positive traits. In contrast, practitioners of the big round hand, even though they might achieve high military rank, could simply come across as uninteresting, unimaginative drones.

Graphology is very much like fortune-telling, pure speculation totally disconnected from the facts on which it claims to rely. According to one graphology site on the internet, crossing *t*'s with a stroke that slants upward from left to right signals a disposition that is optimistic, or ambitious, or independent. Look out for a variable slant with wavy baselines, irregular writing, and uneven pressure, all signs of excitability, mood swings, and impulsivity to the point of going out of control. On the other hand, small letters, monotonous rhythm, and a regular, light pressure indicate a reserved, unassuming manner, a follower rather than a leader, a person with few interests who accepts authority and lacks initiative, creativity, and willpower. Couples with such contrasting handwriting and personalities are not normally compatible, though the analyst acknowledges that the couple whose writing produced the foregoing analysis lived and worked together for many years (britishgraphology.org).

Graphologists claim that handwriting can reveal the potential for criminal activity, something of particular interest to employers and the police. An online demonstration of Handwriting Analysis Software for Windows says this about the JonBenet Ramsey ransom note: "The handwriting...shows evidence of possible organic brain syndrome which could be a result of substance abuse (i.e., alcohol, cocaine, or marijuana, which have a short-acting effect on the brain)" (writinganalysis.com). Another site finds a convicted murderer pressing aggressively on his downstrokes. Even worse, we're told, "his writing also shows an excessive slant to the left, suggesting he is 'mother-oriented.' In graphological terms, a slant to the right would indicate a tendency towards his father, the future, and a more out-going personality" (britishgraphology.org).

A *USA Today* article points out that terrorists like the person behind the anthrax scare that gripped the United States in 2001 don't type their threats, they write them by hand. The newspaper consulted the graphologist Mark Hopper, who ventured that handwritten threats are more personal, more human. After looking at copies of several envelopes containing anthrax spores,

Handwriting of the convicted murderer Craig Belcher, slanting ominously toward the left. Courtesy of Erik Rees, britishgraphology.org; used by permission.

Hopper concluded that the block printing and awkward word placement is "characteristic of bombers and people who send anonymous poison-pen letters" ("Experts" 2001). Unfortunately, block printing is also characteristic of people who didn't take well to penmanship in school, and that probably covers an even greater number of writers.

A more-detailed analysis of one anthrax letter appears on the website handwriting.com. The accompanying "expert" analysis of the anthrax letters finds that the writer is probably suicidal, severely depressed, rigid, neurotic, male, single, self-employed, and "not scientifically trained." Not only that, but the anthrax letters are "likely written by a person with some but only limited familiarity with American style script....In fact, it excludes writers from countries that teach alphabetic forms: Europe, Mexico, etc. but does not exclude writers from the Middle East, China, etc. which do not teach the English style lettering" (handwriting.com). The description does not generally fit the government scientist whom the FBI eventually identified as the likely perpetrator of the attacks, though he did wind up taking his own life before he could be officially charged with the crime.

It's only a short step from this sort of retrospective analysis—we know that the letter writer is a killer or a bomber or a poisoner, and his hand-writing shows it—to prediction: this person may have done nothing yet, but the handwriting reveals sociopathic tendencies. The certainty with which graphologists make such pronouncements has convinced many employers

The envelope containing anthrax sent to Sen. Tom Daschle. From www.fbi.gov/headlines/anthrax_evid6.jpg (U.S. Department of Justice).

The letter to Sen. Daschle. From www.fbi.gov/headlines/anthrax_evid6.jpg (U.S. Department of Justice).

to sample the handwriting of prospective employees in order to determine whether they have the qualities of honesty, creativity, or ambition that the job requires. Handwriting analysis is not as invasive as drug testing, and applicants for jobs need never know that they didn't get the job not because of their qualifications, but because of the slant of their writing.

Handwriting.com is one of many graphology sites that offers such psychological profiling online:

> Founded in 1983, Handwriting Research Corporation (HRC) has provided corporations, individuals, and the media worldwide with psychological profiles produced entirely from handwriting samples. Utilizing the latest in computer technology, HRC can provide you with insight into an individual or team which cannot be obtained through subjective interviewing, self-reports or testing. Reports from one to fifteen pages are available and include professional consultation with each analysis.

And it's no big jump to thinking that, since handwriting reveals personal flaws, simply changing a person's handwriting will go a long way toward correcting them. At myhandwriting.com, a site that flogs such "as seen on TV" books as *Handwriting Secrets of the Rich and Happy*, one testimonial from a satisfied graphology student describes how she modified her handwriting so that it would show attention to detail, a characteristic that she found valuable. Another student tells how consciously changing his handwriting by writing with a slant makes him more optimistic, even when things aren't going all that well. If the murderer whose handwriting sample we saw above had only slanted his writing toward the future, he might still be walking around free.

Another graphology site, for the impressively named Institute for Integral Handwriting Studies, actually promises that changing handwriting can be life altering:

> Your handwriting is a graphic reflection of your thought habits. By making specific changes in the way you write, you are able to release self-sabotaging attitudes, step into life with self-confidence and clarity, and redirect your life. (iihs.com)

Many graphologists sell handwriting analysis courses so that once their own handwriting is analyzed, users can hang out a shingle and go into the business for themselves. But the goal of IIHS combines money making with altruism: "Our mission is to spread healthy handwriting globally, and by so doing increase the possibilities of world peace." The graphologist who runs this site also sells a vegetarian cookbook for people on the go, and she has designed a special alphabet to promote her ideals. She will even sell customers who don't want to bother learning a new alphabet to change their lives a set of special computer fonts (available for both Windows and Macintosh) so that their computers can make those changes for them, a curious instance where handwriting experts join with the digital revolution to become complicit in the decline of handwriting.

▪ ▪ ▪ ANECDOTE: ALTERING EGO

I couldn't resist the offer of one graphology website to have my handwriting analyzed for free online. The procedure is both simple and painless, and the results are instantaneous. Following their simple directions, I first copied a thirty-word passage from the screen onto a piece of paper and signed my name. Then I answered questions about the appearance of different strokes and letters in my writing sample. As soon as I clicked the "submit" button, I received a personalized analysis that informed me,

Handwriting is really brain-writing. It is an exact neurological projection of your subconscious thoughts onto paper. That's why more and more people are insisting on seeing someone's handwriting before they date or marry them. Employers are even using handwriting analysis as a basis for hiring or not hiring employees. (free-handwriting-analysis.com)

The graphologist analyzing my writing sample, who signed herself "Cheryl" but was probably a computer rather than a person, reported that I was neither intense nor flighty; I have sound judgment; I keep my feelings inside; I am slow to anger; I'm ruled by self-interest; I'm stubborn (she suggests I'll need to change this); I don't pay attention to details; and I was angry when I dotted my i ("What are you angry at?" she asks therapeutically). I can adapt to the people around me. I'm sarcastic. I'm lazy. I have the characteristics of self-made millionaires (even though I'm lazy?). I'm a take-control person and shouldn't marry someone who crosses *t*'s the same way I do. I'm also a loner, and my large capital *i* suggests that I think highly of myself.

Cheryl assures me that her analysis is very accurate and urges me to work on character traits that need attention. Plus she offers to teach me the basics of handwriting analysis in less than two hours. The starter kit is only $39.95, and in addition to a deck of handwriting flashcards, I will receive a copy of *The Secrets to Making Love Happen* (not available in stores), which claims that "using handwriting analysis and neuro-linguistic programming can and will improve your love life!"

If I become a graphologist, Cheryl tells me, I can be the life of the party, earn $100 an hour analyzing other people's handwriting, and hire myself out as an expert witness. Cheryl signs the report in digitized script, the letters sloping ever so slightly upward in what must be the optimistic hope that I will buy the starter kit. She's right that I'm sarcastic, but wrong about my spending habits.

The notion that handwriting is individualized—like fingerprints—led to the fortune-telling practice of graphology, but it also led to handwriting analysis as a method for authenticating signatures, letters, and other handwritten documents. Unlike graphology, which is a scam, handwriting analysis doesn't profile writers to determine what they have done in the past or what they might do in the future. Instead, it tries to establish, by comparing handwriting features, whether a document is genuine or forged. It may also help to track down the author of anonymous documents. Handwriting analysts look at some of the same characteristics that graphologists concern themselves with: slant, pressure, placement, and spacing of letters and signature. Sometimes using the more elevated job title "forensic document examiners," handwriting analysts determine the validity of contested wills, solve problems in literary authorship, and authenticate autographs for collectors. Handwriting analysts determined that the anthrax envelopes were most likely addressed by the same person. They use words such as *most likely* rather than *definitely*, because, while it is more exact than graphology, handwriting analysis is still fallible. Sometimes the mistakes these analysts make wind up in the headlines. In the 1980s, handwriting experts readily authenticated a set of Hitler diaries that later turned out to be a blatant forgery.

▪ ▪ ▪ THE HANDWRITING ON THE SCREEN

The digital age is narrowing the scope of handwriting even more than the typewriter did. No one can disagree that many documents once written by hand are now being keyboarded instead. But at the same time that computers are eroding our already compromised handwriting skills, they are carving out new spaces for handwriting in the hopes that we will use computers even more than we already do.

After typewriters took over the bulk of our professional writing, so that a big round hand was no longer needed in the office, the rules of etiquette dictated that some documents, like personal letters, invitations, and expressions of sympathy, be handwritten. The handwritten letter was perceived as more direct, more polite, more personal, than the typescript. And handwriting was essential in situations where typewriters were unavailable, impractical, or just too noisy.

Now that computers have replaced typewriters, email has become *the* way to send a personal letter, one reason that postal revenues are down. In addition, some of the other genres of personal writing are shifting to the keyboard: more and more invitations are electronic; birthday cards are increasingly virtual; even the diary is going digital, and its outgrowth, the web log, or blog, is an entirely new virtual genre. Ten years ago, although Americans were well into the email revolution, the *New York Times* reported that condolence notes were still handwritten (Napoli 1997), but when there was a death in my family a mere three years later, I received more email condolences than conventional sympathy cards.

American schools are starting to catch up with this shift to virtual writing, teaching less handwriting and more keyboarding. While the nostalgics complain about this refocusing of classroom time, one fan of computing actually wrote to his local paper to complain that teaching cursive writing—like teaching French, he adds—was a waste of money in a time of tight education budgets (Krampitz 2003).

Handwriting has become the concern not of clerks and teachers, but of antiquarians and those few remaining idealists who see in good penmanship a reflection of one's inner nature. Asserting that older writing technologies are more natural, as Roszak does, won't make much of an impact on computer users, particularly those students today who came of age surrounded by computer technology.

But even the rest of us have come to see the personal computer as a natural part of the writing landscape, so that any computerless work surface will seem strikingly spacious and empty. The more we get used to any writing technology, the more natural it becomes. The computer has already become naturalized as a writing tool for many writers, and one correspondent even writes in a letter to the editor that the computer is actually a more natural writing tool than the pen: "For many seasoned computer users, the brain seems to be more at ease in sending signals to one's fingertips to pound the keyboard rather than sending instructions to the same fingertips to write on a piece of paper" (Kasim 2003).

Despite these claims, or the pretensions of the writing instrument industry, technology is not in fact natural. By definition it is artificial, a device fashioned for a purpose. Pens are no more natural than keyboards, penmanship no better at reflecting the human spirit than digitized text. But for those of us who have gotten used to keying in our words, working with pens and pencils has already begun to seem less natural, less automatic, less of a direct connection from mind to text, than going online.

Ironically, now that penmanship is about to become a forgotten skill, the same hardware and software designers whose computers turned handwriting into an endangered practice are shifting their attention to digitizing script.

The handwriting may or may not be on the wall, but it is certainly becoming more common on the screen, with an increasing variety of handwriting fonts available for computers. Advertisers think customers will respond more positively to their computer-generated mass mailings if they appear to be handwritten, and therefore more personal. And nostalgics may even be tempted to combine their love of the old with the attractions of the new by purchasing a handwriting font for their digital literary creations. The website texashero.com sells computer fonts of seventeenth- and eighteenth-century penmanship, encouraging customers to "write like they used to." The company offers a digitized font mimicking the handwriting of the Declaration of Independence and another copied from Sam Houston's letters.

Houston Pen Font based on the handwriting of Sam Houston. It's not clear whether the "inkblot" is also computer-generated, a graphic designed to add that touch of authenticity. Houston Pen™ ©1998, 2006 by Brian Willson; image courtesy Three Islands Press (www.3ip.com).

Another site, killerfonts.com, sells fonts based on the handwriting of "outlaws, brainiacs, maniacs, and rock and rollers," including Lizzie Borden, Billy the Kid, John Dillinger, Napoleon, and Genghis Khan (who certainly didn't use the Roman alphabet and was probably illiterate). But for those who don't want "to write hate letters in the actual handwriting of the killers of your choice," as the *Chicago Tribune* reviewer of this site put it (Warren 1997), another site promotes handwriting fonts as "the best way to humanize your computer" (pro.wanadoo.fr). Other font designers offer customers the option of turning their own handwriting into a digital font to further combat the perceived impersonality of the computer. One site advertises, "Fill out a one page form for a very realistic (but neater!) font of your handwriting and signature!" (signaturesoftware.com). The software produces a slightly uneven line and four different representations of each character in order to create an artificial irregularity that will appear more authentic to readers.

When in the course of human events it becomes necessary for one people to dissolve the political bands which have connected them with another and to assume among the powers of the earth, the separate and equal station to which the Laws of Nature and of Nature's God entitle them, a decent respect to the opinions of mankind requires that they should declare the causes which impel them to the separation.

Thomas Jefferson

A demo of a more natural handwriting font, based on Thomas Jefferson's handwriting. ThomJeff font and image provided by vLetter, Inc. at vLetter.com; © vLetter, Inc. 2008; used by permission.

But the emphasis on providing a font that is neater than the writer's own handwriting pushes us back in the direction of the Palmer method and the attempt to make handwriting as uniform as possible. What the computer adds is just a pinch of regular irregularity to humanize the appearance of the digitized text.

Handwriting fonts are intended for two kinds of buyers. One group, ranging from direct mail advertisers to individuals sending computerized birthday cards to their friends, hopes that by substituting a script font for the ubiquitous Times New Roman, readers will feel that the message is personal in spite of its obvious mechanical generation. The other group, as one website puts it, consists of "all the egomaniacs who want to type in their own handwriting" (chank.com), an echo of the notion that handwriting projects personality.

The machine-generated individuality of handwriting fonts probably won't lead to a renewed interest in penmanship—these fonts work by displacing the actual pen-writing that they imitate. But the growing desire of some computer users to bypass their keyboards is leading in a direction that even Theodore Roszak and Bill Henderson might appreciate.

The current debate over handwriting versus keyboarding is going on at the same time that hardware and software developers are devoting significant resources to getting computers to accept handwritten as well as keyed input. Many readers will be familiar with the PDA, the personal digital assistant, where characters conforming to a special script are drawn by stylus on a touch-sensitive screen. It's not a perfect system. Nineteenth-century office clerks proficient in the Spencerian hand or the Palmer script might have interfaced smoothly with a PDA, writing perfect Palm Pilot Graffiti every time. But the Palm Pilot frequently misreads the intended strokes, or, worse still, it displays nothing at all while users frantically scribble characters with the stylus.

The PDA has become a popular device despite the fact that its usefulness as a note-taker is compromised by poor character recognition and by the slowness of the data entry process. Although work-arounds such as portable PDA keyboards are an option, users typically download information directly from their PC rather than entering it by hand. Or they switch to BlackBerry-style gadgets that combine some functions of the PDA with those of the cell phone and permit data entry using a miniature keyboard (the iPhone touch screen allows users to type while they play music, show videos, and surf the web).

Perhaps more promising in the technological convergence of longhand and digitization are developments such as the digital pen, which records hand movements for later downloading to a PC, and the new tablet computers. Like PDAs, tablet PCs still require users to learn a proprietary script, but unlike the PDA, writers generate streams of continuous prose, entire words and sentences, across the full, touch-sensitive computer screen, just as they would on paper, instead of tracing individual letters in the small window allotted to them on the Palm Pilot.

All successful writing technologies require writers to adapt, but the technologies adapt in turn to the demands writers make on their tools. If tablet computers are to succeed, they will need to recognize more of the variations inherent in human handwriting, while at the same time pushing us to make our handwriting more standard.

▪ ▪ ▪

National Handwriting Day was a lost cause from the start, but handwriting itself is far from dead. Just as a twenty-first century Thoreau would probably busy himself with cramming more memory onto a microchip rather than taking the pencil to the next level, no one would expect a modern-day Shakespeare to use a quill pen to write his plays or his shopping lists. Writers in any age use the tools at hand, whether they are bits of graphite tied to wooden sticks or line editors, like the first computers, machines so poorly adapted to the demands of writers that they made clay tablets seem high-tech.

5

■ ■ ■ Writing on Clay

I grew up writing by hand. Most of the students in the classes I teach used pencils and pens at first, as I did, but many of them came of age in the digital age, and with a keyboard in hand, they're ready to write. Even those who didn't start using a computer until high school have become so used to the technology that they don't bother looking at the manuals when they get new hardware or a new program. They just press the 🔘 switch, click an icon, and start working. When asked whether computers or traditional writing instruments seem to provide a more direct connection between brain and page, more of them pick the keyboard than the pencil.

It's not surprising that those of us who grew up with ink-stained fingers think of computers as harder to master than ballpoints. Nor am I surprised that, when I ask my students to write on clay tablets, they find the ancient technology unnecessarily complex and cumbersome, and they feel relieved when they're allowed to go back to their writing tool of choice, the keyboard. That's because, once we have mastered them and use them regularly, our word technologies—both apparently simple ones like pencils and clearly complex ones like word processors—become automatic and invisible. We don't notice our writing machines until something goes wrong:

- The pencil point breaks.
- The lights go out.
- The computer freezes.

There's one thing we can depend on with word technologies: like any machinery, they are sure to fail at a critical juncture, at which time, to echo Willy Loman's wife, Linda, attention must be paid:

- The pencil must be sharpened.
- The candles must be located.
- The unsaved file must be reconstructed from human rather than digital memory.

Sometimes repairs aren't in the cards, and we have to go to Plan B. Of course, if we were already on Plan B when the disk crashed....

We learn from our word technology failures. Once burned by a lost file or a darkened house, we take precautions, at least for a while. After the disaster, we back up our work on the computer every five minutes. Or we make sure that there are batteries and matches, flashlights and candles stashed where we can actually find them next time.

Everyone has lost a digital file or an important piece of paper, and with any writing technology, archiving doesn't always seem worth the time and trouble. With computers, as with paper, one's intellectual life becomes risky business, ever at the whim of power surges, equipment failures, and magnetic storms, and we know that technology still leaves us vulnerable to the loss of our words.

We don't need spilled coffee and bursts of static discharge to remind us how fragile those words are, and we don't have to wait for a word technology to fail in order to remind us that we depend on it. A less stressful way to consider how automatic our customary ways of processing words have become is to try writing with an unfamiliar technology.

Before paper, before parchment, before papyrus, writing on clay was one of the main ways that writing got done. Initially, accountants in ancient Iraq kept their "books"—records of inventory and sales—on both sides of clay tablets the size of credit cards. Later still, Sumerian scribes began recording contracts, laws, inscriptions, and, eventually, more narrative sorts of legal, historical, sacred, or literary texts on larger tablets, many of them about the size of the writing paper that we use today (Robson 2007). But nowadays, while some people still carve words in stone, nobody writes on clay. Even though backyards around the world are full of clay that could be made into cheap, serviceable writing tablets, contemporary writers don't want to deal with the messiness of digging up the clay, getting out the impurities (not to mention the earthworms), and adjusting the moisture content. Of course writers don't make their own paper either, preferring to go out and buy it. Since writing-quality clay is not available at most office supply stores, and considering the issues that surface when I ask my students to write with it, clay doesn't seem poised to make a comeback as a major writing medium.

A cuneiform clay tablet from Sumer, ca. 2041 BCE. Unlike writing on paper, where the color of letters and background contrast, clay writing, like all carving, is essentially monochromatic. With letters and background the same color, the light source must be positioned to create contrasting shadows, thereby increasing legibility. Photograph courtesy of the Spurlock Museum, University of Illinois at Urbana-Champaign.

In the box on the next page is the assignment that I give to my students in our writing-on-clay workshop (the students work in groups of three or four, but readers are invited to try this by themselves, at home).

Though a few of my students throw pots or sculpt, most of them haven't used clay since they were children, and they think of it primarily as something to play with. For the exercise, I give the students modeling clay that comes in brightly colored sticks. The students, perhaps momentarily transported back to the carefree days of preschool, spend some time choosing the color they

WRITING ON CLAY

Each person will receive 4 ounces of nontoxic modeling clay; a short, pointed wooden skewer; and a length of a 3/4" hardwood dowel. There is wax paper to protect the surface of the table. Use the premoistened towelettes to clean your hands when you are done.

First, prepare a clay tablet to use as a writing surface. Then, with the stylus provided, or any other implement you may have on hand, each member of the group should try the writing assignment. Each group will be given a different exercise from the following list:

1. Transcribe the following passage (just the Latin, not the English translation):

   Caesar exspectavit dum legati ad castra venirent. Antequam legati ad castra venirent, legiones eduxit. Caesar legatos laudavit, quod ad castra venissent. Caesar legatos laudavit, non quod ad castra venissent, sed quia legiones exspectabat. Legatos laudavit, quippe qui socii fideles essent.

   [Caesar waited for the envoys to come to the camp. He led out his legions before the envoys could come to the camp. Caesar praised the envoys because they had come to the camp. Caesar praised the envoys, not because they had come to the camp, but because he was waiting for his legions. He praised the envoys since they were faithful allies.]

2. Draw a map showing how to get from where you live to class. Make sure that you label streets and landmarks, and give any directions that a visitor might need to follow that route.

3. Write a short clay-mail to a friend describing how to prepare a clay surface for writing.

4. When Hamlet asks, "To be or not to be, that is the question," what exactly does he mean?

5. Create a short, illustrated advertisement for your favorite soft drink.

want to work with even before they begin. Occasionally there's friction if a participant doesn't get his or her first-choice color. That in itself is a reminder that, given the chance, writers will focus on the artistic elements of writing as much as on the content. Perhaps Shakespeare favored a certain kind of No. 2

quill? Perhaps the scribe who carved the Rosetta stone patronized a particular chisel maker?

The writing-on-clay workshop brings into relief several other aspects of the writing process that writers normally take for granted. As they go about their assignment, students consider these issues:

- how writing—whether on clay or on computers—forces them to deal with the technology at the same time that they are trying to get the writing done;
- how technology affects the content of their writing as well as the writing process;
- how the type of writing they are doing influences the technology they are using;
- and finally, how the technology affects the way that they read a document or text.

▪ ▪ ▪ FORMING THE PAGE

The first task the workshop participants face is to prepare a writing surface— something writers using contemporary word technologies don't have to think about: paper, disks, and LCD monitors come ready-made and ready to use.

Despite efforts to recycle, contemporary writers tend to treat paper, so easy to come by, as disposable. However, clay, while abundant, is not a renewable resource. Reforestation provides new trees and eventually, more paper, but creating new clay is not really an option. The earth's clay deposits form slowly from the weathering of many kinds of rocks. Even if the process could be accelerated, the supply of rocks on earth remains finite. This really isn't anything to be concerned about, even in the long run. It would take a lot of clay writing to use up the available supply, but a planet whose inhabitants wrote on clay instead of paper or computer disks could, in some wild science fiction scenario, find itself literally written out of existence. Of course, earthlings would run out of room to store all those clay tablets long before we ran out of clay to write on.

Unlike paper, clay doesn't come ready-to-write. Workshop participants receive their clay in the form of a stick about the size of a quarter-pound of butter. When using an unfamiliar word technology, writers tend to model what they do on their experiences with more conventional technologies, and workshop participants first flatten out their clay to form a writing surface that resembles a sheet of paper, insofar as a lump of clay can be worked to look like paper. For the same reason (i.e., we expect the new to connect to the familiar), most writers didn't switch to computers for their text processing until those machines were able to mimic the black-on-white typed page that writers were used to.

Some clay writers flatten their clay with the heel of their hands, then roll it out as if preparing dough, using the dowel as a rolling pin. Others apply dowel to clay without flattening it first. They have to press much harder to do this, but initial hand-flattening gives the clay less of a squared-off shape: the choice appears to be an easy-to-form circle, which then needs squaring to look like paper, or a rectangle requiring more physical pressure and less tinkering later on. Occasionally a student will use a straight edge to replicate lined paper in clay, only to find that the lines, which for paper keep the writing even and enhance its legibility, get in the clay writer's way and make reading much more difficult.

While some clay writers seem content with a rough approximation of a quadrilateral, others labor diligently with dowel and stylus until they've crafted a paper-thin sheet with a smooth surface, straight sides, and right angles at the corners. A particularly artistic participant may scallop the edges of the page. Just as some writers take shortcuts when using familiar writing technologies in order to get the writing over with, there are a few students who streamline page preparation by stomping on the clay, then writing on the flattened, irregular surface that results (they do flip the clay over so the sneaker treads are on the back). Of course, new word technologies prompt experimentation as well as mimicry, and there's usually one student in each class who exploits the unfamiliar medium by creating innovative shapes to write on (a fish, a triangle, a miniature computer screen) or forms the clay into a stele, an engraved column, a plaque, even an inscribed Grecian urn.

▪ ▪ ▪ TECHNICAL DIFFICULTIES

The next problem workshoppers face is using the stylus to incise letters, numbers, and shapes into the clay, which is generally more difficult for them to do than conventional writing, where ink or graphite is painted onto a paper surface. Sumerian scribes wrote cuneiform (literally, "wedge-shaped") letters using a reed stylus that was wedged at one end and pointed at the other, a system better adapted to clay writing than the modern English alphabet, and so far no student has succeeded in retrofitting the alphabet for clay technology. Workshoppers do report that straight lines carve more easily and that print works better for clay than script. Cursive writing on paper minimizes interruptions of the written line, but notwithstanding the promises of National Handwriting Day, carving in the dense and sluggish medium of clay is physical labor requiring frequent lifting and repositioning of the stylus.

Finally, carving the clay raises shards, chadlike bits of clay that some workshoppers carefully remove from the edges of their letters, since they interfere with reading and ruin the overall aesthetic of the tablet. Cuneiform writers, who pressed their clay instead of carving it, didn't have to deal with such excess clay removal, a tedious process that can also blur the inscription. This problem is exacerbated by the fact that the workshoppers tend to craft small letters that are easily obscured. They do this for two reasons: small is their normal pencil-and-paper printing style; plus they're trying to fit the entire text onto one clay page that's about half the size of a piece of writing paper, so that they won't have to bother taking another stick of clay and forming a second clay surface. Writers, as they discover during this exercise, can be very practical.

Writing on computers initially presented technical difficulties that writers also had to deal with. Line editors, the rudimentary word processors available on early mainframe computers, gave writers a surface to work on that looked nothing like a page: a line of text on a screen, or on a sheet of thermal printer paper, instead of a continuous stream of prose. The text was not visible in its entirety until it was formatted—a process separate from text entry—and printed out.

Early typewriters were even worse in terms of letting the writer monitor the text as it was being formed: "understrike" typewriters, of the kind made by manufacturers such as Sholes and Glidden beginning in the 1870s, relied on gravity to return the type bar to its resting position. The illustration of the Yost 4, a popular understrike machine first built in 1887, shows that the type bar struck the paper from below, which meant that the typist couldn't see what had been written without either lifting up the carriage or rolling the paper forward through the machine. Using a more complex arrangement of levers, "visible" typewriters began to appear in the 1890s. They allowed the typist to see the text as it was produced, though understrike typewriters continued to be made and sold alongside the new "frontstrike" models for many years, perhaps because their simpler mechanisms were less prone to jamming.

Computers and typewriters, much as the original eraserless pencils, did not provide for correction at the outset: they are designed with the unrealistic expectation that the writer will not make a mistake. Even more recent typewriters, marketed as "self-correcting," like the IBM Selectric, were not able to handle "cut-and-paste" revisions without extensive retyping. But clay is reusable. Evidence from early clay tablets shows that unbaked clay was inscribed, then smoothed over and re-inscribed by students using them for

The Sholes Remington understrike typewriter (1873). Remington's first typewriters were decorated with decals, like its sewing machines, perhaps with an eye toward domestic as well as office use. Image courtesy of the History Center of Tompkins County (New York), used by permission.

writing practice, by writers correcting their mistakes, and perhaps also by anyone needing a scratch pad for their less permanent texts. In addition, sun-hardened clay tablets could be softened with water, reformed, and used again (Robson 2007).

That's not to say that writers will take reusable clay-based shopping lists to the store anytime soon, or that clay tablets offer the cut-and-paste revision techniques that make computers so attractive to today's writers. The clay writers in my workshops, like users of eraserless pencils, quickly learn to think before they write, since errors engraved in clay can't readily be crossed out or erased. Correction involves smoothing out the clay and starting over. It's difficult to smooth out a word or phrase without effacing nearby text as well, and new text can't be added without disrupting the surrounding text. It's always possible that early Sumerian schoolmasters used quick-drying clay so that, like stone carvers, their pupils would not have the luxury of changing their minds.

The Yost 4, 1894, another understrike typewriter, shows a clearer view of the understrike mechanism. The Yost had three sets of keys, one each for capitals, lowercase, and numbers. The shift key, eliminating the need for extra rows of keys, would be introduced later. Machines like the Sholes and the Yost don't jam, but the typist has to roll the paper forward in order to read the text. Image courtesy of Richard Polt.

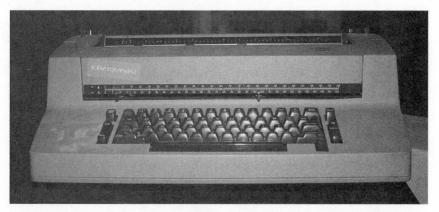

Selectrics came on the scene in the 1960s. The IBM Selectric III, introduced in 1980, was a "self-correcting" typewriter, allowing relatively precise correction of a letter, word or short phrase, although major corrections still required retyping one or more pages. While it is only about thirty years old, and used or reconditioned machines are still available, the Selectric is already an antique. As the green inventory tag shows, the machine above is being scrapped. Photograph by the author.

▪ ▪ ▪ THE WRITING ASSIGNMENT

The Latin transcription exercise emphasizes the difficulty of writing not just in an unfamiliar technology, but in an unfamiliar language as well (very few of my workshoppers have had any Latin). The exercise is not intellectually taxing in the way that composing a few off-the-cuff sentences about the meaning of *Hamlet* would be, but it is slow work that replicates what many scribes and keyboarders often do: copy a text that they did not create themselves, and whose contents may be a mystery to them. It's easier to make mistakes copying such an opaque text, and harder to catch transcription errors when proofing.

The other three writing exercises involve more familiar school-based composition tasks: providing straightforward information about something the writer knows, analyzing a literary text, or creating a display involving text and graphics. For these tasks, workshoppers don't struggle with the genre so much as they adapt it to the constraints of the medium. For example, SparkNotes notwithstanding, even an infinite number of scribes won't discover the meaning of Hamlet's soliloquy in a way that fits on one side of a small clay tablet. It may not even be possible to explain Hamlet's words using an infinite number of monkeys seated at an infinite number of workstations. But for each of these topics the writer must deal with planning, drafting, and revision in a medium that is really meant not for outlines and trial runs but for finished products alone. The clay writers are forced to adopt more of a think-before-you-write approach, and they show less of a tendency to make major revisions once they've started in a particular direction.

▪ ▪ ▪ TWENTY-FIVE WORDS OR LESS

There may be a lot of clay in the world, but there is only a limited amount in the workshop assignment. Writers on clay quickly realize that they have to maximize the amount of text they inscribe on the clay surface. They can't turn the clay over to expose a new blank page without obliterating what they wrote on the first side. Spilling over to a second page requires additional clay (I'm always ready with more, but no one seems to want any), and it takes additional prep time as well. So workshoppers economize on words and skimp on the "white space" surrounding the words they do use.

Whether they are writing on computers or typewriters or sheets of lined paper, experienced writers develop the ability to fit what they have to say into a given space, either by adjusting the margins or by expanding (or in some cases, contracting) the size of their writing. Writers who feel that they don't have enough to say on their assigned topic may pad their papers by adding useless words and needless repetitions, widening their margins, scaling their fonts, or, for those who try to be more subtle about it, choosing a large font such as Arial instead of a smaller one: a ten page, double-spaced paper in Arial 12 pt. type comes to only nine pages in Times New Roman 12 pt. (obviously, the word count remains the same).

Writing on clay challenges the scribe to estimate what will fit in the space available. Journalists are used to this kind of preplanning, learning to fit their words into the appropriate number of column inches, and certain kinds of journalistic writing—for example, news stories—are designed to be cut from the end so that they can fit into a page layout without sacrificing essential information. But that kind of writing assumes at least two copies of the text: a draft and a final version that has been cut to size.

Not much is known about the writing process of the ancient clay writers. Perhaps they too worked from drafts that could be reused after they were copied onto a final tablet that was then dried for preservation. Perhaps they planned the text in their heads, rehearsing it till they got it right and then committing it to clay. Or maybe they just wrote extemporaneously, keeping

The high-tech version of an old probability favorite: place an infinite number of monkeys at an infinite number of text processors, and eventually they'll type out, not *Hamlet*, but HAMBASIC. Cartoon by the author.

corrections to a minimum, letting stand any large chunks of text they may have had second thoughts about, just because correction was difficult. And maybe they stopped not when they reached a logical conclusion, but when they ran out of prepared tablets.

My clay writers don't have time to make a rough draft of the text on paper or on another piece of clay, editing it before they copy it onto their clay tablet. Nor are they adept at forecasting what will fit on the clay tablet they have

Hieroglyphic text from the Egyptian Book of the Dead, on papyrus. It is not easy to correct errors on papyrus. The sign indicated by the arrow, which seems to be a scribal error, may have gone unnoticed, or the scribe may have thought it not worth the trouble to correct. From the Book of the Dead of Amun Paenwiaenadj. 21st Dynasty, 1070–946 BCE; Aegyptisches Museum, Staatliche Museen zu Berlin; used by permission, Bildarchiv Preussischer Kulturbesitz / Art Resource, New York.

made. If they don't write enough they can always pad the text with extra details or simply cut off the extra clay. Shrinking text after it's written in clay isn't easy: it requires smoothing out the clay and starting over—and in the absence of a separate outline or draft text to copy, it assumes that the writer can remember what was written before it was obliterated.

▪ ▪ ▪ BUT IS IT ART?

My workshoppers clearly associate clay with art projects, not text. That may explain why many of them embellish their writing with decorative flourishes. But many writers like to experiment with the aesthetic variables of whatever medium they are using. Workshop students form their clay into interesting shapes—occasionally, three-dimensional ones like the obelisks they've seen in museums. Others combine colors to vary the backgrounds. Students who finish early sometimes decorate their clay as an afterthought, sticking appliqués of clay flowers, cute animals, or geometric designs onto the surface while they wait for the rest of the group to complete the task.

Even writers who think of handwriting as a chore may pay special attention to their penmanship for this exercise, practicing a kind of clay calligraphy to produce not just letters, but actual inscriptions worthy of display. The most artistic writers sign their work, though they must adapt their signatures to the new medium. A bold John Hancock dashed off with a pen becomes slow and awkward when the writer must form it while fighting the resistance of the clay medium.

Although there are always writers who ignore the aesthetic elements of their clay as much as possible, plowing rapidly through the assignment just to get the words down so they can move on to something else, aesthetics plays a role in all writing technologies. About half the writers I survey acknowledge consciously developing a distinctive signature for their handwritten documents, and many pore over the various computer fonts at their disposal, balancing the demands of their document against mood and personal preference.

Even the choice of writing instrument can be aesthetic as well as practical. To readers who remember them, typewriters may have been little more than utilitarian machines for writing, as interchangeable as the various brands of No. 2 pencil. But for some writers, choosing what to type on was as personal a decision as choosing which fountain pen to use, and as we saw on page 78, some early typewriters were built as objets d'art, with decorative decals and fine wood cabinets.

In contrast to the fine art that went into designing fountain pens or early typewriters, later, mass-produced typewriters were much plainer in design: they were, after all, office tools, not home decorations. Although by the 1970s typewriters were sold in a variety of colors, the first personal computers of the 1980s were thoroughly plain in their packaging. They were utilitarian machines, or at least they would become utilitarian once users figured out how to work them. The popular IBM PC offered one color choice and one cabinet style—like Henry Ford's promise to build the Model T in any color the customer wanted, so long as the color was black, only IBM chose a non-descript taupe.

A working IBM PC. The original model 5150 was released in 1983, housed in the simple metal box that symbolized the plain vanilla approach to personal computing. The 5150 came with one standard 5.25-inch floppy drive, 64 kb of RAM, and a green monochrome monitor. A second floppy drive was optional. This machine above has been upgraded with two 3.5-inch floppy drives and a 20 mb hard drive. The display screen shows an early version of Microsoft Word. Courtesy of the Department of Electrical and Computer Engineering, University of Illinois; photograph by the author.

The earlier PCs kept that homemade, Heathkit look. Even twenty years later, with personal computers an essential part of the well-appointed home as well as the office, PC design has focused on the inside more than the outside. Though color choices have expanded a bit (they come in black now), body type has remained fairly boxy. There is one glaring exception to lackluster PC design: Steve Jobs is said to have put his first computer together in his garage, giving it a very homemade look, but Apple Computers now hold onto their market share at least in part because of the flair they give to their packaging.

Packaging may sell the product, but document design in the end is the most important aesthetic quality that writers attend to, even writers who see their writing tools as merely tools. Whether it's a drop-down menu or the hands-on physical shaping of text, all writing technologies present options that allow writers to determine the look as well as the content of their text. Just as the clay workshoppers quibble over who gets which color clay, some writers prefer colored inks to Model T black (the default ballpoint ink is actually blue), and tinted papers instead of plain-vanilla white, though they may reserve these options not for school assignments or business reports, but for more personal writing.

The first Apple computer (1976) in a furniture-quality wooden case. Image courtesy of the Smithsonian Institution; used by permission.

The distinctive design of the discontinued PowerMac G4 Cube, introduced in 2000 by Apple, and its 17-inch flat panel display contrasts sharply with the simple casing of most personal computers. Newer Apple models continue to focus on appearance as well as performance. Photograph by the author.

Writers like to control the aesthetics of the letters they make as well as the medium on which they write. As we saw in the last chapter, many writers who put pen to paper don't produce penmanship worthy of calligraphy, but some do manage enough control over their handwriting to produce special effects. One student I know perfected her script to the point where she was able to pick up extra cash addressing wedding and bar mitzvah invitations. Another, whose penmanship was realistic rather than artistic, and who also had an ear for parent-speak, created passably convincing "Please excuse my daughter from P.E." notes and sold them to her high school classmates.

Typewriters never offered writers much flexibility in the way of document design. Until IBM came out with its Selectric typewriter in 1961, with its replaceable type ball, typists were pretty much confined to the Model T font that came with their machine:

Something that looked like this (though this is actually a computer font called "American Typewriter").

As I've mentioned more than once, new technologies often get a foothold by allowing us to do what we are used to doing with older technologies, only better. It was the personal computer's ability to mimic typing that first attracted users who were not technologically sophisticated, those writers who weren't really thinking about information processing so much as they were looking for the next big thing in typewriting. Once computer writers discovered they could replicate not just typing, but print as well, the widely used newspaper font Times New Roman became the standard. But the more recent explosion in the availability of computer fonts has given these users a machine that allows the kind of control over the appearance of a document that writers on clay, pen and ink writers, typists, and even typesetters only dreamed about. Today even the most mundane emails and instant messages come adorned with designer fonts, pictures, sounds, and even animations.

Like beginning clay writers, writers new to the computer are quick to focus on the design aspect of their text, decorating it because they can, not because they should. I once spent several days in the mid-1980s designing a sig.file, the signature that can be attached to an email. This was before text and graphics could be merged, and getting a picture on an email required crafting it out of letters, numbers, and punctuation marks. I was obsessed with exploring my newly acquired computing skill, and I proudly attached this protographic to all my emails only to learn that my carefully worked visual, created on a DOS machine, displayed as complete gibberish on any Macintosh computer.

Computers, as they improved over two decades, began offering design options that allowed writers to personalize and professionalize their writing. These new choices in turn led to a proliferation of overcomplicated document presentations. The creators of personal web pages and PowerPoint presentations, two of

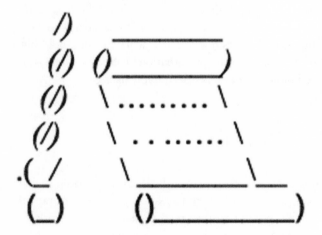

My first sig.file, made by arranging keystrokes and spaces, represented a quill pen, inkpot, and scroll, an ironic homage to an old-style word processor.

the newest genres spawned by the new word technology, had a particular tendency to go overboard on the special effects: scrolling banners, marching ants (a moving border resembling an old-time movie marquee), sound effects, lurid text, and background colors created a busily rococo effect that shouted, "Hey, look what I can do." Overproduced commercial emails may also avail themselves of these techniques. Nothing is more disconcerting than clicking open an ad or following a web link only to come up against a sudden wall of flashing lights and sound that makes everyone else in the office look up to see what happened. Fortunately, most texts tap the computer's potential more tastefully as writers integrate illustrations or even video clips at appropriate points in a document to reinforce or go beyond the typed words themselves.

Students produce almost all their schoolwork on computers these days, but they don't seem to be as adventurous in their academic writing as they are either with clay or with their web-based writing. Instructors may have feared an onslaught of digital versions of the classic middle school paper, heavily illustrated with clip art instead of the traditional technology of pictures cut from magazines, but what usually happens is that student writers don't experiment very much when designing their school assignments. Occasionally they will escape the plain vanilla of Times New Roman and try out Monaco or Verdana, but most of them just go with Microsoft Word's default fonts and margins.

It's not just students and teachers who are more aware of formatting these days. Typography has become a cultural phenomenon, and computer fonts are the new wine. Although cuneiform eventually developed more than six hundred symbols, it's not clear that the first clay writers discussed the merits of fonts. Typists probably didn't, either. Until recently *font* was the kind of obscure word that might appear on the SAT or the *New York Times* crossword puzzle. But today it's not unusual to come upon knots of people heatedly debating the qualities not of a fine wine, but of a bold **New Century Schoolbook,** a peppy but unpretentious Futura, a subtly scalable, slightly sophisticated Palatino, or an art-deco Papyrus.

▪ ▪ ▪ PROCESSING THE TEXT

Writers in the clay workshop have little trouble reading what they wrote themselves, but when I ask them to exchange papers—or tablets, to be more exact—they find it's not easy to read their neighbor's work. For one thing, unlike print, typing, or paper and pencil writing, writing on clay is monochromatic, and readers need to position the clay tablet so that shadows throw the incised letters into relief. They must also adjust to the unfamiliar linear shape that stylus writing forces on the letters, and to the fact that many writers cram words together, making it hard for readers to sort out where words and sentences begin and end.

Early writing is not known for its readability, either. Audience awareness wasn't a high priority for the first clay writers, who didn't have the benefit of freshman composition. The fact that writing initially had no punctuation and didn't necessarily use spaces to separate one word from the next suggests two likely explanations:

1. These early writers crammed as much as they could onto each writing surface because preparing new clay tablets, animal skins, or papyrus was slow, costly and labor intensive.
2. As Plato suggested in the *Phaedrus*, writing served as a reminder rather than an attempt to present new information: scribes were recording words on clay as a mnemonic or memory aid, either for themselves or for readers who were already familiar with the text.

Squeezing too much text onto a page, scroll, clay tablet, or stone slab makes it easy for readers unfamiliar with the message to lose their way, and even when writing materials are scarce, one sign that a writer has moved away from writing-as-reminder to the presentation of new material is the increased use of white space, word breaks, punctuation, headings between sections of text, comfortable margins, and other design features that facilitate comprehension.

Clay tablets are fragile: unbaked they are easily torn, while dried clay becomes brittle and prone to cracking or crumbling (according to Robson [2007], clay writing tablets were dried in the sun, not fired like pottery). Writers in the clay workshop don't have access to a kiln or a hot desert sun, and since the clay we use doesn't dry out, they face a transportation problem if they want to take their work home with them. One workshopper rolled up her clay text in wax paper, jelly-roll style, and she reported later that it survived the trip home in her backpack reasonably well. But she couldn't figure out how to display her schoolwork on the refrigerator. If she had a refrigerator with a computer in the door, she could have uploaded a digital photo of her project for display. But her campus landlord wasn't going to spring for an amenity like that, and in the end she did what most workshoppers have done, she balled up the clay, played with it while watching TV after dinner, and eventually threw it out.

Early clay writers also faced the problems of transporting, storing, and retrieving their heavy tablets. While they may have greeted with skepticism and suspicion the newer technologies of writing on parchment made from dried animal skins or papyrus, a precursor to modern paper made from the papyrus plant—both materials were less permanent than clay or stone, and each presented its own difficulties in terms of preparation and use—enough writers recognized that it was a lot easier to write on these paintable surfaces than on clay. In addition, they were both more pliant and more portable than clay. In the end, writing on hard and heavy substances such as clay and stone was relegated to ceremonial text as writers made the switch to parchment, paper, and, ultimately, to pixels in their quest for the newest and most flexible writing mediums. But the conversion to digital text wasn't an easy one: the first computers, which did a great job of processing numbers, presented daunting obstacles to writers wanting to process words.

6

▪ ▪ ▪ When WordStar Was King

Writing on clay was not the last word technology to drop off the screen. The market for parchment dried up in the late Middle Ages, and while papyrus continues to be sold as a souvenir in Egypt (Roemer 2007), paper has become the universal medium of choice for writing on soft and pliant surfaces, though thanks to computers those surfaces have become "hard copy." Typewriters are quickly moving toward extinction, though they're not dead yet. Although the machines have become increasingly rare in the United States, typewriters are still manufactured and sold around the world. But it is hardly a stretch to claim that sooner rather than later the people who are still typing will join the digital age and retire their machines in favor of the computer.

In fact, computers so dominate writing today that it may be difficult for the growing number of writers who have never known anything but Microsoft Word to understand that writing on screen once posed many more challenges than writing on clay. It was so difficult to write with the first digital computers that their later impact on writing would have been hard to predict. In this chapter, we will look at word processing in that pre-Word era to see how a technology that was developed without writers in mind quickly came to be used more for writing than for just about anything else.

▪ ▪ ▪

Mainframe computers have been around since the 1940s, when the U.S. Army sponsored development of the Electronic Numerical Integrator and Computer, or ENIAC, at the University of Pennsylvania, but the computer was originally designed to replace the adding machine, not the typewriter. ENIAC reduced from days and hours to mere seconds the tedious and repetitive arithmetic calculations needed to create ballistics tables for aiming artillery shells and dropping bombs, calculations previously performed by rooms full of human "computers" working mechanical comptometers.

ENIAC replaced the human "computers" who created firing tables for the army by working adding machines such as the Comptometers shown in this office photo. From the Early Office Museum; used by permission.

ENIAC was programmed not by software, but by switches and cables that had to be manually reset (Weik 1961), and the computer was so numbers-focused that it had no text entry capability at all. Some early machines were actually capable of limited word processing, but they focused their power on military and scientific calculation instead. For example, UNIVAC, developed in 1951 as the first commercially marketed computer, helped compile the U.S. Census and successfully predicted the 1952 presidential election (www.computermuseum.li/Testpage/UNIVAC-1-FullView-A-htm). But although the first UNIVAC permitted data entry by means of an alphanumeric keyboard, it wouldn't actually accommodate word processing. Even twenty-five years later, the "interactive text editor" introduced in 1977 on the UNIVAC 1100 was intended not for writing as such but for "symbolic data manipulation, for correction of compiler input, data preparation and performing runstream editing" (Borgerson 1977).

Even the personal computer, introduced in the 1980s, was intended to crunch numbers, not words. When *Time* named the PC the "machine of the year" for 1982, the magazine touted the PC as a "work processor," not a word

The ENIAC, or Electronic Numerical Integrator and Computer, which went online at the University of Pennsylvania in 1946, had nineteen thousand vacuum tubes and cost close to half a million dollars. But so far as writing was concerned, the computer was decades behind the typewriter. From the John W. Mauchly Papers, Rare Book and Manuscript Library, University of Pennsylvania; used by permission.

processor (Friedrich 1983), and the programmers who shaped what the computer could do still preferred pencil and paper as they figured out how to run their machines.

It took some time, though only a blip in the long history of writing technologies, to be sure, for the computer to become the writer's tool of choice. Today in the United States the computer has effectively taken over most work, school, and leisure writing, but like other writing technologies, computer writing does have a history. Understanding that history will help us put the impact of the computer on reading and writing practices into the broader perspective of the five-thousand-year history of writing and its technologies.

As the application for the ENIAC patent makes clear, science had advanced to the point where a powerful computing machine had become a necessity (Weik 1961). What the computer's developers hadn't considered was that writing had reached that point as well. The line editors that came with ENIAC's early successors allowed for rudimentary text entry and got the attention of the more daring writers. Then WordStar, a program able to harness computing power for text creation, came on the scene in 1978, and over the next few years, growing numbers of curious and daring writers began to unplug their electric typewriters and plug in their PCs. WordStar quickly went from relative obscurity to the top of the software charts, although that program eventually lost some market share to challenger WordPerfect, which attracted its own fan club. Then came Word, in 1983, and before anyone knew it, Bill Gates got richer still and the clunky word processing of the pre-Word era was wiped from our collective memory.

■ ■ ■ ANECDOTE: BUT EVEN BEFORE WORDSTAR, THERE WAS...

When I was looking for a teaching job in 1971, there were no personal computers to help me create print-quality letters and résumés. The task of typing applications was well beyond my skill level, and paying someone to type them for me was not an option. But photocopying a letter was out of the question as well. In the employment world, hand-typed letters, ones where each keystroke left a distinct imprint on the paper, signaled a job candidate's drive, dedication, and personal character. At least, that's what every job seeker was told. Photocopies were for losers.

Luckily my problem was solved by a new machine that could mass-produce an individualized-looking job letter: the word processor. The term *word processor* first appears around 1970, although machines capable of word processing—the electronic creation, storing, editing, and printing of documents—first came online in 1964, when IBM introduced a magnetic tape storage system for its Selectric typewriters. Five years later, just in time for my job search, the tape was upgraded to a magnetic card that could hold a full two-page letter, which was fine for my purposes though well below the capacity of the earliest computer floppy disks.

When typists used the mag card Selectric to type a form letter, they could start and stop the operation long enough to type in a name and address, a salutation, and some personalizing details to convince the recipient that the letter had been made to order. Even though the Selectric had a light touch, it left subtle indentations in the paper. There was never any doubt that this automated letter was hand typed.

The automatic typewriter wasn't easy to master—even professional secretaries who knew their way around office machines had to be trained in its intricacies. But using the machine took me far less time than typing the individual letters myself. It was also a lot cheaper, and far less embarrassing, than paying a professional typist to copy my pathetic pleas for work, one of which eventually paid off.

Memory typewriters, a tantalizing and expensive innovation forty years ago, are now mostly memories themselves, although Brother and Nakajima still make electronic typewriters with small display screens and the capacity to store a short letter. The mag card typewriter was a technological sidetrack: not quite the blend of typewriter and computer that would result in the PC, but a move in that direction. It adapted the typewriter to the newest demands of the American workplace. However, it proved to be more than just the word-processing equivalent of eight-track tape. IBM had shown writers that electronic storage could transform the process of creating, revising, and printing their work. Today, the PC makes preparing job applications a snap, though no machine can ease the pain of dealing with the rejections most job applicants experience.

▪ ▪ ▪ UNFRIENDLY MAINFRAMES

The automatic typewriter did for writers what the mainframe computer could not. Those mainframes that could handle text were not well-adapted to the task. For one thing, users could type either in caps or lowercase, not both. For another, mainframe software was unforgiving. Writing on these computers daunted all but the most stubborn writers: all in all, writing with a mainframe, or even with an early PC, made writing on clay seem pretty easy.

Anecdote: A Writer Takes the Plunge

I was an unlikely computer writer. I'd heard of FORTRAN and COBOL but I'd never written a line of code. The only computer I'd ever seen was on *The $64,000 Question*, a TV quiz show that debuted in 1955. Each week America watched in fascination as a new contestant picked a category—boxing, or spelling, or opera—and the show's onstage computer spit out a pack of questions for host Hal March to ask. Viewers were told that the computer was selecting a group of questions at random from its memory bank. But three years into the 1950s big-money quiz show craze, it came out that the randomness was fake, that some quiz show contestants were being fed the answers in advance. The *$64,000 Question* computer turned out to be only a prop, nothing but an IBM punch card sorter whose elaborate and impressive bells and whistles were nothing but a sham.

The "computer" shown on the set of *The $64,000 Question* turned out to be little more than a card sorter like the IBM 082 shown here. It could deal up to two thousand cards per minute into twelve bins, with a thirteenth bin for rejects. Each week the faux computer "selected" questions whose answers had already been given to some of the contestants. From Columbia University Archives; used by permission.

The early popular image of the computer depicted a machine that was either hopelessly complex or, in the case of that popular quiz show, the high-tech equivalent of three-card monte, and as I came of age in the 1960s and '70s, I voiced my share of skepticism about the creeping computerization of American society. Little did I know how quickly I would become a convert to computers. I didn't wind up eating my words, but I did have to digitize them.

It was the spring of 1983, and while I still clung tenaciously to my fountain pen, for more than a decade I'd been doing all my real writing, from first draft to final product, on electric typewriters. I don't remember where or when I first heard about writing with computers, but I recognized from the start that they were going to be the next tool of choice for writers.

Electric typewriters weren't particularly cheap in those days, but an IBM personal computer was an even more expensive proposition, so before investing more than $6,000 on what could easily have been a disastrous economic sidetrack in my personal writing history, I decided to try out writing on the university's VAX mainframe.

To facilitate my experiment, the Computer Services Office at my university lent me a "dumb terminal" to take home for a week. It looked like a typewriter with the typing parts left out. There was a keyboard and a platen, but no type bars and no ribbon. Dumb terminals with screens were available only in the campus computer labs. Instead, my portable terminal printed text that I entered with the keyboard or downloaded from the mainframe onto a roll of thermal paper, so that I could see it.

These portable terminals came with a pair of rubber cups into which I placed the handset of my home telephone. If I didn't remember to disable call-waiting, the beep that signaled an incoming call would kick me off the VAX. Connecting to the mainframe was fairly straightforward—not too many people were dialing up in those days, so the dial-in ports were never jammed. But writing online proved more challenging. The prospective writer had to master two thick, mimeographed instruction manuals, one for writing on the VAX, the other for printing. VAX stands for Virtual Address eXtension. Knowing that made me feel part of a new community of insiders. But when I cracked the manuals, I began to realize just how much of an outsider

The portable dumb terminal consisted of a keyboard, thermal printer, and an acoustic coupler, a set of cups where a telephone receiver was placed for connecting to the mainframe. Photograph by Jed Donnelley; used by permission.

I really was. Reading the instructions, I found myself suddenly in a land where the brand of English being spoken definitely called for subtitles.

VAX users wrote with a line editor, which worked as advertised: I could enter text one line at a time, just like I could on a typewriter. But unlike the typewriter, each line of VAX text was numbered and stored as a separate file in the computer. To edit a line after it had been stored, I had to go back and call up that specific file, and I spent a lot of time at my dumb terminal reloading lines I'd already written—sometimes guessing till I got the right file number. I also had to remember the gist of the lines that came before and after, since the terminal's printer would only display the line I had recalled from storage. Revising involved a routine of load-edit-save; load-edit-save; load-edit-save.

Lines didn't wrap when they got too long, as they do on today's screens, and paragraphs didn't automatically reformat to account for additions and deletions. Printers in those days could only handle eighty characters per line, the number of columns on an IBM punch card, so if a line was too long, I'd have to clip words from the right margin and put them at the beginning of the next line, adjusting the paragraph line by line till I reached the end. Otherwise my prose would print out like some formless ultramodern poem.

Visual feedback is important to writers, and I was challenged by the line editor's inability to display large chunks of what I was writing. Line editors weren't quite as bad as the first understrike typewriters, which hid the text beneath the platen and made typing an act of faith. But with the VAX I had to rely on my memory of what the text should look like, because the visual feedback available to VAX writers was extremely confusing. My keystrokes printed out on the thermal printer as I entered them, but corrections resulted in overstrikes, which made the printout unreadable. Loading lines for reediting destroyed the continuity of the text on the printer, so I could only get a sense of the line or paragraph I was working on, not its place in the larger document.

Even when the text was reasonably clean, the output on the thermal printer was disappointing, useful only for rough drafts. For final copies I sent my first computer "job"—a five-hundred-word book review—from my terminal at home to a printer in a campus computer lab some distance from my office. There it waited in a print queue for an unpredictable amount of time, usually a day. When it was done I could pick it up, assuming that I could locate the lab and remember the job number it had been assigned.

Each time I retrieved my "final draft" from the printer bin, I found new things in the text to correct. It eventually took me several days of entering lines, storing them, retrieving them, revising them, and reformatting them, and several trips to the lab that housed the printer, before I produced a document that I could show to my editor without embarrassment.

The Horror …

Once I got the knack of writing from home and became reconciled to the reality that my text existed not on a piece of paper in front of me, but on some magnetic tape on a machine miles away under someone else's control, I decided to try writing at a terminal in the computer lab. The advantage of the lab was that the terminals had monitors, so I could see my text. The lab also had an attendant who could help when the technology proved too overwhelming.

The disadvantage was that I had to write next to other people who were computing. Even though I was just working on a fairly pedestrian book review, not a great American novel, a soul-baring confessional, or a deep philosophic tome, I had always considered writing a private act. Writing in the lab was anything but that. I tried not to notice the other writers, but I couldn't help myself. I certainly couldn't help noticing when the man sitting next to me jumped up from his terminal screaming, "Stop! Help! Stop!" As he watched in horror, the words he had been typing vanished from his screen, replaced by row after row of horizontal lines. Bystanders gathered around as one does at an accident, some speechless, others offering futile advice, or still others just staring at the twisted wreckage.

I knew, abstractly, that the electronic forces at work within the bowels of the computer could wreak havoc with a text, but this was my first real glimpse of the malevolent, implacable, and nightmarish computer netherworld. But the amazing disappearing text turned out to be just an illusion, a byproduct of the mainframe's primitive screen capabilities. The writer had marked a block of text to be underlined, and the monitor, which couldn't display both text and underlining at the same time, was doing its best to show him that the command was being carried out. A couple of clicks by the lab attendant and the text was back on the screen—it hadn't disappeared from the mainframe's memory tapes, at least not yet.

Working with line editors was painful, but once I tasted computer writing, I wasn't eager to go back to a typewriter. Mine was more than just a fascination with the latest gadget. In fact, I found the mainframe too frustrating. But I knew after wrestling with this new technology that my writing would never be the same. My VAX experience convinced me that there had to be a better way to write, but it also convinced me that the personal computer might just be that way.

■ ■ ■ DEDICATED WORD PROCESSORS

The personal computer craze was just starting in the early 1980s, but even as the PC began to sell, there were few writers among the early converts to the machine. Mainframe computers crunched numbers, not words, and while mainframes carried the first email, it was clear they were never going to become general-purpose writing instruments. But personal computers didn't do much better in the word-processing department. Like the mainframe, these machines were meant for people in the numbers game. Those users hadn't demanded more text capability, and since most writers and typists considered computers too forbidding, PC developers saw no need to develop the text manipulation end of the business. That left room for the hybrids, dedicated word processors such as the Wang 2200 and the WPS-8 that combined the stand-alone advantages of the memory typewriter with the flexibility of a computer. Xerox and CPT sold such word machines as well.

For $20,000, the CPT 8000, a dedicated word processor, displayed a full typed page of text. It did less for more, but it did what writers wanted. Photograph by Adrian Graham, from binarydinosaurs.co.uk; used by permission.

The personal computer displayed only a piece of a document at a time, twenty-four lines of type, with the IBM standard of eighty characters per line. Calling the slice of text that appeared on ordinary monitors a "screenful" or "window" fooled no one: it was only part of a page, not a whole one, not very attractive to writers and typists who came out of a centuries-old tradition where pages counted, not lines.

In contrast to the PC, dedicated word processors showed writers on-screen what they were used to seeing on their typewriters, a full typed page with black type on a white background. To further mimic the typewriter feel, some of these machines digitally mimicked other typewriter features such as setting margins. The screen only displayed a single font, not the wide variety that we've now become used to, but most people used just a single font on their typewriters as well. What these word processors did offer besides the full-page display was an image of their document that looked pretty much like the final copy that came out of the printer attached to the word processor.

But these dedicated word processors were pricey—the CPT 8000 sold for $20,000, more than three times the cost of a new IBM PC or Apple. At that price, the CPT wouldn't be replacing electric typewriters anytime soon on the average office desk, not to mention the desks of starving novelists or underpaid academics. And sharing digital documents on stand-alone word processors was limited: like the mag card Selectrics, their proprietary operating systems ensured that data could only be retrieved by other users of the same equipment.

It's a computer industry axiom that IBM, which came to prominence as a developer of business machines and was a major player in the development of mainframes and an early marketer of PCs, seriously underestimated the potential of the personal computer. After playing catch-up for years, the company finally gave up on making PCs altogether, selling the rights to its Think-Pad laptop to the Chinese manufacturer Lenovo. Perhaps one reason IBM failed to foresee that the PC was destined for a place on every home or office desk in America was its commitment to its own typewriter line, together with a conviction that writers didn't want—or need—to change technologies. What most writers do at their desks is create or copy documents, and so far as IBM was concerned, between the pencil and the typewriter, the writers' market was all sewn up. People used computers for numbers, and numbers meant bigger and bigger mainframes, not trim, underpowered desk units. The entertainment potential of the personal computer, particularly in the area of electronic games, boosted its popularity, but factoring in such post-1982 developments as email, instant messaging, and the web, what most people now do with their PCs is process words, and while a lot of word processing still involves copying or manipulating text created by others, more and more writers are taking advantage of the new digital genres to create and publish texts of their own.

Mainframes and dedicated word processors showed those writers and computer manufacturers who cared to look a glimpse of what their future would be. Two things happened that paved the way for the personal computer to become the word processor of choice: PCs became affordable, and they became not just user friendly, but writer friendly as well.

▪ ▪ ▪ THE MACHINE OF THE YEAR

Time magazine named the computer the "machine of the year" for 1982. Image courtesy of *Time* magazine; used by permission.

Even with its primitive word-processing capabilities, the PC was on a roll. In 1982, *Time* magazine awarded its person of the year slot to the personal computer, calling it the "machine of the year." The cover depicted a pale, monochrome man looking at, but not using, a similarly colored personal computer sitting not on a desk, but on a small table, while the other half of the gatefold showed a barefoot woman lounging in a wicker chair and looking off into the distance, with a small desktop computer sitting on a low table to her right. In *Time's* graphic, the humans don't interact with the machines. This, along with the menacing title of the cover story, "The Computer Moves In," reinforced the popular notion that "electronic brains" were on the verge of replacing people.

As the accompanying article reported, PC sales had jumped from 724,000 in 1980 to about 2.8 million just two years later, and futurologists were lauding the PC's role in the information revolution (Friedrich 1983). *Time* acknowledged that gaming was a big attraction for computer users, but the magazine attributed the computer's surging popularity to its potential for education and praised the PC's main strengths as number crunching and data manipulation. By 1982, Fortune 500 companies had already replaced 10 percent of their typewriters with personal computers, but *Time* didn't tout the computer as the next writing machine. Instead, it portrayed the PC as an adjunct to the typewriter that would allow writers to access and sort the information they so sorely needed. The magazine grandly predicted that the personal computer would do for the knowledge workers of the late twentieth century what the assembly line had done for factory workers in the early 1900s—though it didn't suggest that the computer would dehumanize the creation of knowledge as the assembly line had dehumanized the manufacture of goods.

In response to *Time*'s paean to the PC, most writers yawned. So far as word processing went, it turned out that the first PCs may have been a little less unfriendly to use than mainframes, but they still presented major challenges for readers and writers. The early personal computers could not display text that looked anything like the documents writers were used to, and the machines slowed writing down and complicated it in a way that most writers were unwilling to put up with.

It was the age of color television in America, but computer monitors in the 1980s were resolutely monochrome, displaying text in one-size-fits-all, low-resolution fonts, typically green letters set against a dark background, more iron gray than black. Small changes in these displays were heralded as vast improvements. The first monitors to display orange text were greeted almost joyously as a psychological and ergonomic breakthrough, with some users claiming that orange led to a major reduction in eye strain, while others insisted that with orange their words suddenly took on a new vibrancy.

But whether the display was green or orange, the text on the screen looked neither businesslike nor literary. And as with mainframes, what users saw on their PCs bore no resemblance to the printout. On-screen text was filled with strange characters such as ^B or .co that interrupted reading. These "control codes," which told the printer how to format the raw text, interrupted writing as well since they had to be entered manually, either while composing or later, in the editing and revision stage.

Critics today fault the computer for making writing too easy. They worry that entering text has become so effortless that writers don't bother to think about their words, that the speed of computers has led to a decline in the quality of writing. Good writers, these critics warn, need to slow down, to savor their words, to think before they write, to pause while they write, and to reflect on their writing when they're done. Like Shakespeare, they caution, it wouldn't hurt writers to have to sharpen a goose quill now and then.

Maybe so, but new writing technologies always start by slowing writers down. When the typewriter was developed, typists were forced to write slowly, not quickly. Type too fast and they'd jam the keys. Even when design advances alleviated this problem, the typing technology still interrupted writers at times when interruption might not be welcome: there was always paper to change, mistakes to correct, and, just when it was most inconvenient, a ribbon to replace.

The demands of handwriting put a brake on our words as well, not just because writers had to sharpen their pens or correct errors, but also because they had to take pains to make their letters legible. Write too quickly, and legibility loses out to sloppiness. Write too slowly, and one's train of thought is lost. People often lament that they think faster than they can write, whether they write with a pen or a typewriter, and the first clay writers probably complained that dragging a stylus through what was essentially wet mud didn't do much for their own thought processes.

Computers were no different in slowing writers down. Despite the high speed we associate with digital communication, computers impeded writing even more than typewriters, clay tablets, or quill pens did. The PC's keyboard introduced extra keys to confound touch typists: the backslash \ and vertical line |, the CTRL, ALT, and DEL keys, the angled brackets < >, grave accent `, and tilde ~, not to mention the function keys, which most computer users still ignore. Unlike typewriters, computers allowed periods and commas to be entered only in lowercase. Another big obstacle for those making the transition from the electric typewriter to the PC was unlearning the habit of hitting the carriage return key at the end of every line.

Even after the keyboarders of the 1980s figured out where to put their fingers so they could work at a reasonable pace, they still had to slow their typing down because their personal computers simply could not process the rapid-fire keystrokes of accomplished typists. The slowest hunt-and-peck typists could actually exceed the PC's ability to keep up. Keys didn't jam when data entry was too rapid, but once the keyboard's small type-ahead memory buffer filled up, any additional keystrokes would be lost. Until these buffers were dramatically expanded, typists were routinely frustrated by loud beeps warning them that they had exceeded the machine's capacity to remember what to do.

▪ ▪ ▪

The reluctance of writers to buy early PCs isn't surprising. Even though new technologies promise the moon, most writers—whether they are creating or simply copying text—wait for a technology to prove itself before changing how they do things. The print shop had to develop in ways that allowed it to mimic the scriptorium, creating a page that readers found familiar, trustworthy, and reassuring before moving on to explore the new possibilities of mechanically reproduced words on any large scale. Typewriters, too, had to conquer the prejudice that machined text was not as real or direct as the handwritten word. In much the same way, writers didn't take to the personal computer in large numbers until monitors were able to display crisp black text on a white background and software allowed them to create the kinds of documents they had cut their teeth on: typed pages. The first computer writers craved what came to be called WYSIWYG—an acronym for "what you see is what you get"—with easily formatted and highly readable text that did what typewriters do, only better. They wanted all this, and they wanted it to be both cheap and easy to learn.

There were other hurdles as well. The fact that texts are stored electronically on a PC involved an act of faith: even though they could hold a disk in their hands, writers preferred their words to be visible on paper and not subject to the whims of stray magnetic fields. Writers still like to see what they write, and they know that even though paper is a fragile medium—it can burn, crumble, mildew, or become lost—it's a lot easier to verify that a text exists on paper than on a magnetic disk or a TV screen.

Computer manufacturers had little initial incentive to make their machines more attractive to writers because computer operators actually scorned the idea of using their powerful number-oriented processors to reproduce mere words. Those writers who braved the clumsy technology and actually began typing messages were condemned either to the line editor or to one of the early word-processing programs. In either case, they had to deal with a system that was hard to learn, maddeningly inflexible, and diabolically slow. A writer could write more text more quickly with a Selectric, or even with a pencil.

Writing on silicon, like writing on clay, slowed everything down, but more of a stumbling block was the fact that the machine constantly called attention to itself, pulling the writer away from the task of composition to attend to the demands of booting up, naming and saving files, formatting documents, making backups, and recovering from crashes. These details were more intrusive than having to sharpen a pencil point or change a ribbon. Plus, when a pencil crashes, it doesn't take the entire document with it.

▪ ▪ ▪ WRITING WITH WORDSTAR

A look at WordStar, which was released in 1979 and soon became one of the most popular writing programs of its day, shows us what early computer writers had to put up with. At the time, writers with personal computers imagined themselves as word crunchers pushing at the frontiers of writing, but now, twenty-five years after personal computers started flying off the shelves, we can see that programs such as WordStar, WordPerfect, and Volkswriter were little more than writing in slow motion.

The cluttered WordStar screen showed that word processors, like line editors before them, were sure to take a writer's mind off content and refocus it on mechanics—not grammar and style, but the details of loading and saving files, not to mention formatting text and correcting inadvertent keystrokes. With WordStar and most other programs, the space allotted to writing—it looked like a little chalkboard—was partly taken up with lists of menu commands, and once writers entered text, their words were obscured by formatting characters that were displayed on-screen and made reading difficult. A competing program, WordPerfect, became popular with some computer writers because its later versions allowed the extensive lists of commands to be turned off, giving writers a blank "page" to stare at (see illustrations).

Working with text required many separate keystrokes to move the cursor, erase text, or mark blocks of words to be underlined, italicized, or relocated—there was no mouse to expedite these tasks. Word wrap, the adjustment of text so that line lengths fit within specified margins, was not automatic in the early writing programs, although it was easier to manage on these "full screen" editors than it had been with line editors. Each time text was revised, paragraphs had to be manually reformatted: in WordStar this was accomplished by typing ^B (read as "control B").

Complicating matters further, printed versions of documents created with software such as WordStar or WordPerfect still seldom matched what writers saw on their computer screens, so page design entailed laborious trial-and-error sessions of print, reformat, reprint. While futurologists enthusiastically predicted the paperless office, computer writers found themselves cranking out page after page till they got it right, and then printing multiple copies of the final product for fear that their files would mysteriously disappear from their floppy disks like alien abductees. Often those fears of disappearing files were justified.

WordStar screen shot. WordStar users wrote their documents in the program's oddly named "Non-Document Menu," which offered writers a list of commands above a blank workspace for composing. Later versions of the program minimized the command list and increased the writing area. Graphic by the author.

Word Perfect screen shot. In contrast to WordStar, WordPerfect 4.1 (1985) allowed writers to hide the command codes (there was, of course, a command for this, as well as one to restore the codes). WordPerfect's adherents boasted that its uncluttered screen offered more of the feel of real writing, but most serious writers didn't gravitate to word processing until monitors were able to display a white background simulating a piece of paper. Graphic by the author.

Even if the technical obstacles to word processing on a PC weren't enough to keep them away from the new technology, writers still had to come up with the funds for an entry-level personal computer, which cost up to ten times as much as a starter machine does today. Only the most determined visionaries considered computer word processing worth pursuing, and even they held on to their Selectrics and their Bics just in case.

▪ ▪ ▪ SOME WORDSTAR COMMANDS

An early WordStar manual demonstrates the control codes for formatting a typed selection so that it will print out an illustration of the cursor and an equation, with boldface type, superscripts, and subscripts. The user was first instructed to type the following text:

^BCombining Special Effects^B. To combine special effects, simply insert one control character after another. For example, your ^BWordStar^B^VTM^V^B cursor may look like this: H^HI^HN^HZ.

|^Ba^B| = /(a^Vx^V^T2^T + a^Vy^V^T2^T + a^Vz^V^T2^T)

The typist would see this on the screen:

WordStar screens were cluttered with formatting codes. Graphic by the author.

which if done correctly produced a printout that looked like this:

To combine special effects, simply insert one control character after another. For example, your **WordStar**™ cursor may look like this:▮.

$$|a| = / \left(a_x{}^2 + a_y{}^2 + a_z{}^2\right)$$

WordStar did permit writers to design their documents—something type-writers weren't much use for. Keyboarders could customize the size and appearance of their document by entering formatting codes. These compli-cated codes set such variables as margins and offsets, as well as the length of the page. They allowed the writer to include headers and footers; to change the character height and width to match the printer's capabilities; to set line spacing, tabs, page numbering, and so on.

Today the commonly used features of word processing programs are more intuitive, or at least easier to figure out, with context-sensitive online help available rather than extensive print manuals. But even so, few writers take advantage of the thousands of features built into their word processors because the programs are inordinately complex and the online documentation often remains hard to find and far from helpful.

▪ ▪ ▪ THE WORD MACHINE COMES OF AGE

What made it easy to ignore the computer's many shortcomings was the fact that writing with a PC offered writers something that typewriters could not: the ability to cut and paste, to revise and correct, to make change after change in the text, and, extraneous codes not withstanding, still have clean copy staring back at them from the screen or better yet, from the printed page.

The ease of revision was what really made the first computer writers put up with a steep learning curve and all the false starts and instabilities that go with any new technology. But most writers didn't get in on the ground floor when it came to writing with computers. They waited until the process got easier still. It took some time before computer manufacturers realized the potential that their technology had both to improve and to complicate the lives of ordinary people who had ordinary writing tasks. But computers did improve, and ordinary people gradually joined these early adopters of the new technology to become part of the computer revolution. More than the pencil, much more than the typewriter, the computer was turning America into a nation of writers.

▪ ▪ ▪ THE GUI: GRAPHICAL USER INTERFACE

The second generation of DOS-based word processors made a giant leap toward showing writers on the screen what their printed text would look like. The improvements were modest, but they made the text easier to write and easier to read: paragraphs reformatted automatically as corrections were made; italics displayed as slanted letters; and bold text appeared brighter and thicker than plain text. As a result, a few more writers made the jump to the computer.

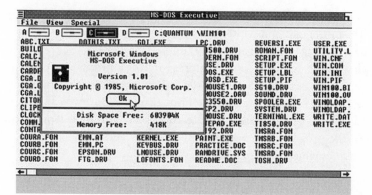

Screenshot of a DOS 1.01 menu from 1985 offered a list and did
not accommodate a mouse; there were no icons to click on, and all
commands had to be typed. Notice, too, the small disk capacity and the
minuscule computer memory (in kilobytes, not megabytes) compared to
today's high-capacity machines. Graphic by the author.

But what really did the trick in terms of user-friendliness was the graphical
user interface, the GUI, which allowed users to work with a mouse, making
their choices by pointing and clicking on icons and menus instead of entering keyboard commands that had to be memorized or looked up every time
they were needed. It was the advent of the GUI that signaled the end of the
typewriter industry as we knew it.

Computer graphics were nothing new. In the early 1960s, a decade before
the invention of the microprocessor paved the way for personal computers,
programmers began creating pictures on mainframe computers, and the first
computer games followed almost at once, both on mainframes and on dedicated gaming machines such as the Odyssey, introduced by Magnavox in
1966. Nor was combining words with pictures an innovation in the history of
text production. Many of the first written signs were stylized pictures of real
world objects, and writers have been actively merging words with pictures
at least since the days of the hieroglyph. The decorated medieval charters of
eleventh-century England are a perfect parallel to the computerized graphics
that became all the rage a millennium later. But as with earlier technologies,
the blend of text and graphics that the GUI enabled brought about innovations not just in document design, but also in the kinds of documents users
would create.

The first GUIs were created by Xerox at the Palo Alto Research Center in the 1970s, but they didn't spread to the world of the PC until 1983,
when Apple introduced its LISA office machine, which sold for $10,000,
and Microsoft offered its first Windows program (illustration). Once the

technology enabled writers to produce ordinary documents such as business letters, novels, term papers, and reports, ordinary writers were willing to give it a try, and the increased demand for PCs and competition among PC manufacturers forced prices down. In addition, developments in the chip industry and advances in magnetic storage led to a dramatic increase in PC power. Manufacturers began offering newer, faster machines at such a breathtaking pace that new generations of machines came out every eighteen months, and wags quipped ruefully that a new PC was actually obsolete the moment it came out of the box. But that didn't stop sales.

As more people jumped on the bandwagon (or were forced onto the bandwagon by employers who took away their typewriters and put PCs on their desks), some of them began to exploit the computer power that drove these high-tech typewriters. It wasn't long before writers began not just typing, but also designing their texts, drawing from a growing array of type fonts, another benefit of the new graphics-intensive and increasingly powerful personal computers. They inserted digitized clip art as well, or created their own pictures and, later, videos and sounds to go with what they were writing.

And these new computer writers created new kinds of writing that reflected the computer's impact on the ways we communicate: email, newsgroups, chat, instant messaging, the web page, and, most recently the blog, or web log. Each of these represents a new genre, one that owes its birth directly to digital writing technology. And each of these genres has developed its own set of conventions that writers are expected to observe. Each one, too, brings with it complaints: email is destroying the language; instant messaging has taken the place of conversation; the World Wide Web is the source of lies and misinformation; and, as for the blog, well, who would want to read the rants and ramblings of a total stranger? Apparently lots of people: the personal computer has turned us into a nation of writers, and perhaps for the first time since the invention of writing, these writers are having no trouble finding an audience.

Nowadays, fewer people are afraid of using a computer, but many people who use a PC every day at work, in school, and at home are still suspicious of what it can produce. Stories of digital fraud abound. Get-rich-quick schemes from Nigeria fill our email in-boxes. The internet thrives on pornography and phony term papers. Pedophiles and predators lurk in teen chat rooms. The government is recording every click we make. Some fears are justified, others overblown. Having learned to trust the technology, we are now engaged in the process of learning to trust the texts it produces.

7

▪ ▪ ▪ Trusting the Text

Readers have questioned the validity of written documents since the technology of writing first came on the scene. Compounding this skepticism, texts generated by new technologies are often greeted with mistrust by readers preferring the old, tried-and-true to the newfangled, unconventional, and potentially fraudulent. In an attempt to counteract suspicion, new technologies may mimic the look of older ones in order to gain readers' trust. Sometimes this works: the first printed books resembled illuminated manuscripts, a look that worked in part because their illustrations weren't printed, but added by hand; not by the printers, but by artists skilled at manuscript decoration.

Over time, writers and readers have resorted to a variety of authenticators to measure textual reliability. Some of these are internal, found on or within the written document: dates, signatures, and seals, for example, were developed in large part to assure readers that the text was genuine, that its message could be trusted. Other authenticators are external. These may be objective, for example, the physical analyses of paper, ink, or other materials used to create the document. Most readers can't conduct these scientific tests and rely instead on their own previous reading experience, together with the subjective opinions of experts: scholars, archivists, reviewers, document specialists, or simply other readers whom they've come to trust.

Sometimes, however, as in the "Case of the CBS Memos" discussed below, the internal and external authenticators were either inconclusive or contradicted one another. In this case, the question of trusting the text turned not on the documents themselves, but on a messenger who handled them, among other things, a further demonstration that whatever the technology, the text itself exists not simply on paper, but also in the minds of readers—readers who may disagree wildly on interpretation.

▪ ▪ ▪ THE BUSH MEMOS

In September 2004, as the presidential campaign between George Bush and John Kerry heated up, the CBS News program *60 Minutes* announced that it had received four memos "that show President Bush's National Guard commander believed Mr. Bush at times shirked his duties and used his political influence" (CBS 2004a).

Concerns over the nature of George Bush's 1970s service in the Texas Air National Guard had surfaced earlier, in the 2000 presidential race, and the issue had already been raised in the 2004 campaign as well. So it came as no surprise when the president's supporters immediately challenged the CBS memos as fakes created on a computer, not a Vietnam War–era army typewriter. They pointed to internal inconsistencies in the memos to justify their claim. For example, in the May 4 memo, the phrase "111th F.I.S." contains a superscript *th* in the body of the message, while in the letterhead the squadron's number is written without a superscript as "111th." Democrats, looking for equally technical evidence to prove the memo genuine, retorted that the IBM typewriters of the 1960s could indeed produce superscripts, and they noted as well that the superscript in the memo rises above the height of the line, as it would on a typewriter. In contrast, computer-generated superscripts reach only to the top of the line, not above it, as we see when 111th is typed on a word processor. If the memo were computer generated, these believers in the memo questioned, wouldn't there be two superscripts? And wouldn't it be more reasonable to expect such stylistic inconsistency from a typewritten document?

The appearance of the type in the memos suggests the irregular shapes and pressures associated with the typewriter rather than the uniformity of the laser printer, but those wrinkles could result from photocopying and faxing as well as typing. The memos were signed or initialed, but since no one had access to the originals, it wasn't possible to tell whether the signatures were true autographs or copies pasted into bogus documents by means of a computer, or even by hand. Finally, the memos show inconsistencies of style and language, but we don't typically expect attention to detail and careful revision from memos, whether typed on typewriters or keyboarded on computers, because such documents tend to be written hastily and with little concern for posterity. Such inconsistencies didn't prove or disprove authenticity.

Just as it was not possible to tell from internal evidence whether the memos were real or fake, there were also no external validators. The memos weren't notarized, a process used to certify formal documents such as wills, contracts, and affidavits, but not memos. And there were no eyewitnesses. CBS couldn't ask the author to verify the memos: Lt. Col. Killian had died in 1984. Living "witnesses" couldn't vouch for the composition or transmission of the memos, they could only offer opinions. Family members insisted that Killian hadn't written the memos, though they weren't really in a position to know one way or the other. His secretary, now elderly, was certain she hadn't typed them, but although she believed that the memos were forgeries, she indicated to reporters that their contents did reflect her boss's thinking. Some of Killian's military colleagues firmly agreed that the memos sounded like his work, while others were just as sure that they did not.

The Bush memos may or may not be fakes, and it's not my goal to determine their authenticity. What's interesting about the memo controversy is that neither internal nor external validators were conclusive, that the memos were ultimately dismissed as fakes not because of their content or appearance, or the opinions of experts, but because both believers in the memos and skeptics alike came to see that a middleman who had handled the documents was a crook.

Defending the memo's authenticity, CBS news anchor Dan Rather reported that the network had consulted a document expert before breaking the story. CBS News even posted on its website a photo of the document examiner, Marcel Matley, in the act of scrutinizing a piece of paper, ostensibly one of the Bush memos, to encourage confidence in the report. Both Rather and the network defended the memos as genuine for several days, despite the revelation by Matley that he had worked from photocopies, not originals, and had only been asked to look at the signatures, not authenticate the memo's text.

Finally, about ten days after the original story aired, CBS acknowledged that its source, Bill Burkett, had lied about where he got the memos and that their actual provenance could not be verified (CBS 2004b). Without originals, and without an unbroken chain of possession for the photocopies given to CBS, the memos suddenly became worthless as evidence. CBS then broadcast an interview in which Burkett acknowledged lying to the network and showed himself to be both evasive and untrustworthy. Though Burkett still maintained that the memos were genuine, and CBS did not say that they were forgeries, the network issued a statement regretting their use, and Dan Rather apologized on his evening news broadcast for relying on documents whose origins were murky.

In the end, there was no smoking gun, no actual proof that the documents were faked. But what finally sank the memos was the apparent shiftiness of the man who gave them to CBS. Bill Burkett, it seemed to those who watched him on TV, was someone from whom they wouldn't buy a used car, or a hot memo.

The memo incident put an end to Rather's long career, but while Rather eventually went to court to protest his firing by the network, the whole memo issue faded as quickly as it arose, and the inexorable cycle of news moved on to other concerns.

▪ ▪ ▪ IS SEEING BELIEVING?

Many viewers believed Dan Rather's initial story about the Bush memos because Rather, like other network news anchors, had established himself as a public figure worthy of trust, a symbol of accurate reporting who came into their living rooms every evening with the day's top stories. Rather's predecessor, Walter Cronkite, ended each of his broadcasts with the line, "And that's the way it is today..." and for viewers everywhere, the evening news as delivered by the broadcast networks or the cable news channels, or even *The Daily Show*, has become "the way it is." But when people finally saw Bill Burkett on CBS, they saw him to be a liar. Seeing for ourselves is often a way to determine trustworthiness, whether of a memo or a person. Seeing, after all, is believing. Or is it?

Since its invention in the nineteenth century, the visual technology of photography was often equated with truth and realism: pictures don't lie. But there has always been a parallel strain of suspicion associated with modern visual arts like photography, film, or television, which rely on technology not simply to record, but also to mediate the visual world. Technologies let us recreate the world and also lie about it.

In Sir Arthur Conan Doyle's novel *The Lost World* (1912), the aptly named Dr. Illingworth expresses the prevailing skepticism that photographic evidence is no evidence at all, that only the naked eye can discern the truth. The story's narrator summarizes Illingworth's objection to pictures proving that dinosaurs had been found living in a remote area of South America:

> The corroboration of these wondrous tales was really of the most slender description. What did it amount to? Some photographs. Was it possible that in this age of ingenious manipulation photographs could be accepted as evidence? What more?...It was understood that Lord John Roxton claimed to have the skull of a phororachus. He could only say that he would like to *see* that skull. (Doyle 1912, 181)

Almost as if to prove Illingworth right, the BBC's television version of *The Lost World* places live actors alongside computer-generated dinosaurs, but it doesn't take a big operation like Pixar or Industrial Light and Magic to doctor a picture. William J. Mitchell (1994) explained how off-the-shelf software and a run-of-the-mill personal computer can create a photograph of Marilyn Monroe and Abraham Lincoln that never existed in the original (see illustration).

Computers allow us to manipulate images in ways that make forgery undetectable. We recognize the picture of Abe and Marilyn as fake because Lincoln's eyes seem focused in an unlikely direction, considering his companion, and because we know that Monroe had a taste for Democratic presidents, not Republicans. It helps to remember, as well, that she and Lincoln lived at different times. But because the seams of this concocted photograph were finished at the level of the individual pixel, no amount of magnification will reveal the editing to a skilled document examiner.

The image of Lincoln and Monroe reproduced here, which appeared on the cover of *Scientific American*, was created with an early version of Photoshop and an off-the-shelf personal computer. From Mitchell 1994; image of Marilyn Monroe by Howard Frank; image of Abraham Lincoln from a photograph by Alexander Gardner now in the Corbis collection; used by permission.

▪ ▪ ▪ ANECDOTE: PHONY AS A THREE-DOLLAR BILL

Mitchell is correct that it's easy enough for an amateur to produce a fraudulent document, even a complex one, on a computer. Although I have only a smattering of knowledge about computer graphics, I created an image of a three-dollar bill on my own computer, using the same program Mitchell used, a low-end scanner, and an inexpensive digital tablet.

In contrast to the photo Mitchell produced for his *Scientific American* article, my own attempt to create a three-dollar bill by scanning a two-dollar bill and retouching the image with elements scanned from a C-note is amateurish, with visible seams and inconsistencies of color and resolution that are easily detected by the naked eye and that jump out at the observer with any degree of magnification.

But despite my clumsy efforts, which took all of an hour, when I project the image on a screen during a lecture it gets some double takes from the audience. After all, we have become so confident that the money in our wallets is real that we seldom take the time to examine it closely. We know that counterfeits exist, and we may have read stories about college students caught cranking out bogus twenties on color laser printers in some administrative office. Surely we've noticed tellers or store clerks testing big bills with special pens or passing them under black light. But such precautions just remind us that the U.S. Bureau of Engraving and Printing employs a variety of safeguards to ensure the validity of the currency it prints. Anyone who happens to wind up with a phony bill has to absorb the loss, but because that happens very rarely, the chances of our being left with the hot potato are remote; and other than counting it, we don't pay all that much attention to the money as we put it in our wallets.

▪ ▪ ▪

My own clumsy attempts at photo manipulation notwithstanding, we're more suspicious of printed text than paper money, despite the fact that the paper

Phony as a three-dollar bill. Graphic by the author.

money is often worth more, both in real and symbolic terms. If I stood on a sidewalk and handed out poems, most passersby would avoid eye contact and refuse my offer. I suspect it would be harder to give away poetry than incriminating memos about presidents, even if I were standing outside the CBS News building on West 57th Street in Manhattan. But if I were handing out ten-dollar bills, then I'd have to fight off my newfound friends who couldn't wait to get their hands on some free dead presidents. Of the few people who actually might take the free verse, most would throw it away in disgust once they saw it wasn't a discount coupon or an ad for adult entertainment. In the post 9/11 era, someone might even alert the Department of Homeland Security about my suspicious activities. But so confident are we in the authenticity of the money supply that no one would give the banknotes I was handing out more than a cursory glance before stuffing them away. Perhaps the scenario I've just outlined sounds far-fetched, but my point is not: How many of us take the trouble to actually "read" the money we so readily accept from total strangers where we bank and shop every day?

In fact, learning to trust paper money was a slow and difficult process, one in which many people were left holding worthless or devalued notes. As paper money began to circulate in the United States during the nineteenth century, there were few conventions that established the size, appearance, or even the denomination of individual bills. Like many written documents, banknotes employed both graphics and text, including signatures, both to convey information and to serve as authenticating devices. Though today few people "read" their money, as David Henkin (1998) has shown, recipients of these early bills examined the text closely to determine their money's genuineness.

The greenback has become a symbol of global capitalism, but that's hardly surprising since the first paper money was an exercise in a kind of textual free enterprise. American banks in the 1800s began printing their own paper currency (hence the term *banknote*). According to Henkin, by the time of the Civil War as many as 1,500 financial institutions, not all of them solvent, were issuing bills, and many forgers were cashing in on a money system that was only marginally stable. Nevertheless, the American economy grew increasingly dependent on banknotes instead of coins for transacting business. Henkin adds that, since far too many of these notes were only as good as the paper on which they were printed, merchants and bankers cross-checked the currency they received from customers against frequently updated lists of worthless or counterfeit money before accepting it. Eventually, in 1863, the federal government stepped in to centralize and regulate the production of a uniform national currency, and Americans learned to trust their money more and read it less.

▪ ▪ ▪ THE TECHNOLOGY OF FRAUD

But back to the Bush memos. Aside from their role in the dirty trickery of a presidential campaign, one in which Republicans had already produced ads claiming that John Kerry's military service, including his Purple Heart, was more faked than real, the Bush memos show us that after millennia of dealing with written texts, and despite the essential role that documents play in our daily lives, they can still be problematic, even untrustworthy, unless we know where they came from or who really wrote them. A text, for us, remains only as good as the paper it's written on or the person behind it, if that person can be found. The Bush memos were initially suspect because, even though they show some signs of being typed, it was also easy to think of them as computer generated. It may have taken a long time, but we eventually learned to trust handwriting, print, and typewriting. The Bush memos are another story. Given the complicity of computers in the juggling of visual images for good or ill, the jury's still out when it comes to our willingness to trust the digitized text, at least when it's deployed in a political campaign.

All new writing technologies bring with them the potential for fraud. In the early days of writing, few people trusted any sort of text. Even though writing had been around for several thousand years, until the Norman Conquest, writing in the British Isles consisted mostly of Bibles, prayer books, and the occasional poem or saint's life. Some literature was written down, along with some history, and admittedly much of the early written record, which could have included such ephemera as to-do lists and personal notes, has been lost. But day-to-day business in England was still conducted orally, not in writing, and the records of such transactions were preserved in people's memories, not in written ledgers or office filing cabinets.

When the Normans came uninvited to England in 1066, they brought with them not just regime change, but also a change in business practice. The Normans wrote everything down, and that was something that the Anglo-Saxons had some difficulty accepting. The historian Michael Clanchy (1993) chronicles the shift in business practices in eleventh-century England from reliance on the spoken word to written documents, and his phrase, "trusting writing," is particularly apt to the present discussion of how we respond to digital text.

As Clanchy reminds us, the Anglo-Saxons were used to recording ownership and property transfer through word of mouth: a purchaser might tender a verbal offer for land or goods; a parent might tell the children what part of an estate they would inherit. The Normans had already switched to written documents for recording such gifts and transfers, and since Normans were now in charge, they wanted their English subjects to do the same.

In contrast, Clanchy notes, the Anglo-Saxons were used to verifying property claims orally, by asking questions and listening to whatever individuals who had witnessed a transaction might remember, or if no witnesses survived, what the other members of the community recalled hearing about that transaction second- or thirdhand. Even in the absence of the polygraph, spoken assertions could be trusted as an accurate record of the past, though if a witness failed to answer questions well (as in the case of the Bush memos), they could be dismissed as untrustworthy or untruthful. Written documents couldn't answer questions the way living witnesses could. The veracity of witnesses could be tested, their memory of events compared with other people's recollections. Skeptical readers couldn't look a written text in the eye and see if its gaze wavered or it looked guilty. Speech was interactive while letters on a page—as Socrates told Phaedrus—were unresponsive. They were literally dumb. Who could be trusted more, the skeptics asked, a respected elder of the community or some marks inked on an animal skin?

Adding to the problem posed by documents that challenged the authority of human memory was the fact that, because few of the English could actually read, they had to take someone else's word for what a charter said. And since that someone was usually a Norman, it's not surprising that the English perceived writing as just a nasty Norman trick to steal their lands. In many cases, they were right. But despite initial mistrust and resistance, documents proliferated in twelfth-century England just as paper money spread in United States in the nineteenth, and, as with paper money, not all the documents were false. Everyone new to the written word has to learn to trust the text. So, like it or not, as they had once learned to test the truth of witnesses, Anglo-Saxon readers and nonreaders alike now had to learn to assess the validity of a piece of writing.

To make that task easier, writers adopted conventions of text production that could encourage acceptance of their documents. Even the illiterate among the Anglo-Saxons, who had been converted to Christianity by missionaries centuries earlier, had seen priests using Bibles and prayer books. As Clanchy observes, some of the new charters were drafted with illuminated initials and red rubrics to resemble these trusted documents. But such ornamentation was an expensive and tedious option, and for their less ceremonial documents, writers had to come up with more practical ways of convincing the reader that a text was genuine.

We see two such authenticators, crosses and seals, in the eleventh-century Anglo-Norman charter reproduced from Clanchy's book (see next page). The document contains three crosses, each signaling the consent of a participant in the land transfer being recorded. The cross is a Christian symbol used by illiterates in documents of this era to attest authorship. Signing with a cross was tantamount to taking a religious oath.

Charter and seal of Ilbert de Lacy. Three annotated crosses and a seal authenticate the document. From Clanchy 1993, plate 1, p. 346; used by permission.

As Clanchy describes the document, the first cross represents the English king, William Rufus, or William II. He was the second son of William the Conqueror and had inherited England, his father's second most important possession (the most important possession, the Duchy of Normandy, went to Robert, the Conqueror's eldest son). The second cross is that of the donor of the parcel of land in question, Ilbert de Lacy. And the third is that of Ilbert's wife, Hawise.

In addition to the three crosses representing the persons of the King and M/Mme de Lacy, appended to the charter is Ilbert de Lacy's wax seal, identifying him as the principal author of the document. Seals or other symbolic objects such as small knives were attached to documents as authenticators so that readers would recognize them as the property of the author. Clanchy reports that Ilbert's is one of the earliest English knight's seals to survive. The cross and seal say, essentially, "I am Ilbert de Lacy. This message has been approved by me."

De Lacy was, as his name suggests, a Norman, and his carefully authenticated charter, which announces the donation of a manor house in Buckinghamshire to an abbey in Rouen, and which Clanchy tells us may actually have been drafted by a Norman monk, is a fine example of what the English feared most from written documents, the transfer of their wealth to the continent.

It's noteworthy too that both King William and his vassals, the de Lacys, were illiterate—none of them actually signed the charter. It's also not likely that William inked the cross that stands for his name, and, according to Clanchy, it's possible that the de Lacys relied on a scribe to make their crosses as well. While the Normans expected written records to accompany important transactions, literacy itself was not widespread in medieval England or in Europe. The Norman aristocracy, like the general public, depended on a small scribal class, typically clerics, to do their writing and reading for them.

In the centuries that have passed since Ilbert de Lacy exported a little bit of England back across the Channel, literacy has become the rule rather than the exception. Today we expect the few illiterates left in our society to certify documents not with a cross, a mark that was trusted in Christian Europe during the Middle Ages because of its religious significance, but with an *x*, which masks its own faith-based origins behind a letter of the secular alphabet—the *x* originally stood for *chi*, the first letter in χριστοσ, Greek for Christ. And while most readers today rarely encounter a document signed with an *x*, we all know that anyone signing that way will need to have their mark witnessed—and countersigned—by someone who can actually read and write.

Of course, not all of the texts that we produce for ourselves or others need signing: people don't sign their shopping lists or diary entries, and even more formal writing such as a book manuscript or news article, while it bears the name of the author, doesn't require that person's signature. But the absence of a signature where one is required, for example on a check or a contract, or on the back of a credit card, can void a transaction or invalidate a document. In most cases, particularly for documents with legal implications, we now expect not a seal or cross but an actual signature, preferably a bold and unique one, to authenticate an author's words for the reader.

In the most famous signing ceremony in American history, John Hancock used his signature to stick a metaphoric finger in a monarch's eye. According to the popular story, the president of the Continental Congress made sure his name was large on the Declaration of Independence so that King George could read it without his glasses. Perhaps Hancock simply did it because he

John Trumbull's 1817 painting of one of the most publicized signings in history, that of the Declaration of Independence, hangs in the Capitol Rotunda and is reproduced on the back of the two-dollar bill. Based on sketches drawn from life, Trumbull portrays John Adams, Roger Sherman, Thomas Jefferson (presenting the document), and Benjamin Franklin standing before John Hancock, the president of the Continental Congress.

The original Declaration has faded, as we can see from the John Hancock signature reproduced here. From the National Archives. www.archives.gov/exhibits/charters/declaration.html.

thought it might secure his place in history, or because he was the first to sign. In any case, the other signers wrote in a smaller hand, with the result that Hancock's has become the best-known signature in the United States. In fact, the name "John Hancock" has become an informal synonym in American English for any autograph or signature.

Since Hancock's time we have come to invest a lot of meaning in a signature—it carries the identity and the individuality of the author in ways that an *x* or a seal cannot. While a signature may not be as foolproof as a fingerprint, many people work to perfect their own signatures in the belief that this written token carries part of the writer with it, not simply like the DNA we might leave at a crime scene, but something with actual life and personality. Like the little holograph of Princess Leia in *Star Wars*, a signature is an accurate stand-in or replacement for the person behind the message. As a means of validating a written text such as a credit card receipt or a love letter, it's the next best thing to being there.

Barring name change, illness, accident, the reduction of fine motor skills that may come with age, or the deliberate alteration of one's personal trademark, people's signatures remain remarkably consistent over the course of their lives. Because of the individuality and consistency of signatures, we use them to verify typed and printed documents as well as handwritten ones. We sign everything from personal and business letters to checks and applications. Signatures are essential on wills, passports, and driver's licenses. Unsigned forms are summarily rejected, and during critical election campaigns, poll watchers scrutinize voter petitions looking for evidence of fraudulent signing.

Signing letters is a way both of finalizing their content and adding the personal touch that means so much to recipients. When letters are produced in bulk, politicians, celebrities, and executives, faced with the problem of signing hundreds or perhaps thousands of these automatically generated documents, turn to signature machines. Automated Signature Technology, which makes signing machines that use real pen and ink rather than rubber stamps or computers, assures customers of the effectiveness of the machine-generated personal touch:

> Studies show that personally signed letters will be read more frequently, kept longer and generate substantially more activity than letters signed with digital, scanned, or printed signatures. By decreasing the amount of time a single executive, manager, or VIP signs his [*sic*] name by just 15 minutes a day, a signature machine can pay for itself in just a short time. The written signature gives personal value and meaning to your documents. Organizations that use our equipment understand the power of a personal signature. (signaturemachine.com/products/products.html)

Thomas Jefferson is said to be the first U.S. president to take advantage of such automated writing technology. He used a machine called a polygraph, a version of the pantograph familiar to draftsmen, that harnessed two pens together and allowed him to copy a letter at the same time that he was writing the original.

The polygraph shown in the illustration, which is on display at Jefferson's home at Monticello, is not suitable for making multiple copies, and nineteenth-century office documents continued to be copied either by hand or with a device called a copy press until the perfection of carbon paper, which was invented in the early 1800s but did not become widely used until later in that century. Polygraphs—today we call them autopens—could not produce presidential signatures on a large scale until they became mechanized.

The greeting card shown on the next page, sent to a relative of mine in response to a small campaign contribution, may have been signed by an autopen, which is not all that different in conception from the one that Jefferson experimented with, or it may simply have been printed—it's apparent that the Clintons did not sign such mass-distribution cards personally. At least one autograph hound has accepted the fact that the rich and famous aren't likely to sign their own correspondence, and he has turned to collecting less-lucrative

The Hawkins & Peale polygraph uses two pens yoked together. A writer grasps one pen to write the original, and the machine's levers manipulate the second pen to create a copy. The polygraph required constant adjustment, and even when the levers worked smoothly, both pens had to be dipped in ink repeatedly. Despite Thomas Jefferson's enthusiasm for the polygraph, the machine's manufacturers lost money on the product. Special Collections, University of Virginia Library; used by permission.

*Our family
wishes you and yours
a joyful holiday season
and a new year
blessed with health, happiness,
and peace.*

Greeting card signed by the Clintons, presumably using an automatic signing machine. Photograph by the author.

An autopen version of Richard M. Nixon's signature. From geocities.com/~sbeck/ autopens/ap-rn.htm.

but easier-to-obtain autopen signatures, such as a machine-generated version of President Richard Nixon's autograph.

A signature can be enabling as well as authenticating: signing, to use the popular *Star Trek* command, can make it so. Presidents may sign greeting cards as a feel-good gesture to constituents, but they sign laws to give those laws force, both legally as well as symbolically. Although there is no record that John Hancock used multiple quills when he signed the Declaration of

Independence, presidents today will sign new bills using a different pen for each letter of their name, then give the pens to key supporters as souvenirs of the occasion. (In an homage to the days of prepaper technology, the official copy of every new law is printed on parchment.)

Signatures themselves can serve as souvenirs. The autographs of the significant or famous can become the objects of adoration and desire. Sports figures sign baseballs, basketballs, and footballs for fans, sometimes for a fee, and reproductions of their signatures decorate collector cards and athletic paraphernalia, authenticating them for consumers much as Ilbert de Lacy's seal authenticated his charter—"I am Willie Mays. This fielder's glove is approved by me"—and thereby adding to their value.

A quick check on September 28, 2007, showed that there were more than 33,706 autographs for sale on eBay, the internet auction site. Most were the signatures of sports or entertainment figures, some were reprints rather than originals, not all were genuine, and a few were even names I recognized: a Ronald Reagan signed photo for $5; an Eva Peron letter from the 1940s for $200; and an Elvis Presley that the seller admits is printed rather than hand-signed, for the curious sum of $4.60.

On the same day, on their own websites, professional autograph dealers were offering the signatures of such historical figures as Gen. George Armstrong Custer ($5,500); Albert Einstein ($9,000); and Martin Luther King ($12,900). A John Wilkes Booth letter was going for $15,500, and an Abraham Lincoln for $22,900. Booth letters are rare. After the actor assassinated Lincoln, most of the people that he had written to destroyed the correspondence, fearing guilt by association. As a result, when Booth letters are offered for sale they may draw even more than a Lincoln signature does, a fact that suggests some collectors may not have their priorities straight. A week after I checked autograph prices, a signed John Wilkes Booth letter sold for a record $68,000 at a Boston auction, topping the previous record for Booth's John Hancock by $30,000. In contrast, an original John Hancock, whose value is clearly more symbolic than commercial, had just gone to a happy buyer for only $4,950.

Despite advances in literacy since the Middle Ages, and the occasionally inflated value we place on autographs and the pens that produce them, we still approach words on paper ambivalently. We trust the familiar handwriting of friends and family and those whose authority has been established beforehand (a supervisor, a teacher, a physician, a government official), but we can remain skeptical when strangers sign things; and we are downright suspicious when they don't.

A sign in the local post office warns that patrons presenting unsigned credit cards will be asked to provide two additional forms of official identification before their payment will be accepted. Salesclerks check credit card receipts against the signature on the card itself (though many skip this step if they think management isn't looking). And most American merchants require photo identification before accepting personal checks. The signatures on such papers as marriage certificates and wills need to be witnessed or the documents are not considered valid. Deeds, depositions, and some documents that are signed outside the presence of their intended recipients must be notarized, a process whereby a public officer called a notary witnesses the signing and attests to its legitimacy (that's just for the signature; as was the case with the Bush memos, the actual contents of the document may require additional verification).

Sometimes it takes more than a signature to authenticate a document, whether Norman or modern. A certificate given to me in the sixth grade looks much grander than the simple commendation for picking up litter that it is. Its designer invoked a number of features that we have come to associate with charters, diplomas, and other documents suitable for framing in an effort to dazzle the recipient and his parents: Old English type, calligraphic

A mid-twentieth-century document bearing various kinds of authenticators. Photograph by the author.

hand lettering, inflated language (I already knew as a sixth grader that picking up crumpled paper and gum wrappers from the school hallway hardly constituted "meritorious services"), a background image of the great seal of the City of New York bearing the Latin legend SIGILLUM CIVITATIS NOVI EBORACI, a gold-foil-embossed seal of the New York City Department of Sanitation (no Latin on that), and a mix of autograph and printed signatures of city and school officials. Unfortunately, someone at P.S. 144 in New York City forgot to fill in the school's name, considerably lessening the impact of this good-citizen award, not to mention its resale value on eBay.

▪ ▪ ▪ QUESTION AUTHORITY

Although documents replaced oral tradition as a way of doing business, and despite the many safeguards that we have developed to certify writing as valid, we still run into handwritten texts that may not record the past as it really happened. Even after centuries of dealing with manuscripts, experts were duped by the sixty-two handwritten notebooks of the so-called Hitler Diaries, forged by Konrad Kujau and sold by his accomplice Gerd Heidemann to the German magazine *Der Stern* for two million dollars. When *Stern* announced the discovery of the diaries, a bidding war ensued as *Newsweek* and other publications sought to get in on the action. In a dramatic gesture, the British publishing magnate Rupert Murdoch hired the historian Hugh Trevor-Roper, who served on the board of a rival newspaper, to authenticate the diaries. Although Trevor-Roper was fooled, other experts exposed the notebooks as amateurish fakes, crafted from modern paper and ink and full of obvious factual errors, and both Kujau and Heidemann were jailed for their scam.

Signatures and seals, photographs and thumbprints, serial numbers, specially formulated inks, and perfumed papers serve to authenticate official documents such as certificates, licenses, and paper money or, in the case of the Hitler Diaries, to trick experts into declaring such documents genuine. Today's readers look for other indicators to establish the bona fides of the more mundane texts—the books, newspapers, magazines, and reports—that we encounter every day. When we pick our reading material we rely on everything from the cover, to the paper, to the reputation of the author or the recommendation of a reviewer to tell us what to read or how to read it.

Anglo-Saxon readers managed to get past Normans' deceptive practices as they learned to put at least some trust in writing, and, despite contemporary forgeries like the Hitler Diaries, today we readily value type or printed text over the individually penned document. Certainly printed fakes like my three-dollar bill or the infamous "Protocols of the Elders of Zion" do exist, and some people are taken in by phony money or spurious books. But even though treatises on etiquette remind us that a handwritten note is always preferable, and while a handwritten text is as valid, legally, as anything typed or printed, today we are more likely to accept the writing of strangers if it's machine generated.

The primacy of print didn't happen overnight. Just as the Anglo-Saxons had trouble negotiating the new document-dependent culture that was imposed on them, Europeans had to learn to trust the printed books that slowly began to circulate in the fifteenth century. It was no accident that the first printed books were Bibles and prayer books. Just as some early business documents in England copied the format of religious manuscripts, early printed Bibles, such as the Gutenberg Bible, were hand-decorated with elaborate initials, rubrics, and numbers to make them look more like the illuminated manuscript Bibles that readers were already used to. Even so, printed books, like manuscripts before them, were greeted with suspicion.

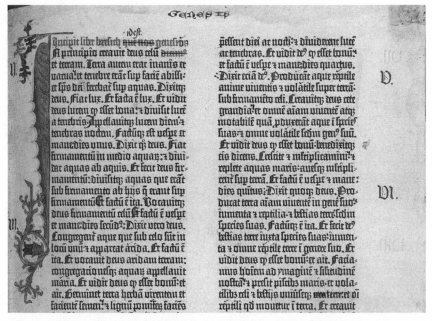

The upper portion of a page showing the beginning of the Book of Genesis, in Latin; from a Gutenberg Bible printed in the 1450s. Rubrics, numerals, illuminations, and other decorations were added after printing by scribes and skilled artists, and for more than two centuries it was common practice to illustrate or correct printed books individually, by hand. Courtesy of the Harry Ransom Center at the University. of Texas; used by permission.

One critic of the new printing press complained that paper wouldn't survive more than a couple of centuries, while parchment lasts one thousand years and vellum, made from calfskin, would last twice as long (Clanchy 2007). Just as I knew in 1971 that typed job applications were superior because the type bar actually engraved its image into the paper, while photocopiers essentially sprinkled some toner onto its surface, one medieval critic praised the pen for carving out its message on parchment, like a plow planting wisdom instead of seeds, while the printing press merely painted ink onto the paper's surface:

> Peter the Venerable, abbot of Cluny, had likened the act of writing to work in the fields: "The pages are ploughed by the divine letters and the seed of God's word is planted in the parchment."... The scribe is understood to incise the words of Scripture into the parchment with the point of his quill pen, whereas the abbot of Sponheim criticizes printing as an essentially superficial process which stamps text onto perishable paper. (Clanchy 2007, 195)

Early printed books were the products of a new and developing technology, and not all of them were produced with the care or expense that accompanied Gutenberg's Bibles. More run-of-the-mill printed works—using woodcuts for illustrations rather than hand-painted miniatures—were seldom as attractive as manuscripts. But printed books had some advantages that readers were quick to notice: they were still expensive, to be sure, but much less expensive than manuscripts. And books were literally cranked out by printers more quickly and in greater numbers than manuscripts, which meant that more people with means could actually get their hands on one. In the long run, books achieved acceptance—and that meant sales—not by imitating manuscripts, but by trading on the reputation of authors and presses, factors which even today move us to choose or reject a printed work.

Looking back, it's easy to see the printing press initiating a revolution in writing and reading practices. Elizabeth Eisenstein (1980), in her extensive history of printing, establishes the reputation of the press as an agent of change. But the "revolution" caused by printing was actually very slow in coming, and the changes heralded by Eisenstein took several centuries to become firmly established.

Both literacy and printed books began to proliferate in tandem, but their greatest impact occurred not in the 1450s, with the invention of lead type and the building of the first presses, but with the industrial revolution, some 350 years after Gutenberg, when the market for print really exploded. And even with the huge increases in book, magazine, and newspaper production that took place in the nineteenth century, the daily written work of the factory and the office remained dependent on pencil and pen rather than moveable type until the twentieth century, when the typewriter and adding machine began to revolutionize the business practices of industrialized countries in Europe and North America.

Today we associate manuscripts with error: as we know from personal experience, writers make mistakes when they're creating or copying text, and handwritten copies differ one from another often in significant ways. In contrast, we've come to think that because books can be reproduced mechanically, all copies of a given title will be identical. Anyone who buys a new car knows that although each vehicle coming off an assembly line looks like the one before it, on closer inspection each one exhibits variations in fit, finish, and even performance. Similarly, as Adrian Johns (1998) has shown, printed texts, particularly early ones, were hardly clones of the first copy that was run off. Even more than cars, early books exhibited a great degree of variation. Paper was expensive, and as Johns reminds us, authors were often expected to pay for the paper that was used to print their books. Time was clearly money even before capitalism came into its own, so print shops wasted as little as possible of either, binding sheets with errors in them into the books even as they reset corrected pages for their next trip through the press:

> The first sheets of a print run would…often be checked as the rest were being printed off. In such a case, books would inevitably be made up of sheets in different states of correction. The consequence was that no two final copies out of a given edition would necessarily be the same. (Johns 1998, 91)

It's true that the eighty-four fourteenth-century manuscripts of Chaucer's *Canterbury Tales* differ significantly from one another, but it's also true, as Johns points out, that no two copies of the 1623 First Folio of Shakespeare's plays are identical—some 228 copies of the First Folio's original print run of about 750 still exist, according to Anthony James West (2001). The state of both Chaucer manuscripts and Shakespeare printed texts makes it difficult if not impossible for scholars to agree on authoritative versions of these authors' work. Even more astonishing to those who think of books as somehow more dependable than manuscripts, there were an estimated twenty-four thousand variations in so standard a text as the King James Bible—also called the "Authorized Version," a name which itself all but guarantees some uniformity—between its initial publication in 1611 and 1830 (Johns 1998, 91). Even today, with production techniques more standardized and efficiency improved, printers silently introduce subtle variations in books between print runs.

Even so, print has come to inspire confidence not just because it can be relatively uniform, but also because we've learned that much of what gets published undergoes editorial scrutiny and a winnowing process in which inappropriate or deficient material is rejected and only the best content makes it to the press (at least that's what's supposed to happen). In addition, once accepted for publication, such text is vetted before it reaches its audience. Someone, a copy editor, publisher, manager, or authority of some sort has fact-checked and proofread the document, authenticating and certifying the text before passing it along to us.

▪ ▪ ▪ SIGNING OFF

As soon as computers allowed us to generate digital versions of conventional texts, skeptics began to question the authority of those texts, not just controversial documents such as the Bush memos or obvious frauds like the Abe Lincoln–Marilyn Monroe liaison, but the mundane documents of everyday life, the emails that threatened to supplant the telephone call and the digital orders and receipts traversing the World Wide Web without their customary signatures.

It was just a few years ago that most people considered online shopping a reckless endeavor, but today e-commerce is big business and getting bigger. Americans are not just buying from internet versions of familiar stores, but also from virtual stores with no bricks-and-mortar presence at all. Most recently, person-to-person online shopping has exploded, with individual buyers and sellers trading goods through the mediation of such entrepreneurial sites as eBay, Amazon, and Craigslist, all actively pumping up the national garage sale mania.

So prevalent is online shopping, trading, banking, and bill paying today that the signature, the long-trusted validator of documents ranging in import from declarations of independence to greeting cards and personal checks, and the one last survivor of the decline in handwriting, may soon go the way of clay tablets and quill pens. Even such basic identification documents as driver's licenses and passports are moving toward new ways of validating authenticity to back up, and ultimately supplant, the written signature and photo. After all, signatures can be forged, pictures faked—and neither can compete with the latest technological identifiers: the thumbprint reader, which has started to appear in the workplace, and the more "scientific" eyeball scan and DNA analysis, all of them mediated by the computer and promising more accuracy than a John Hancock ever could.

The impending death of the signature is just one of the new wrinkles that the computer has brought to the process of creating and evaluating the written word, wrinkles that will occupy us for the rest of this book and for many years to come.

8

■ ■ ■ Writing on Screen

■ ■ ■ FREQUENTLY ASKED QUESTIONS

1. Are email, texting and instant messages destroying the English language, killing the art of conversation, and rupturing social relationships?
2. How can I use email, texting, and IM to enhance my communications skills, cement business and personal relationships, and increase profitability, while at the same time protecting my privacy?

The first question is often raised by alarmists who don't trust digital texts and are anxious to find something wrong with the new technologies of communication, and its answer seems to be "No." English survives, conversation thrives online as well as off, and on balance, digital communication seems to be enhancing human interaction, not detracting from it. The second question is more likely to be asked by those who want to trust the new media and are anxious to learn how it might be useful for them, while making sure these new ways of doing things with words won't blow up in their faces. The answers to the second question are too complex to be rendered in a sound bite. But as we see in the chapters that follow, both questions reveal a lot about how digital communications are changing our lives and how we're responding to those changes.

Now that writing has established itself as *the* way to do business in the modern world—not just the business of trade and commerce, but that of governance, education, culture, and the arts—we find ourselves facing new textual challenges posed by the computer, that upstart successor to the pencil, the printing press, and the typewriter. Our day-to-day experiences with reading and writing online require us to learn how to trust not just the familiar texts that computers reproduce for us so quickly and efficiently, but all sorts of new and unfamiliar kinds of computer-generated texts as well, ones whose value and reliability go unquestioned by their enthusiastic practitioners, but which prompt serious objections from the vociferous technophobes who still long for an imaginary "good old days," a golden age that never really was, when texts were simpler and more reliable. For the rest of us, these new genres— email, instant messaging, texting, and blogging, to name only some—pose a continual challenge as we look for ways to evaluate the digital texts that we read and to make credible the digital texts we write.

While much of the impact of the digital revolution in processing the written word expands horizons, presenting us with new information and new ways of packaging that information, it is also important to remember that like the telephone, the computer is a technology that sometimes lets us roam free and sometimes keeps us on a leash. For example, despite advances in wireless networking that allow us to take a laptop and curl up, more or less, on the couch or on the rug, as we were wont to do with a good book, computers are generally useless at the beach or in the bath. But more than one acquaintance of mine checks the morning email in bed the way the idle rich were shown to peruse their paper missives along with morning coffee on a tray in old Hollywood films, and a few even turn to their laptop, with its warm batteries, to read themselves to sleep in those same beds on a chill winter night. But they're not reading novels or self-help books online; they're chatting, watching videos, and catching up on the news.

Advances in telephony connect the caller and the called in ever-expanding ways and locations. In particular, the mobile phone brings private conversations into public spaces and permits the outside world to intrude on our most intimate moments. Advances in writing technologies are also redefining public and private, connecting writers and readers in new ways and places, facilitating communication while at the same time letting not just well-defined audiences but also a fluctuating set of anonymous observers read our screens and record our keystrokes. The computer, like the writing technologies that preceded it, is revising how we think of public and private writing.

The mobile phone lets us carry along with us two-way access to everyone we know, plus a raft of strangers. With it, we are present to all who care to call, and whether they are near or far, friend or stranger, we are free to intrude on anyone else who has a phone as well. No activity is safe from interruption. Campaigning in the 2008 presidential primaries, Rudy Giuliani, who as mayor of New York City was a strong supporter of gun control, took a cell phone call from his wife—possibly planned to defuse the tension—while he was addressing the National Rifle Association. But what was most amusing about the incident was just how ordinary it seemed to everyone in the audience. After all, phones go off in restaurants and bathrooms, at lectures and funerals, on crowded city streets and in remote wilderness refuges, and no one at the NRA rally took aim at the candidate for this particular gaffe.

The increasing miniaturization of the mobile phone is speeding us toward the *Star Trek* reality where anyone can speak with anyone using a two-way communicator that doubles as a piece of jewelry. No dial, no buttons to press, no "hello" necessary. Just tap and talk. An audience awaits. In a similar fashion, writing on screen makes everyone an author. And finding readers presents no problem for our newest writers. Any scribbler with a computer, a Wi-Fi card, and a place to sit at Starbuck's has immediate access to the universe of plugged-in readers, many of them eager to devour all manner of digital text they would never touch in printed form. Writers using conventional technologies may spend their lives desperately seeking an audience, but on the web, if you write it, they will come. All a cyberauthor needs to do is upload a bit of text and there's an instant readership—a small niche audience or a vast and very general one—eager to consume every virtual word.

■ ■ ■ VIRTUAL GENRES

And those readers will read just about anything, from the latest attempt at the great American novel to a shopping list. Today all my students are on Facebook, and many have MySpace accounts as well, but ten years ago, when people first began putting up personal home pages, only two of the students I surveyed had an online presence, one of them because it was assigned in a computer technology class, and the other—let's call him George—because it seemed to him that it might be fun. On his page George posted pictures of his family and his cat; a list of his favorite songs; a link to a pro basketball team that he liked—the kinds of things that users of older technologies might have put in a scrapbook intended for personal use only. It seemed to me at the time that no one but a doting parent would read such a web page. When I asked George about this, he answered, "You'd be surprised." His own relatives didn't use computers yet, but his hit counter showed about a dozen connected readers a day clicking on the trivia of his life. Those were early days, and many early personal web sites were poorly designed and carelessly maintained. But what goes into the popular Facebook and MySpace pages of the present are essentially updated variations on George's cat photos and playlists.

The personal web page is no longer a novelty, and it remains a creative force alongside the more uniform Facebook and MySpace templates. While many of these pages still have an exhibitionist quality about them, their content often runs a lot deeper than "here are my favorite top ten lists this week." As a genre, this sort of page encompasses a wide range of material from the very local—the latest snapshots of the kids for the growing numbers of web-enabled grandparents—to things that might actually interest both a broad and a targeted readership: reviews of movies, music groups, and TV shows; opinion essays; artistic and literary dabbling; job résumés; and lists, lists, and more lists, all of them clickable. And then there are the corporate pages, like tide.com, which we discussed earlier, whose goal is to portray the company positively and enhance profitability.

As the web page evolved into a genre, a variety of self-identified experts began creating an aesthetic of dos and don'ts for individuals who wanted to design their own. Programs such as Frontpage and Dreamweaver promised to idiot-proof the process of creating a web page by providing users who didn't want to learn HTML programming with templates and prefabricated modules into which they could drop their own content. And of course there are books on the subject: even the most accomplished computer users resort to traditional printed books to show them how to use the presumably user-friendly web design software they have just installed, because the "help" utility that comes with almost every kind of software simply doesn't help enough. But all of this—the innovation, the formulation of standards, the how-to-do-it instructions, and the prefab formats for those who can't or won't try DIY—is part and parcel of genre development.

It isn't often that new writing genres evolve. The last major literary genre to develop before the computer revolution was the novel, which came on the scene in the seventeenth century (though some scholars date it earlier or later). It too was facilitated by a new technology. The novel might exist without the printing press, but it clearly became the dominant western literary form in part because improved press technologies enabled the mass production of reading matter. Books and readers increased in a supply–demand spiral from the sixteenth to the nineteenth centuries in the West. This reflected changes in the status and lifestyle of the middle class. There was more that had to be read at work and more leisure time for reading at home. The printing press provided reading materials in quantities sufficient to address both needs. And in doing so, this new technology of literacy helped reading and writing become more of a daily event.

Like the novel, the newspaper is a technology-dependent genre. While the news was propagated both in manuscript and print formats in the seventeenth and eighteenth centuries, newspapers and magazines, like novels, owe their improved circulation to the hand-operated press, and even more to the automated printing presses introduced in the nineteenth century. But while the novel has so far resisted the migration to computers, newspaper circulation in the United States has been in decline for many years, and as more and more people get their information from screens instead of kiosks, newspapers have been quick to digitize in the hopes of improving readership and the advertising revenue that keeps these digital "papers" afloat.

▪ ▪ ▪ :) WHEN YOU SAY THAT, PARDNER: EMAIL AND THE TAMING OF THE ELECTRONIC FRONTIER

Besides the web page, computers have spawned a number of other new genres: email, which is neither phone call nor letter; instant messaging, which goes a step beyond email; and the latest, the blog, a kind of web page on steroids. We've had the rare opportunity of watching these genres form in our own lifetime—it's a little bit like being present at the birth of stars. Like stars, each new genre emerged from an initial chaotic state and coalesced over time, developing its own structures, conventions, and standards as its community of users grew and began both to organize and regulate itself. Email was one of the first digital genres, and it has had a tremendous impact on our communication practices.

While many readers of this book wouldn't dream of starting the day without email and a latte, the early days of email were rough and uncivilized, a virtual electronic frontier where not just fancy coffee, but any hint of food or drink was strictly banned from the computer clean room.

There wasn't much email in the mornings either. Email in those days was still a long way from replacing the standard ways of keeping in touch, letters and phone calls, not just because it was new, but also because, like the first phone calls (and, presumably, the first letters as well), it was at best a very clunky form of communication.

As I noted earlier, mainframe computers were designed to run numbers, not words, and the first computer prose was written despite, not because of, the technology. Computer keyboards resembled typewriters, only not quite. Text was all lowercase or, sometimes, all uppercase, because some early computers didn't allow shifting on the fly to create the occasional capital letter the way typewriters did. (To be sure, the first typewriters didn't have shift keys either.) Worse, digital text was almost impossible to revise, so typos went uncorrected. And there were plenty of typos, since even the best touch typists were tripped up by the computer's not-quite-familiar key arrangements. Given the technical limits of computers back in the 1960s, it's no surprise that spelling didn't count for much in informal documents like the messages that programmers sent to one another while they waited for their programs to compile, or that the conventions of grammar and punctuation were only loosely observed.

Considering the circumstances under which they were produced and read, the first electronic messages were quick and dirty, short and not always particularly sweet. The format of email, such as it was, was informal too: there were no greetings or farewells—messages just began and ended. When names were used, it was first names only. The idea was to get in and out fast, take up as little bandwidth as possible, and get on with one's life.

At least that was the image that the early emailers wanted to project: theirs was a shoot-from-the-hip prose that identified them as a new breed of men (and they were mostly men) on the cutting edge of a technology that was about to remake the world using language dressed just like they were, in t-shirts, jeans, and sandals. Walt Whitman, the nineteenth-century American poet who celebrated just this kind of unbuttoned language, would have been proud to see the early emailers rejecting schoolmarmish letter-writing rules in favor of an imaginary frontier style that branded them as mavericks, thinly disguising what they really were: slide rule–toting nerds at last taking their revenge on the refined, Eastern literary world.

But there is another side to the story of early email: the pin-striped, corporate communications side where letter-writing rules mattered, where vice presidents and account executives, not rogue programmers, sent polite and well-punctuated email memos announcing meetings or discussing projects over company intranets, clusters of computers that had been linked together for the use of employees only. These white-collar emailers favored conventional spelling and usage; they keyed in the customary forms of letter writing such as the salutation and the polite close; they kept to the memo format so faithfully that our sophisticated email programs still begin every message with *to:*, *cc:*, and *subject:* fields; and they revered the do-and-don't authority of rulebooks.

Unfortunately, there's not much except people's memories to tell us just how many of the emails of the 1960s took the law into their own hands, stylistically speaking, and how many were indistinguishable in tone and form from conventionally typed interoffice correspondence. Access to mainframes was limited and expensive—it would be a good twenty years before the personal computer turned email into a mass medium. Besides, email, like the early phone call, was considered a fleeting and impermanent form of communication. It wasn't typically printed out or even saved on computer tapes, those being reserved for the most important data (floppy disks, a more personal and portable form of storage, would come later, but email programs are still configured in a way that makes saving emails to an archive less than user-friendly).

But even if many of the first emails were pressed and pin-striped, not wrinkled and lawless, the perception grew that email was the new voice of the electronic frontier. No matter if you commuted to the wild, wild West of Cupertino, Redmond, and Austin, or to the wilds of Rte. 128 just west of Boston, the renegade image of email prevailed. This was a genre whose convention was to flout convention, and emailers could earn their spurs by intentionally misspelling, omitting commas, and choosing vocabulary that was more rough-hewn than businesslike.

Then a combination of developments—analogous to the coming of the railroads—turned Silicon Gulch into Silicon Valley, and thus began the closing of the electronic frontier, at least so far as email was concerned. Favorably priced and easy-to-use personal computers tempted more people to jump into word processing, and it wasn't long before these newcomers discovered email. A new breed of dudes and city slickers came to cyberspace with their conservative textual conventions intact, and they proceeded to set up housekeeping on the internet.

Immediately, feuds began to break out between the experienced computer users and the newbies, the contemptuous label given to those who had just begun to use WordStar or Volkswriter, who knew the importance of effective business correspondence, and who, discovering Eudora, wanted to do email *right*. While it wasn't exactly cow punchers versus sheep ranchers, the lawless email pros quickly found themselves outnumbered by eager newcomers anxious to obey the laws of the new writing community that they were joining, so they wouldn't look like amateurs.

It did no good to explain to these newbies that the electronic frontier preferred its own rough justice to the rules of Strunk and White. For them, bad spelling, like uncombed hair and casual dress, had no place in the computerized corporate office. On top of this, crusading newspaper op-eds lambasted click-and-send, spell-as-you-go email for destroying the English language and lamented the fact that computers were turning the nation's youth into mindless hooligans who would rather email than write a book report for school.

Critics quickly warned that the speed and easy availability of email encouraged haste, made people lazy with their words, and was—paradoxically—both completely impersonal and overly informal. Such complaints persist today. A recent report issued by the National Commission on Writing quotes one government official complaining,

E-mail is one of the leading causes of miscommunication....The sender is composing on the spot. You might do a spell-check, but you can't do a "thought-check." It's like blurting out something without thinking it through, or considering how it's going to be understood by the recipient. (National Commission 2005, 5)

Another critic cited in the report dismisses email as "just a higher order of Instant Messaging," despite the fact that IM's popularity is more recent than email's:

> The use of e-mail has had a negative effect on writing clarity....
> Punctuation has disappeared. Nobody uses a period. There's no
> capitalization anymore. It's more like a stream of consciousness and often
> hard to follow. (National Commission 2005, 10)

But the Luddites have no need to fear that email signals anything as momentous as the death of civilization, or even the end of book reports as we know them. Second-generation emailers, who quickly became the majority, were concerned with the niceties of format, style, and usage, and "netiquette" guides began to overrun the web. *Netiquette* was the new term coined to describe the Emily Post–style discussions of proper email. Here's part of one newspaper reporter's list of the dos and don'ts of the new genre:

- Don't shout. Whenever you type in capital letters, it's considered "shouting" on line because it's exceptionally hard to read, just like real shouting is hard to listen to....You wouldn't think of shouting, flying off the handle or repeating everything everyone says in polite company, now would you? Yet some of you never think twice about doing just those things—and more—on line.
- Keep your missives short, to the point, and tightly directed.
- [Don't] fire off a hasty note....The rule to follow: engage brain, THEN engage fingers. [Here the reporter unabashedly violates her own rule against writing all caps, showing that even on the internet, rules are made to be broken.]
- [Don't] quote the other person's entire message—especially if your response is merely "I agree."
- Don't...stuff the bottom of [your] messages with everything from cute quotes to every phone number [you] have. These "signature files"....can get annoying...when there's a two-word message followed by a huge chunk of clutter.
- Do pay attention to posterity. The messages you post...are often saved by the people that receive them....Do you really want someone five years from now reading your note to your mistress? Or your description of your drunken frat party?...Don't put it on line if you wouldn't want to see it on television or in the newspaper. (Newman 1996)

Manners weren't all that mattered on email. Spelling counted too. Suddenly the electronic frontiersmen were doffing their buckskin and worrying about such niceties as whether *email* can even be a verb; whether a plural form, *emails*, is permissible; whether *on line* should be one word or two; and whether *internet* and *Word Wide Web* are capitalized (and if so, does that mean *web page* must become *Web page?*).

The "correct" spelling of the word *email* itself was up for grabs, with lexicographers at Merriam-Webster and the *American Heritage Dictionary* opting for the hyphenated *e-mail*, while the *Oxford English Dictionary* chose solid *email* for the noun and hyphenated *e-mail* for the verb, without explaining this apparent inconsistency.

One clear sign that convention was taming the web appeared in 1996 when the technology journal *Wired*, known for its radical and freewheeling prose, published *Wired Style*, a guide for writing in the digital age. The manual's introduction, taking a cue from the likes of Walt Whitman, celebrates "not the clear-but-oh-so-conventional voice of standard written English....[but] the voice of people who write the way they talk" (Hale 1996). But despite protestations that its judgments are based on "actual usage, not rigid rules," *Wired Style* presents what is essentially a list of rules, a set of dos and don'ts that have little to do with write-like-you-talk and everything to do with write-like-I-want-you-to (or is that *as-I-want-you-to-write?*). These are only some examples of the magazine's hipper-than-thou diktats that could just as easily come from Strunk and White's *Elements of Style*, Fowler's *Modern English Usage*, or any of the other style bibles that insecure writers have come to rely on:

> **Darpa** (Defense Advanced Research Projects Agency): Pronounced "darpah" and spelled with an initial cap. Neither Darpa nor Arpa takes an article.

DARPA is the U.S. government agency credited with establishing the internet as a way for people engaged in military research at universities, labs, and military installations around the country to share their work quickly and securely. It's not clear why *Wired Style* uses only an initial capital for the acronym. Merriam-Webster prefers the more common all-caps DARPA that is customary with acronyms, and the DARPA website always spells the agency's name in caps: "WELCOME to DARPA" (www.darpa.mil). *Wired Style* itself spells other acronyms all-caps as well, as the entry for ENIAC shows:

> **ENIAC:** Pronounce it "ee-knee-ack" but don't say "the ENIAC computer"; it's redundant. Some claim that the "C" in ENIAC originally stood for calculator, but go with computer.

In its entry for *plug-and-play*, *Wired Style* opts for formal usage over informal. After all, *Wired* isn't *Rolling Stone*, and writing isn't rock 'n' roll: "**plug-and-play:** If you must use it, at least don't say plug-n-play." So much for writing the way one talks, or even talking the way one talks. In contrast to such categorical rules, the entry for *readme* begins by acknowledging that linguistic variations will occur when people write the way they talk. But when such variants rear their ugly heads, read the editor's lips: fahgeddabowdit. *Wired Style* will choose the best form to use—after all, that's what style manuals are for:

> **readme:** A file containing vital information about a software program or file. Some companies use README, others Readme, and others Read Me! Keep it simple: readme.

Wired Style urges writers to treat *data* as a singular, rejecting the advice of other usage guides that English *data* must be plural because the word is plural in Latin (the Latin singular, for a single bit of information, is *datum*). But even as the manual makes this liberal recommendation, *Wired Style* stresses the importance of getting things right:

> Should you ever use the singular of **data**—that is, datum? Once there was a day when datum was singular and data was plural. That day is past. Datum is beyond vestigial. Combine data with a singular verb. And you didn't ask, but get this right: Data travels *over* wires or lines, not *through* them.

But get this right? So much for the light touch. Despite their claims to the contrary, neither capitalists nor style manuals are ever laissez-faire. To be sure, *Wired Style* occasionally prefers one variant over another, but less frequently, instead of dictating the correct form, the guide allows readers to choose:

> **mouses or mice?** What's the plural of that small, rolling, pointing device invented by Douglas Engelbart in 1964? We prefer mouses. Mice is just too suggestive of furry little critters. Both terms are common, so take your pick. We actually emailed Engelbart to see what he'd say. His answer? "Haven't given the matter much thought."

Despite the editor's recommendation, actual usage indicates that people are avoiding the plural of this word altogether because *mice*, the normal plural of mouse, seems inappropriate when applied to computer pointing devices, while *mouses*, whether or not it's the "preferred" term, strikes most people as

Screen shot from a 1968 video: Douglas Engelbart demonstrates how to create text on the computer. The mouse, which he developed, consists of a small rectangular wooden box with three buttons on top and does not actually resemble a mouse, *Mus musculus*, as much as today's mice—or mouses—do. From Stanford University Special Collections; used by permission.

downright wrong. If the inventor of the mouse considers worrying about its plural unnecessary, perhaps *Wired Style* should take the hint.

Most emailers don't check with the style manual before clicking the send button, but the proliferation of email usage guides provides an indirect indication that writers of electronic messages do want to be correct. There are two even stronger indicators that email has gone from wild and woolly to domesticated and conventional. Every college writing textbook now includes a section on electronic writing, focusing not so much on how to do it, since college students are assumed to have already mastered the technical side of email, but how to do it correctly. And for a number of years now, all the off-the-shelf email programs have been offering spell-checkers. Some of these mail programs even boast grammar-checkers as well, a sure sign that the emailers, long criticized for their inventive spelling and loose adherence to standard usage, are either preoccupied with correctness or wish to give the impression that they are.

Even those writers who don't fanatically revise and polish their emails and who routinely spell-check before sending, avoid the freewheeling, rough-and-ready, stripped-down email style in which correspondents get right down to business and then move on. So salutations and sign-offs, once thought unnecessary in emails since the email header names both the sender and the addressee, are now more common, even in informal email, because their absence suggests an abruptness that many writers and readers find impolite. And like phone callers, emailers, when they write person to person, often include some chit-chat along with the business at hand to preserve the personal touch necessary to maintain the social connection between writer and reader.

While the first electronic mail may have resembled the telegram more than anything else, its users recognized the uniqueness of the genre and eventually positioned it somewhere between the phone call and the letter. Electronic mail has some of the immediacy of a phone call, yet it is written, like a conventional letter, and delivered to a virtual mailbox from which the addressee can retrieve and open it, discard it, or ignore it; so it makes sense to consider it a form of mail as well.

Electronic mail lacks two key features of the phone call and the letter: readers can't hear—and therefore recognize—an emailer's voice. And the writer can't sign an email to certify it in the same way that writers put their John Hancock on the bottom of a letter. Most people don't worry about the absence of these authenticators, perhaps because they find emailing so much easier and less stressful than either letter writing or calling on the phone. People still use the phone—as the popularity of mobile phones attests. But voice-to-voice communication is not always the medium of choice: people sitting at their computer with a phone nearby often email instead of calling, and increasing numbers of cell phone users are indicating a preference for texting, not calling.

As for writing letters, according to U.S. Postmaster General John E. Potter, while total mail volume has increased dramatically since 1999, there has been a decline in first-class mail (Longley 2005). The increased volume of mail consists almost entirely of catalogs and credit card offers, and the decrease in first-class mail can be attributed directly to the popularity of email. With the increasing number of bills received and paid online, many Americans are finding, to the post office's dismay, that a book of stamps lasts longer than ever.

Unfortunately, like the important letter that cries for attention amidst an ocean of junk mail, the personal email is quickly being displaced by spam. Like its offline counterpart, junk email has become a fact of life as well, along with the escalating spiral of junk mail filters and hacks to subvert those filters. I regularly purge my electronic mailbox of catalog ads, get-rich-quick schemes from Nigeria (a scam that began in the days of snail mail but ported nicely over to the electronic side), offers of cheap drugs and mortgages, political rants, attempts to get me to reveal bank account information, and the inevitable obscenities that have managed to elude my junk filters.

Spam may be inconvenient or annoying, and it may bilk the overly trusting reader out of some serious cash. But some email can actually inflict physical damage. Communication technology, while generally less dangerous than other sorts of technological development (enriched uranium, asbestos, the automobile), always brings with it a certain amount of risk. The telephone can be a vehicle for crank and harassing phone calls, although caller ID and the do-not-call list have gone a long way toward eliminating these downsides of having a phone. Portable and mobile phones expose callers to small amounts of microwave radiation, raising concerns about telephone-induced cancer.

There is as yet no scientific link between brain tumors and these phones, but even so, phones can bring about death and destruction. Alfred Hitchcock's 1954 movie *Dial M for Murder*, based on the play by Frederick Knott, may be the most famous fictional example of a telephone call triggering a death, although the wrong person is killed, but more recently we've seen that real-life terrorists who prefer not to martyr themselves can use cell phones to set off the bombs they leave by the roadside, at the mall, or on a crowded bus.

In the 1954 Hitchcock classic *Dial M for Murder*, Ray Milland phones home to set in motion his wife's murder. Image courtesy of Warner Entertainment; used by permission.

As Ted Kaczynski's exploits demonstrated, the U.S. mail can be a potent vehicle for mayhem as well. Fortunately letter bombs are few and far between, and even at the height of the more recent anthrax scare, when ordinary people donned latex gloves to open their bills and copycats sent missives with flour and talc to stir things up, only a few letters actually contained the deadly white spores.

As for email, unfortunately it's now all too common for messages from friends as well as strangers to deliver electronic viruses that can jam up a computer, render it useless, steal passwords, or convert their new electronic home to a springboard from which to infiltrate or disable other machines. The computer virus has become a genre of software unto itself, and whole industries have sprung up to counter the virus threat. Some computer users install weekly upgrades to antivirus software to protect their data from these poison pill emails.

But the deluge of spam and the threat of computer viruses haven't dampened enthusiasm for email. Even though making contact with an addressee can be almost instantaneous, many emailers find the medium less demanding and less confrontational than either calls or letters. It's more polite, they maintain, to ignore an email than to hang up on a caller or let the machine get it, much easier to defer action until one is ready to reply. Or to blame deliberate inaction on the technology. In addition, since most email users have deleted important emails by accident or lost them in disk crashes, some emailers brazenly say, "I never got your email," or "I think I deleted it," or "Somehow it wound up in my junk folder, and I never noticed it," when in fact all they did was ignore the email in question.

Telling little white lies about lost messages may be no worse than the old ploy of telling a creditor that the check is in the mail. But there are some email gaffes that can make us wish for the good old days when typing or writing on clay tablets really slowed down the communication process. Email can be sent with just a click, and once it's sent, there's no way to undo it, no going back to the way things were just a moment before. Clicking before I should have, I've done all of the following, with predictable results: sent off a nasty email before my temper cooled; inadvertently copied an email to a large group of people who shouldn't be seeing it at all; or forwarded an email without editing out the one sentence in the original message that was not intended for the new addressee. Google has just introduced time delay in its popular Gmail program that gives users five seconds to cancel a message, but five seconds may not be enough time to recall an ill-advised message.

Email has come full circle in one sense. The epistolary novel, begun in the eighteenth century with Samuel Richardson's *Pamela*, consisted of exchanges of letters among the characters. At least two recent novels consisting entirely of email exchanges bring the epistolary novel into the computer age, and there are novels based on instant message exchanges and text messages as well.

▪ ▪ ▪ IM ME TONIGHT

A decade ago my daughter went off to summer camp in Wisconsin. The campers boarded the buses in the parking lot of a Chicago bowling alley, and while some were already deep into conversation with one another, others crowded around the open bus windows and waved to parents and siblings who would soon be left behind. One father, clearly having second thoughts about sending his little girl almost two hours away from home, jumped up and down frantically trying to get her attention. When she finally tore herself away from her friends long enough to notice her distraught dad, he shouted one last request, "Fax me tonight, sweetheart!" This is one high-tech family, the rest of the parents thought to ourselves.

The next year, that all-too-rare fax gave way to email sent by any camper who wanted to use the camp's new computer lab of an evening. Then cell phones were added to the mix. Now the campers bring their own laptops and web-enabled smartphones, and use the camp's wireless network day or night to communicate with one another and with those parents who are educable enough to learn instant messaging.

▪ ▪ ▪

Instant messaging, or IM, which got its start around 1996, is the newest and perhaps the fastest growing genre of digital communication. Some experts see it eclipsing email in the near future. According to one estimate, two years ago there were 860 million people around the world IM-ing, almost eight times more than had used this technology just four years earlier (Biever 2005). According to figures gathered by the Pew Internet and American Life Project in 2005, 87 percent of all American teenagers were using the internet, up from 73 percent in 2000. Seventy-five percent of online American teens were also using instant messaging in 2005 (Hitlin and Rainie 2005; Lenhart et al. 2001). Today that figure is probably closer to 99 percent, and a second Pew study reveals that 42 percent of online adults use IM at work, with one-fourth of them preferring IM to email (Shiu and Lenhart 2004).

IM permits users to have real-time written conversations with "buddies," or to use a more adult-sounding word, contacts, from a user-controlled list. Before IM introduced the buddy system, internet conversations revolved around internet chat rooms that brought people together around common interests, but since chatters could hide their true identities, these digital salons were magnets for strangers pretending to be friends. Sexual predators masqueraded as teens in teen chat rooms, a situation that alarmed parents and police (though sexual predation online is apparently much less common than popularly supposed).

▪ ▪ ▪ ANECDOTE: THE AUTHOR TRIES A CHAT

My own children were proprietary about instant messaging because, though it was created by adults, at the time it hadn't really spread to the adult world. But one day, knowing that I was interested in communication technologies, my son agreed to give me a quick lesson in IM basics and got me my own screen name, a fairly transparent one that didn't hide who I was. But when I practiced my new skill by IM-ing his sister, who was off at college, she immediately became suspicious. "Who is this, really?" she asked in response to my invitation to chat. I tried to assure her it was really me, but she remained skeptical. Even when she accepted the fact that I was who I claimed to be, she commented, "This is too weird," insisting that I sign off and send her an email, a more "traditional" technology best suited for the older generation. Adults, particularly parents, just weren't welcome in the IM space that she regarded as her private digital sandbox.

And she wasn't wrong in her assumption that the instant message belonged to her generation: according to Ashley Pierson (2003), by 2002, sixty million college students were IM-ing. Pierson, then a student at Iowa State, admitted IM-ing her roommate while both were in the same room. Lately the kids have become a little more tolerant about letting the old folks online, though they still prefer to IM their friends, not their parents.

▪ ▪ ▪ THE INSTANT MESSAGE GENRE

Instant messaging is attractive because it works in real time, like a phone call minus the long distance charges, and because it can run in a small window on the computer screen, permitting users to switch quickly between IM and other tasks, so IM conversations are typically interrupted and desultory. One thing that holds them together is the running transcript of exchanges that appears in the IM window. These transcripts can be saved for future reference, so in that sense they are more permanent than phone calls. However, looking back over a number of saved transcripts, I've found that while adult-generated messages seem to have a subject directing the conversation, most of the exchanges between the teens of my acquaintance seem to be relatively content free: there's a lot of touching base—"I'm here, you there? I'm bored, you bored?"— interspersed among the occasional discussion of the social schedule—for example, "Let's do the movie at 7." Empty exchanges like these are far from new, and those who worry that IM is sapping the English language of intellectual content can relax, because such little nothings are triggered by ennui, not by the technology used to express it. As the deathless dialogue created by Paddy Chayefsky for the movie *Marty* (1955) reveals, the empty back-and-forth of conversation captures an important aspect of social interaction:

ANGIE: What do you feel like doing tonight?

MARTY: I don't know, Ange. What do *you* feel like doing?

ANGIE: We're back to that, huh? I say to you, "What do you feel like doing tonight?" And you say back to me, "I dunno. What do you feel like doing tonight?" Then we wind up sitting around your house with a couple of cans of beer watching the *Hit Parade* on television. (filmsite.org/mart.html)

Necessary expressions of boredom notwithstanding, instant messaging, following the lead of email, is both linguistically inventive and rebellious, and it gives users some creative control over the appearance of their messages. IM users may customize their screens, create icons called avatars to personalize their messages, and assign various sound effects to indicate messages sent or received, or buddies signing on or off. While instant messages often seem offhand and throwaway, much thought clearly goes into the composition of IM-ers' away messages, witty quotes or philosophical observations sent to would-be chatters when the user is away from the computer. People stick to their email sig.files for some time, but on IM there's some pressure to come up with ever-hipper messages, as some IM-ers pride themselves on posting a new message each time they sign off.

One aspect of genre development is the creation of mechanisms to evaluate the effectiveness of a particular text and to deal with those writers who violate the conventions established by the community of users. In addition to the informal self-organization that chat groups create for themselves, there's some formal social regulation of IM interaction. Recipients of unwanted or impolite messages may "warn" IM-ers, or ban them entirely after enough offenses. Instant messages tend to be short, with rapid turn-taking, and some IM-ers favor a kind of acronymic shorthand that distinguishes the style of IM: for example, LOL, for 'laughing out loud'; g2g, for 'got to go'; the liberal use of emoticons, iconographic ways to represent emotions such as ☺ and ☹,

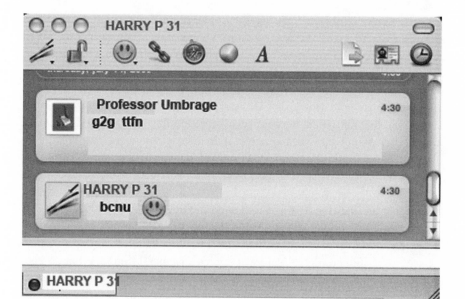

IM screen shot showing customized screen with screen names and avatars for the two participants, IM acronyms g2g, for "got to go"; ttfn, "ta ta for now"; bcnu, "be seein' you,"; and a smiley face emoticon; many IM'ers eschew as too juvenile the stereotypical acronyms, abbreviations, and emoticons associated with the genre (the names of the participants have been changed to preserve anonymity). Screen shot by the author.

called the smiley face and the frowny face, to indicate a happy or sad state, respectively. But many of my students associate stereotypical IM language with preteen wannabes, insisting instead that every word of an IM or a text message be spelled out, and spelled correctly.

IM is now a common grown-up activity as well as a teen one. More and more adults sign on not just at home, but at work as well, often without the knowledge of their employers. While email systems have been tamed by convention-emphasizing mail programs and workplace regulations, IM is attractive in part because it has become the new outlaw genre, operating under the radar of intrusive parents and bosses. Attempts to discourage IM at work, as Citibank initially tried to do, aren't typically successful, and employers now find themselves worrying about the impact of IM on worker productivity. But instant messaging is starting to come out from under cover at the office as IM'ers find that its uses go far beyond chatting or arranging dates. IM, faster than email and, because of the transcript, more permanent than a phone call, quickly confirms stock trades, and it offers the written equivalent of a conference call. So promising is instant messaging for the business world that one business reporter has called it "e-mail on steroids" (Durland 2004).

Email seems to be trumping both the phone and the conference at work—the *New York Times* reported as long ago as 1998 that because of email, "entire days can pass without a single face-to-face meeting" (Hafner 1998)—and it may not be long before IM beats email as the communication of choice. According to one report, 80 percent of businesses use instant messaging in some fashion (Maloney 2004), and management, faced with the reality that instant messaging isn't going away any time soon, has begun to worry about standardizing IM systems and educating employees on the appropriate business use of instant messaging.

IM has legal implications as well: like email, it is discoverable in court, and IM transcripts are covered by rules requiring that certain kinds of business data be stored for a number of years. Also like email, IM is subject to attack by viruses and worms. And instant messaging has even generated its own form of spam, called spim (*Spam*, the brand name, is a word blending *spiced* and *ham*, while *spim* is a blend of *spam* and *IM*). There are other security concerns with IM: employees may divulge company secrets carelessly because IM seems so casual a medium of exchange, or deliberately because many instant messages simply bypass company servers (Goodwin 2004).

Instant messaging is dismissed by critics who see it as one step below email, which they don't like either: in their view, it is mindless communication, if it communicates at all, and it is so careless and unregulated that it's endangering the English language. Teachers add to this their complaint that students are using emoticons and IM acronyms and deformed spellings in their school writing, though when I began teaching more than forty years ago students were writing JMJ (for Jesus, Mary, and Joseph) at the top of their papers or drawing smiley faces on the last page in an effort to improve their grades, and at least the girls were passing notes that ended with TTFN and were "sealed" with SWAK across the back of the envelope. But for the hardened skeptics, there's simply no upside to IM. At best, in their view, the new writing technology lets teens and office workers waste even more time than they already do.

IM occasionally gets some faint praise. Some reluctant fans, who acknowledge that instant messaging has carved out its own space in our writing practices, credit IM with increasing the speed and accuracy of teenage typists, which suggests that these teens are being pointed more toward careers as office clerks, not rulers of the Queen's Navy. But IM does have a core of real supporters as well, who predict that instant messaging will contribute greatly to business productivity, although its ability to increase either worker efficiency or corporate profits has yet to be demonstrated.

Regardless of the posturing of fans and critics, it's clear that instant messaging has had a tremendous impact on writing practice. In less than a decade it has moved from curiosity to necessity for social writing, particularly among teens and young adults, and more recently it has begun to impact business writing as well. The following guide to corporate instant messaging, broadcast on CNN, is one sure sign that despite the critics, instant messaging is a mainstream genre that is here to stay and that is already donning the trappings of conventionality:

1. Check your company's policy on downloading IM software: Some companies offer instant messaging to all employees, but most do not yet automatically provide this kind of software. While most instant messaging software is free, you still need to download it onto your system. Many companies have strict policies about downloading additional software onto company-owned machines.

   This is because downloads can open up company systems to risks such as viruses. Other employers are concerned about potential lost productivity due to instant messaging. If your company does not have a formal policy about instant messaging programs, ask around to see if they are acceptable or not.

2. Use caution: Like other forms of electronic communication, instant message conversations can be monitored by employers, are saved in computer systems, and can be retrieved. Just because it seems like you are having a casual "chat," it doesn't mean you can let your guard down and say whatever you want. You need to be as careful about what you say in an instant message as you would in e-mail.

3. Be aware of viruses and other security risks: Most instant messaging services enable you to send files with your messages. Again, like any other form of electronic communication, be aware of the risks involved. Just like e-mail, you should never open attachments that come from someone you do not know or that are unfamiliar to you.

   Use your status options: Instant messaging programs allow you to tell others what your "status" is. This means you can label yourself as "online," or available to talk, or let others know when you are "busy."

   Use these status options to let others know when you can and cannot chat. If you are swamped at work and need to concentrate, change your status to busy.

4. If you are out to lunch, change your status to "away" so others know you are out and not just ignoring them. Don't feel bad about telling a friend that you have to concentrate on work rather than chatting about your weekend.

5. Be respectful of others' time: Respecting your colleagues' status options is as important as using yours. If you see that someone has

listed their status as "busy," honor that person's wishes and don't try to start an IM conversation.

6. Be responsible: The reason many companies are wary of IM programs is the tendency of employees to use them for personal rather than business purposes. ("Six Rules" 2004)

More and more people are using instant messaging to arrange dates, transact business, or avoid doing work. Sometimes IM proves the next best thing to being there, but it can also be preferable to actually meeting. According to one survey, 31 percent of online teens use instant messaging to write something that they wouldn't tell somebody in person; 20 percent have asked someone out using IM; and 19 percent have used instant messaging to break up with someone (Hitlin and Rainie 2005). As we see from the following exasperated comment that appeared in a traditional print publication, adults also turn to IM to avoid an uncomfortable face-to-face confrontation: "He dumps me on Instant Messenger. I'm not making that up. He IM's me that he is ready to move on and wants a divorce. 'You're breaking up with me on IM?' I typed, lamely" (Allen 2005).

This is also an example—I presume—of the kind of personal use of IM at work that employers worry so much about. While it's not uncommon for people in the same house, or even the same room, to IM one another, the likely response to an online breakup message like the one above makes it reasonable to assume that the writer sent it from a safe distance: another office, or better yet, another building. It's also the kind of message that suggests not much work will get done that day.

▪ ▪ ▪

Email, the web page, and the instant message are three new genres enabled by new word technologies, but not only do these genres show us that technological change produces textual change, they also demonstrate the ways in which the new means of writing work to expand our notion of who is a writer. In the next chapter, we'll look at the impact of yet another new genre, the blog, on membership in the writers guild and see how the explosion of writing made possible by computers leads to attempts to regulate the new kinds of authorship.

9

■ ■ ■   Everyone's an Author

Reading and writing may be two of the basic three Rs in American education, but schools have always emphasized reading over writing, no doubt because there have always been more consumers than creators of text, more readers than writers. But thanks to the internet, that gap may be narrowing dramatically. Each new stage in the history of writing technologies tends to expand the authors club, and the digital explosion seems to have opened that guild up to something approaching universal membership, at least so far as the universe of computer users goes. On the internet, everyone's an author, every scrap of prose a publication.

Whether it's the invention of writing itself or the later introduction of a new writing technology, at the start, only the adventurous and single-minded buy in, working laboriously with slabs of clay, or "the skins of wethers blackened with ink and weighted with a little lump of lead," as skeptical eleventh-century English nobles dismissively characterized a letter from the pope (Clanchy 1993, 261). But as each technology becomes user-friendly and affordable, more and more people learn not just to write, but also to become writers.

The technologies of papyrus, parchment, paper, pens and pencils, the printing press, and the typewriter all wound up making writing cheaper, easier, faster. At the same time, they created demands for reading material and jobs for writers. The current digital revolution extends the potential of writing even further and more quickly: in the time it takes to read this book, yet another digital genre may have been created by the latest and largest generation of scribblers ever.

In the typewriter's heyday, journalists, novelists, scholars, and other professional writers gave up pen and paper to compose at the machine's keyboard. Poets were the last to shift to typing, just as they've been slower to take up composing at the computer. But so clear was the preference of many writers for the typewriter that, as we will see in the last chapter, some educators even saw it as the way to teach children how to write in school. Today, researchers are intent on proving that computers enhance learning.

Despite the machine's promise for improving national literacy levels, attempts to place typewriters on school desks went nowhere, and our schools taught typing not for the benefit of tomorrow's novelists or reporters, but for students who would eventually work in offices. Just as penmanship drill developed the big round hand of future clerks, typing class trained generations of twentieth-century office workers whose job it would be to reproduce complex texts composed in longhand or dictated by other people. Before the computer, writing tools probably didn't create new writers so much as they created new ways for those who were already writers to do their work.

Certainly computers reproduce text as well, and the fact that American offices long ago replaced their typewriters with computers means that anyone working in an office has to know his or her way around these machines. But unlike earlier writing technologies, more and more computer users write for themselves as well as for work and school.

It has always been a challenge for individual writers to put typed text in front of large numbers of readers. Typewriters were superior to printing presses for producing single documents, but for the mass production required to satisfy a growing reading public, printing presses had no real rivals from their invention around 1450 until the present digital age. Even with carbon paper, typewriters could never provide more than a few legible copies of a top sheet.

In the 1950s, the mimeograph machine came to the rescue: teachers reproduced handouts for class, and political radicals unable to storm the radio stations or commandeer the newspapers cranked out their calls for revolution on basement mimeos. The photocopier served the next generation bent on producing limited-edition texts, whether administrative, educational, or political, or copying party invitations or other personal documents. But today all anyone needs to get the message out to the great unwashed, or to a small circle of friends, is a Wi-Fi–enabled laptop. And such messages are going out at ever-increasing rates.

Once they became word machines and not just calculators, computers started out much like typewriters. Their goal was modest—to produce a better way not so much to write as to process words: to fill in forms, to reproduce letters and reports drafted by other people. Computers do these jobs well, but they really pushed the typewriter out of the picture for good when it became possible for computers both to produce business letters and address envelopes into which to stuff those letters.

Even as the computer was becoming the quintessential business machine, something unexpected happened. Instead of merely reproducing texts, office workers began creating their own. Instead of simply keying in their homework (or copying it from a website instead of a printed encyclopedia), students began to spend hours writing voluntarily. And it goes without saying that professional writers, with an exception here or there, traded in their old Remingtons en masse once PCs became affordable. The result of this shift from pencils to pixels is that, in the United States, keyboarding, whether learned in school or picked up on the fly, has become an almost universal skill. And the point of keyboarding is not simply to replicate other people's words, as it largely was with typing and penmanship, but to create original texts.

▪ ▪ ▪ SHOULD EVERYBODY WRITE?

The neo-Luddites may want us to go back to the No. 2 pencil—itself a fairly new tool in the writer's workshop, but in the days before WordStar was king, when humans roamed the earth brandishing their pencils or the styluses that were used for centuries before the pencil was invented, not that many people could read, and fewer still could write. Surely the technophobes who romanticize the pencil don't want to return us to the low literacy rates that characterized the good old days of writing with pencils and quills. Still, a few critics object to the new technologies because they enable too many people to join the guild of writers, and they might paraphrase Thoreau's objection to the telegraph: these new computer writers, it may be, have nothing to say to one another. But the data suggests otherwise: in just a few years, massive amounts of digital text have been generated, and there's even enough digital text online to make Theodore Roszak and other critics of the technology agree that the writers who have put it there are "saying something."

The Slow Rise of Literacy

Like the fourth-century BCE Athenians and eleventh-century Anglo-Saxons, most people initially viewed literacy, and the subsequent innovations in literacy technologies, with skepticism. Rosalind Thomas (1989) argues that although the citizens of Plato's Athens were surrounded by inscriptions on public buildings and were certainly aware of literary texts and written legal and business records, few Greeks actually felt the need to read, and fewer still were engaged in writing. The Greece that we look to as the source of western literacy was never a world of schoolrooms or letters. William Harris has shown that, at the height of Athenian civilization, barely 10 percent of men in Attica were literate. Virgil's accomplishments notwithstanding, Roman literacy numbers were also well under 10 percent (Harris 1989, 114, 22; literacy has always been a gendered phenomenon, and until modern times, figures for women were slightly—sometimes significantly—lower than those for men).

The one literacy event of the ancient world that has drawn the most attention is the destruction of the great library at Alexandria, Egypt. Estimates vary, but the library may have housed as many as half a million scrolls, attracting scholars from throughout the Mediterranean world (Casson 2001, 36), and its disappearance represents a massive loss of knowledge. Accounts, none of them contemporary, suggest that a series of fires ravaged the library building and reduced its collection to ashes. An early fire was set by Julius Caesar, presumably by accident since his goal was to burn ships in the harbor nearby, not books. Subsequent book burnings at Alexandria are attributed to fanatical fourth-century Christians and to seventh-century Muslim conquerors, the latter said to have burned the scrolls to heat water for the city's baths. It's also possible that the lost scrolls were the victims of decay and neglect as much as political or religious strife. But even when the library's collections were the envy of the ancient world rather than collateral damage, compendiums of heresy, or a convenient source of fuel, the average Egyptian did not carry a library card. People then, as now, must be convinced that reading can do something for them before they make the effort.

More recently, during the seventeenth and eighteenth centuries in England, Shakespeare and his contemporaries brought English letters to new heights; the Royal Society oversaw the birth of English scientific writing; Protestant reformers encouraged everyone to read the Bible, newly translated under King James into English, for themselves; and grammars, dictionaries, and usage guides began rolling off the presses. But with literacy rates soaring to no more than 35 to 40 percent of the adult population by the 1770s, the majority of the British public remained skeptical or simply indifferent about the uses of reading and writing, as well as resolutely illiterate (Cressy 1980, 177).

In Europe and America in the nineteenth century, reading and writing—but mostly reading—had firmly emerged as talents necessary for spiritual and professional advancement, and for filling the newfound leisure hours. Presses brought out ever-increasing numbers of books and pamphlets to satisfy public demand, and clerks copied out invoices and letters by hand to ensure that commerce continued to thrive. Literacy rates did rise, but by 1870 they had only reached 80 percent in England: literacy was still far from universal (Cressy 1980, 177). Even today, with literacy considered vital for participation in an information-saturated world, most of the earth's inhabitants remain unable to read or write.

Reading and writing have never manifested themselves equally either in terms of demand for these skills in a given culture at a given point in history or in terms of saturation: Writers deploy their skill far less frequently than readers. From the dawn of text down to the present, literates able to read might also be able to write their names, or copy out letters, but fewer of them actually created original documents, whether personal letters, business records, or literary treasures.

It should come as no surprise, then, that public support for reading always outstrips support for writing. Reading is typically characterized as much more than simply useful. It is edifying, mind-expanding, and in certain cases even liberating. Since the Renaissance, reading has been increasingly encouraged through the proliferation of schools and libraries. However, while writing may also be conceived in positive terms as utilitarian, essential for work, therapeutic, and a necessary part of knowledge creation, writers are frequently eyed with some suspicion. It's true that policies may seek to limit what we read, but writers are always subject to more controls and sanctions than readers.

The idea of every citizen becoming a writer brings with it some anxiety, not just in autocratic states, but in democratic ones as well. Governments, religious groups, businesses, and schools regard writing as a force that must be channeled, censored, even licensed, so that reading materials are appropriately shaped and the public has access only to the approved words of approved writers. Publication may proceed through official channels, like Elizabethan England's Stationers Company, a publishers guild with the authority granted by government charter to search all printing houses and bookshops to determine the legality of their wares, or the Index of Prohibited Books, the list maintained by the Vatican from 1559 to 1966 of all titles forbidden to Roman Catholics.

These controls may be semiofficial, like the Hays Office, a Hollywood group that operated from the 1920s through the 1960s to remove sexual or political content from screenplays before filming and from movies before they could be exhibited. Or the controls may be conventional rather than governed by law, like the peer review required before manuscripts can appear in learned journals or the editorial budget meetings that decide which stories will run in the daily paper.

While such mechanisms are put in place ostensibly to provide readers with appropriate and reliable texts, these systems of control mean that writers must always pass muster, whether it's the nod of a teacher or boss, the acceptance of an editor, the endorsement of a reviewer, the approbation of popular opinion, or the eye (and as often as not, the "nay") of the censor. Today's technology adds to that the V-chip, the rating system for popular music lyrics and video games, and the web filter. At the extreme, writers who persist in their efforts despite a failure to satisfy established criteria, or who evade the traditional paths to publication altogether, wind up on the wrong side of the law and find their books denounced, banned from school curricula, ripped from library shelves, even burned. If official readers get angry enough, writers find themselves the objects of fatwa, with a price not on their books, but on their heads.

Technology and the Authors Club

The call for the regulation of writing often comes from quarters where a new communication technology is viewed with concern rather than acceptance. The increase of books in late-fifth-century Athens brought opposition and criticism (Thomas 1989, 34). Similarly, as I discussed earlier, writing as a means of conducting business produced a skeptical response in eleventh-century England, but not because it was new. Bibles and prayer books were familiar to the Anglo-Saxons, who had been converted to Christianity centuries earlier, and while the average Brit, being unable to read, received the word of God by word of mouth from priests, these examplars of the written text were venerated, not scorned. Rather, the English suspected business writing because they thought that the motives of a new class of writers—Normans drafting charters, deeds, and letters—might be less than aboveboard.

Later technologies of printing, typing, mimeographing, photocopying, and telephoning also eventually led to an increase in the numbers of people who could communicate. The products of these technologies were greeted cautiously at first, because with them, new writers and, in the case of the telephone, new speakers—whose bona fides had yet to be established—seemed to arise from nowhere. These upstarts took advantage of the destabilization produced by the new communication machines in order to take text and talk in new directions, but they and their contributions were not always welcome.

An early critic of the telephone argued that it allowed total strangers, who would be turned away should they knock at the door, to enter one's home unannounced simply by putting a nickel in a pay phone (cited by Marvin 1988). Just as the phone increased the number of people who could initiate a conversation, advances in literacy technology widened the door to the authors club in ways that led readers to seek some seal of approval before allowing these unfamiliar voices to enter their homes. One way to ensure the trustworthiness of text was a mechanism for prior review by editors and publishers.

Another was licensing by state or church. Yet a third was workplace control of speech and writing. All have come into play as the growing community of literates learned to regulate itself and to accommodate new literacy technologies and practices.

Writing itself was never so easy as reading, either to acquire or to practice, and so while the ranks of writers inevitably grew as literacy rates rose, writing did not explode in the same way reading did. While even in the ancient world there was always too much to read (Nunberg 1996, xx), and while the increase in office work in the nineteenth and especially the twentieth centuries meant more people than ever used writing on the job—huge sales of cheap pens and pencils attest to this—the authors club remained a subset in the world of literacy practice. Membership in this guild was restricted; upstarts, renegades, and malcontents could be dealt with in ways that sought to limit their readership. If necessary, there were ways both social and technological to silence writers.

Until the digital explosion, that is. For with computer creation and dissemination of text, writers can now bypass many of the long-established winnowing and qualifying procedures that we have come to associate with writing. In the computer age, the term *aspiring writer* is meaningless. Just as texts have freed themselves from the constraint of traditional publishers' imprints, writers no longer need to carry a guild card. Anyone with the right tools can ignore the traditional routes to publication and set himself or herself up to be a writer. "Readers wanted" seems the catchphrase of every *.htm* launched on the internet, and the itinerant laptop user's away message now reads, "Have text, will travel." Lastly, and most disturbing to those who would control this explosion of writers, since cyberspace is international, digital technology has brought us a cyberworld of writers without borders.

With writing so apparently out of control, we see the predictable backlash. "Computers are destroying the language," cries one lament, as teachers strain to keep the lingo of email and IM out of student prose. "The internet is full of lies and misinformation," cries another. But neither complaint resonates with writers, as more and more of us see our writing in a seamless continuum that stretches from pencils to pixels. In addition, as readers, more and more of us get our information not from traditional print sources or from conventional media such as television, but online.

Literacy technologies provoke cycles of new practices accompanied by new complaints. We've seen these in the past, and they are coming to a head again, as teachers ban smiley faces and IM acronyms from book reports or employers banish email and instant messaging from a workplace that now embraces them—or drag bloggers through the courts, for it's the blog that has become the latest digital battleground.

▪ ▪ ▪ DEAR DIGITAL DIARY...

Instant messaging may be just the ticket for teenage boredom and angst, witty one-liners, or a rapid-fire exchange of meaningless smileys over the internet. And now that the business world is embracing as a capitalist tool what it once trivialized as the high-tech equivalent of passing notes in class, IM may be the perfect vehicle for quick and efficient exchanges in re the latest corporate transaction. But the blog, or web log, is exactly what the digital doctor ordered for those people who are more comfortable composing introspective diary entries at a leisurely pace, yet are exhibitionist enough to put their innermost thoughts, ramblings, and musings on public display.

A few years ago I surveyed my students to find out how many of them kept diaries and how many kept those diaries on a computer. About a third of the students, mostly women, confessed to writing in a diary or journal on a regular basis, but at a time when all my students were writing their papers and doing their homework on computers, only one—a male—kept a disk-based diary. For most of those students, diaries still meant special little books that could be locked and hidden away from siblings and roommates, books in which one wrote with a special pen, perhaps choosing an ink color to match a mood. The students assured me that a computer wasn't inviting enough, or secret enough, for the kinds of thoughts that went into diaries. What if my little brother or my roomie read my disk? they worried. Computer diaries seemed a recipe for blackmail.

Today students still keep their secret diaries in locked quarto-sized notebooks hidden under mattresses. But the computer has become the instrument of choice for writing and publishing the increasingly popular genre of public diary known as the blog. All of my college students know about blogs. A few read them. But only a couple of them maintain blogs in college: blogging is a phenomenon they associate with political commentators such as Matt Drudge or the Daily Kos, but even more with high school students, particularly girls. That perception seems accurate: nineteen percent of American teens aged twelve to seventeen write blogs, twice as many read them, and at least initially, significantly more girls than boys are involved in blogging (while the girls were blogging, the boys were busy downloading music and videos; Lenhart and Madden 2005). In contrast, 8 percent of online American adults keep blogs, 39 percent—57 million people—read them, and the latest report shows men and women blogging in equal numbers (Lenhart and Fox 2006). And blogging, perhaps more than any other internet genre, has become the way to join the authors club. Lenhart and Fox (2006) report that 54 percent of the bloggers they surveyed have never published their work before.

While the date of the first blog is hard to pin down, the term *web log* appears in 1997 to describe a practice that had been underway for a couple of years, and its blended form, *blog*, comes on the scene two years later, in 1999. Definitions of what constitutes a blog vary, though most people agree that blogs are whatever we want them to be, so long as they are published in serial form, and that blogging as we know it started up slowly in the mid-1990s, though it has exploded in the last couple of years. The percentage of adult blog readers almost quadrupled between 2004 and 2006 (Lenhart and Fox 2006).

The popularity of the blog demonstrates that writers are not as reluctant to share their innermost thoughts with a wider audience as one might have thought. According to a count by *Business Week*, there are more than nine million currently active blogs, with some forty thousand new ones appearing every day. Perseus, an observer of web trends, estimated that there were 31.6 million hosted blogs (those on sites such as Xanga and LiveJournal) in 2005 and an unknown number of private-server blogs ("Blogging Geyser" 2005). My students aren't blogging—they're too preoccupied with Facebook, which I'll discuss in the next chapter—but everybody else seems to be busy writing or reading blogs. When I began this section on blogging over a year ago, I didn't have a blog. Now I do: the Web of Language is not a confessional blog, but one devoted to discussions of language policy. I began to blog simply as a way to find out how blogs work, so that I could write about them. But the activity became so compelling that I continued writing the blog itself, and I'll even be teaching a new course in which students study language policy by blogging on the subject.

As a genre, blogs blend the diary with features of the scrapbook and the top ten list. Blog posts are brief, typically a few paragraphs focused on a single theme, arranged in reverse chronological order, with the most recent appearing first. Blogs are updated regularly—or at least genre rules suggest that they should be—and readers may consult archives for earlier entries. In addition to commentary, blogs often showcase the blogger's favorite websites, and while blogs tend to be monologues, many bloggers invite their readers to post comments, setting up at least the possibility of a wider conversation. Just as bloggers can control the flow of feedback, they can also restrict who has access to the blog by setting passwords and requiring subscribers to register. But most blogs don't bother with gatekeeping. Instead, balancing the needs of the poseur and the voyeur, they are available to anyone who wants to look.

Reading blogs requires knowing where to find them. Readers can sort through the millions of blogs on the internet using a variety of specialized search engines or by visiting aggregators that collect links and summaries of new blog posts in one convenient cyberlocation, and feeds that will send updates to subscribers as they are posted are also available.

Blog subject matter ranges from the dreary, unexpurgated minutiae of a single blogger's life—reality TV with the boring parts left in—to tightly focused political and commercial campaigns whose goal is to sign up readers for a cause or lighten their wallets. In between these extremes are those blogs with enough merit to attract large numbers of readers and even encourage new bloggers to put in their two cents.

Not every blogger writes confessional kiss-and-tell posts or records the dinner menu—the blogosphere is not all blogorrhea and mystery meat. Current events often bring bloggers to their computers to report, comment, rant, and harangue. Patriotic blogs blossomed after the 9–11 tragedy. Eyewitness blogs gained prominence during the Iraq War. Milblogs, the diaries of American soldiers in Iraq, offered some counterpoint to government press releases and news reports about the war. Bloggers pursued U.S. Senate Majority Leader Trent Lott for his racist comments, and they hounded Dan Rather for his sloppy reporting on the Bush national guard memos. Political blogs flourished in both the red and the blue states during the 2004 American presidential race, when blogging entered the public consciousness full force and Merriam-Webster named *blog* as its 2004 word of the year. Bloggers funneled news and pictures about the 2007 Myanmar uprisings to the outside world, or at least they did until the government pulled the plug on Myanmar's internet. And there are both gushing and caustic blogs that discuss every new film, TV show, pop culture icon, and music group.

Search engines such as the one provided by LiveJournal allow readers to find blogs by key word, topic, blogger's (purported) age, location, or other characteristics. Like web crawlers, these search engines are necessary because there really are all sorts of blogs to sort through, from the kind that one commentator calls WBC blogs—for whine, bitch, complain—to those whose goal is to convey information, like the newsblogs published by the *Guardian* and the *Washington Post*.

A variety of specialist groups have found blogging to be a useful way to communicate. Linguists have turned to blogging to discuss the language issues of the day. Librarians have their own blogs for discussing such professional topics as the value of blogs, and I'm not the only educator looking for ways to incorporate blogs into courses. Graduate students blog to warm up for writing dissertations, or to lament their writer's block. And an enterprising techie is even taking the blog back to its roots by turning Samuel Pepys' *Diary* into a blog (the latest Pepys daily post, together with linked background material on this seventeenth-century British diarist, can be found at www.pepysdiary.com).

What raises the numbers of blog sites well into the millions, though, are not these specialist blogs, but the many personal web logs that all seem to attract at least some readers. The blog has created a phenomenon that industry analysts at Perseus call the "nanoaudience," the small group of readers who follow particular blogs. According to a 2003 Perseus survey, the average blog has 250 readers, "far smaller audiences than any traditional one-to-many communication method" ("Blogging Iceberg" 2003). Blogs created specifically for friends and family, on the analogy of those annoying annual holiday missives that recount in excruciating detail the events of the past year, have fewer readers still. In practice, according to Perseus, "many blogs have no more than two dozen readers" ("Blogging Iceberg" 2003).

Half of all blogs are written by teenagers, for whom the blog has become almost as indispensable as the cell phone and the screen name (Nussbaum 2004). Teens blog for an audience of their friends, and they read blogs written by those friends (Lenhart and Madden 2005, 8). A random search of recently updated blog posts on LiveJournal produced the following selection of actual blog entries, ranging from the personal to the political:

Ok. . I am a big fan of Dr. Pepper. Great fan…But this…This is something I am going to frame when I finish…It is a name only the most honored, luckiest beings may speak in company of the same calibur…Hold on to your butts everyone. . The name. . Of the greatest off-brand in the world is…

DR. WOW!!!!!!!!!!!

Omfg!! It was amazing!!! [from the blog called poetrywheniweep]

▪ ▪ ▪

This morning my toes seemed fine, they just hurtalittle. Now one of my toes is purple and all swelled. It doesn't hurt that bad to walk, but I haven't tried walking in shoes yet. It better get better before band camp, or band camp is gonna be hell for me. [mcponiel]

▪ ▪ ▪

Emotional relief

ok…i have this major issue…with people that is…~smiles sheepishly~ when don't i??….but anyways…i like to hum…and sing…and all sorts of things along that line but in my house every time i do Jim yells at me…yes Jim….the man who claims to be practically deaf in one ear complains that he can hear me hum at a whisper two rooms away from him and that it bugs him…and since that is the case i get yelled at quite a bit…go figure…but here's the deal…to me singing is not just singing….it is a way to express myself in a way that i can do anything with…i know i don't have the best voice but hey…not everyone does…at least i stay on key…but when i am denied my right to sing…i am being denied a bit of myself…[whiteprophecy]

■ ■ ■

so our friendship officially ended tonight because apparently 90% of the things i say to him pisses him off and vice versa. so all the girls out there that like him you can have him. do whatever the hell you want with him. i don't care. i took you out of my phone, erased you from my myspace and my buddy list. it's over. i can't do this anymore. i gave you so many chances to just be my friend but that's never gonna happen. you and i will never have a normal relationship therefore we can't have one at all. go get a new girl and get over me. i'm not that great. i'm not great at all. you should hate me. go find a better girl for yourself cuz all i do is upset you. it's over. don't try to talk to me, it's best this way and you know it. so goodbye for good [shortie716]

■ ■ ■

The Man You Love To Hate

in case anyone missed it last night…on TVLand they did the Top 10 Characters You Love To Hate, and Larry came in at #4! I don't know who ranks them, but I'd say at least the top 4 were fairly close to what I would have ranked as well. I won't spoil it because knowing TVLand, they'll probably show it again 18 times in the next week, so there'll be plenty of opportunities to catch it again.

one good part was a direct quote from Tony Danza: "I think it's the funniest show on TV today", so that was cool. [from the fan blog, "larrydavid"]

■ ■ ■

Terrorism is a natural outgrowth of capitalism and globalization. There are two ways in which this works. First, there is the usurpation of global networks and connections which, when hijacked by insurgent forces, facilitate the ability for terrorists to wreak maximum damage with maximum ease. [from the aptly named blog, "The Political Rant"]

■ ■ ■ DISCIPLINE AND PUNISH

Given the large number of new writers pushing out blogs as well as the wide range of blog content, it's not surprising that of all the new genres facilitated by digital technology, the blog is the one that brings the loudest calls for regulation. One indicator of the impact that blogs are having on our communication practices is the growing number of bloggers who get in trouble for what they write. Many bloggers are teenagers, and just as school principals have always tried to control what students write in the school newspaper or the literary magazine, administrators are starting to take action against bloggers who aren't sufficiently true to their school (Schaarsmith and Kalson 2005).

Blogging out of school has come under attack as well. The American Civil Liberties Union successfully defended a student at an Ohio high school who criticized the school administration on his personal blog, and a Pittsburgh high school senior suspended for a send-up of the principal on the popular student blog site, MySpace (Paulson 2006). At least one negative comment on a private blog resulted in a fight the next day at another Ohio school. Fearing the new digital genre as a source of unrest, and continuing the long-standing school tradition of regulating student speech, several Ohio school districts now forbid student blogging in school (Roduta 2005).

So common is the practice of attacking students and teachers online that it now has a name: cyberbullying. One study in Alberta, Canada, reported that one quarter of the seventh-graders surveyed had experienced online attacks (Gillis 2006). In Chicago, three AP (advanced placement) students at Taft High School were suspended for making obscene and threatening remarks about a teacher in their blogs. One student later retracted his remarks online, adding, "I didn't know our Xanga's were being monitored. I should have expected it. I thought it...was freedom of speech, but it's not" (Ihejirika 2005). Editorializing on the incident, the *Chicago Sun-Times* cited a Supreme Court ruling which states that students may lose their First Amendment rights if their speech is potentially disruptive.

That Supreme Court decision, *Tinker v. Des Moines* (393 U.S. 503 [1969]), covers speech in school or on campus, and while the high court has not ruled on students' personal, out-of-school, blogs, lower courts have supported school censorship and punishment for threats to their peers or to school personnel made on personal blogs. Applying the so-called Tinker test, such language "materially disrupts classwork or involves substantial disorder or invasion of the rights of others" and may therefore be censored or punished (EFF n.d.).

The Taft High School community in Chicago was split over the blogging issue: there's still a sense among teachers, students, and parents that off-campus speech is none of the school's business. It's much easier to rally support for blogging clampdowns by focusing on the internet as a threat to America's youth. Newspapers don't like to be in the position of supporting the regulation of anybody's speech, and the *Sun-Times* editorial quickly jumped from the free speech issue to the more sensationalist dangers of internet weirdos and the need to protect students from "all the sick prying eyes out there" ("Kids Learn Lesson" 2005).

Private schools exercise greater control over students' off-campus behavior than public ones. Even so, Kieran McHugh, the principal at a Catholic high school in New Jersey, caused a stir when he ordered all students to stop blogging and take down their MySpace and Facebook pages, social sites that function differently from blogs but which, like blogs, open writers' private worlds to prying eyes. McHugh was concerned about sexual predation, but in a clarification of the blogging ban, school authorities explained that their goal wasn't just to keep students safe from lurking predators, but also to regulate student prose: not all blogs were banned, just those over which the school couldn't exercise direct control (Koloff 2005). McHugh further insisted that his goal was not censorship but "teaching common civility, courtesy, and respect" (Parsley 2005), traits that have little to do with protection from sex crimes. As part of that civics lesson, later the same week the principal expelled a student for calling the football coach a name on his blog. One teacher in a Catholic high school opposed the school's MySpace ban in his own blog because he felt that blogging helped his students develop their writing skills. Adding his own tough-love lesson, the teacher explained, "I'd prefer literate, insightful, bullied kids far more than ignorant, inarticulate, 'safe' kids" (Eden 2005). It was the coach, not a student, who was being "bullied," but that kind of implicit support for cyberbullying could get the teacher, who blogs anonymously, in trouble with the diocese as well.

A number of Washington, DC, area elite private schools have also clamped down on student bloggers, forbidding them to use their school email addresses to register on Facebook, MySpace, Xanga, and similar sites. This essentially prohibits students from using the sites, which require a school email address for registration (Bahrampour and Aratani 2006). One student was actually dismissed for violating a school policy prohibiting the use of "technology...that defames individual members of any community." Administrators from several schools in and around Washington warned students not only about dangerous stalkers and predators, but also about college admissions officers and potential employers who could read personal information and "inappropriate material" from students' Facebook and Xanga posts. The Electronic Frontier Foundation similarly cautions student bloggers that,

> whatever you post on a public blog can be seen by your friends, your
> enemies, your teachers, your parents, your ex...the admissions offices
> of schools and colleges to which you might apply, current and future
> potential employers, and anyone else with access to the internet and a
> search engine. While you can change your blog post at any time, it may
> be archived by others.... Although a school has little power to punish you
> for off-campus speech, it can still use your blog against you as evidence of

other rules violations. For example, several underage college students were recently punished for violating their school's alcohol policy after they posted pictures of themselves drinking. (EFF, n.d.)

While it's typically high school students who get in trouble for what they write in their online diaries, college students don't exactly get a free pass when it comes to web logs. One student at the University of New Hampshire was banned from class "for writing violent sexual comments about his teacher in an on-line journal" ("Student's Blog" 2005), and a Marquette University dental student was suspended for criticizing unnamed students and instructors online (Twohey 2005). Blogging is an international phenomenon, and so, not surprisingly, schools in other countries have also been taking a tough stand on bloggers. In May 2005, two Russian students were expelled from their universities for blogging. One of them allegedly posted nasty comments about her professor on LiveBlog.com, Russia's most popular blog host service (mosnews 2005). At around the same time, a Singapore government agency threatened to sue a Singaporean student attending an American university for allegedly defaming the agency on his blog. Anxious to avoid an international incident, and perhaps a caning when he got back home, the student shut down his website, even though it resided on a U.S.-based server ("Singapore" 2005).

Prospective students also need to watch what they post. A creative but indiscreet blogger, outraged that his name had been misspelled in the letter of admission he received from my university, posted some sarcastic comments about the graduate program's director on his web log. Perhaps the student was merely venting and just got caught up in the free-for-all insult style characteristic of many blogs, but the program director read the comments as a serious threat when they came to his attention, and the would-be student's letter of admission was quickly withdrawn. In other cases, subjects of blog attacks haven't much recourse: a *Washington Post* columnist writing about the unpresidential-sounding name of one of the candidates was greeted by insult and invective from conservative bloggers who clearly didn't appreciate the article's gentle satire. Not everyone online is committed to civil discourse, and this instance of the new phenomenon of shock-blogging was simply shrugged off by the *Post*'s editors as one unfortunate cost of doing business in cyberspace.

Job applicants have begun to worry that their network indiscretions are causing the employment office to skip over their candidacies, and bloggers who are already in the work force, older though not necessarily more mature, run the risk of getting fired if they criticize employers or coworkers, whether or not they're doing it from company-owned computers. Googling "blogger fired" will turn up reports of companies that have dismissed employees whose blogs offended the boss: Delta; Wells Fargo; the bookseller Waterstones; several newspapers, where freedom of the press apparently doesn't include freedom to blog about the press; and a number of high-tech companies one might think to be blog-friendly such as Microsoft, Friendster, and search giant Google.

Google actually owns Blogger.com, a blog-hosting service, but that hasn't stopped the company from canning employees who complain about work online. Reporters for the *Houston Chronicle* and the *St. Louis Post-Dispatch* have been fired or suspended for personal blogs critical of the newspapers (Westhoff 2004). One instructor at for-profit Devry Institute was abruptly terminated for what she characterized as digital "water-cooler kvetching" (Spohn 2005), and assistant professors who keep blogs are starting to wonder if their online comments, even ones related to their research, could be held against them. When a political scientist at the University of Chicago failed to get tenure, the educational press was quick to point out that, after all, he kept a blog. A U.S. senator fired an aide for blogging about her sex life. Maintaining that sexual hanky panky on Capitol Hill should come as no surprise to anyone, the ex-staffer retaliated by turning her blog into a novel. And speaking of sex, teachers, like their students, need to be careful about what they say online. A former journalist and part-time instructor at Boston University lost his job after only two weeks for blogging that one of his students was "incredibly hot."

Blog firings are common enough that there's even a word for them: *getting dooced*, "losing your job over something you said on line," was coined by Heather Armstrong after she was fired from her web design job for writing stories about coworkers in her blog, dooce.com. Blogs can also inflict damage on others: a university president lost her job, not because she kept a blog, but in part because of an anonymous blog that repeatedly criticized her administrative style (Barwick 2006).

▪ ▪ ▪ IT'S A FREE COUNTRY

Blogs are making their way into our dictionaries as they become part of our everyday experience, and as they spread we begin to see challenges to their reliability. Even the courts have started to consider the special character of the genre. In October 2005 the Delaware Supreme Court dismissed a libel suit by a local politician who sought to unmask an anonymous critic writing in a local newspaper blog. In his opinion, Delaware Chief Justice Myron

Steele found that no defamation had occurred because blogs are interactive forums for the expression of opinion, not fact.

In law, only text interpreted by readers as factual can be libelous. Although enough lawyers are blogging for law blogs to warrant their own subgenre (see, for example, scotusblog, a blog about the Supreme Court), Judge Steele concluded that no one reads blogs for their factual content, and so the genre cannot be defamatory: "Blogs and chat rooms tend to be vehicles for the expression of opinions; by their very nature, they are not a source of facts or data upon which a reasonable person would rely" (*Doe v. Cahill* 2005).

Steele, who had never been attacked by a blogger, further found blogs to have no real sting. They are essentially harmless sites where mistakes are immediately correctable:

> The internet provides a means of communication where a person wronged
> by statements of an anonymous poster can respond instantly, can respond
> to the allegedly defamatory statements on the same site or blog, and
> thus, can, almost contemporaneously, respond to the same audience
> that initially read the allegedly defamatory statements. The plaintiff
> can thereby easily correct any misstatements or falsehoods, respond to
> character attacks, and generally set the record straight. This unique feature
> of internet communications allows a potential plaintiff ready access to
> mitigate the harm, if any, he has suffered to his reputation as a result of
> an anonymous defendant's allegedly defamatory statements made on an
> internet blog or in a chat room. (*Doe v. Cahill* 2005)

Blogs may be getting bad press in court, but blog readers prefer to judge for themselves. A 2004 survey reports that 86 percent of them consider blogs useful or extremely useful sources of information. In contrast, conventional news sources actually flunked the information test: 82 percent of those surveyed found TV news worthless or only somewhat useful for news or opinion, and slightly more than half said the same about newspapers and magazines ("Blog Reader" 2004).

For now, *Doe v. Cahill* protects political speech online, specifically shielding bloggers from libel charges, but that ruling won't keep people from losing their jobs—getting dooced—for dissing the boss online or for blogging when they should be working. Blogs may be easily corrected texts, but the courts have typically sided with employers seeking to dismiss employees for digital posts that can be viewed as insulting, disruptive, bad for morale, or—worst of all, in the boss's eyes—useful to economic competitors.

In extreme cases, bloggers can find their safety threatened. In some parts of the world, bloggers are subject to arrest. This tends to happen in totalitarian countries with histories of acting against any sort of speech officially viewed as insulting, disruptive, bad for morale, and useful to political competitors. In addition to Myanmar's recent suspension of the internet to hide the government's violent response against protestors, Bahrain regularly arrests bloggers and shuts down dissident blogs, which quickly pop up somewhere else (Mac-Farquhar 2006). China pressured Microsoft to shut down a Chinese blogger writing about "a high-profile newspaper strike" (Barboza and Zeller 2006), and Yahoo turned the e-records of journalist Shi Tao over to the government, which promptly sentenced him to ten years in jail for revealing state secrets (Zeller 2006; Sabbagh 2006; "Google se plie" 2006). There are online reports of blogger arrests in Iran, China, and Egypt. In November 2005 Paris police detained two bloggers "for inciting harm to people and property over the internet" (Plunkett 2005). French *blogueurs* were actually divided over the extended violence that occurred in France that fall, some egging on the car bombers and others urging restraint.

Worse than arrest, bloggers can actually get themselves killed. Steven Vincent, an American freelance journalist who wrote about the Iraq war for the *New York Times*, the *Wall Street Journal*, and the *Christian Science Monitor*, published a web log about his war experiences that he later turned into a book. Continuing his blog, he had begun posting complaints about insurgents infiltrating the Iraqi police. In August of 2005 Vincent was kidnapped in Basra and shot to death, presumably to silence him and shut down his blog (Wong 2005).

▪ ▪ ▪ BLOGGING RULES AND REGULATIONS

Despite the fear of disgruntled employees ridiculing the company or outing trade secrets on their blogs; a legal opinion defaming blogs as information-free or, at best, information-lite; and an initial reluctance to recognize that blogging constitutes a new and extremely popular way of writing, the business world has now begun to embrace the web log just as it has warmed to the instant message. Some businesses have even begun to formulate blogging guidelines for their employees. For example, IBM doesn't want its people to use their blogs for business writing: "IBM regards blogs as primarily a form of communication and relationship among individuals. When the company wishes to communicate publicly as a company—whether to the marketplace or to the general public—it has well established means to do so." However, conceding that blogging isn't going to go away anytime soon, IBM published a set of rules discouraging rude comments, warning employees not to disclose information useful to competitors, and reminding managers that "A blog is not the place to communicate IBM policies to IBM employees" (IBM n.d.). Below is IBM's "executive summary" of its rules:

1. Know and follow IBM's Business Conduct Guidelines.
2. Blogs, wikis and other forms of online discourse are individual interactions, not corporate communications. IBMers are personally responsible for their posts. Be mindful that what you write will be public for a long time—protect your privacy.
3. Identify yourself—name and, when relevant, role at IBM—when you blog about IBM or IBM-related matters. And write in the first person. You must make it clear that you are speaking for yourself and not on behalf of IBM.
4. If you publish a blog or post to a blog and it has something to do with work you do or subjects associated with IBM, use a disclaimer such as this: "The postings on this site are my own and don't necessarily represent IBM's positions, strategies or opinions."
5. Respect copyright, fair use and financial disclosure laws.
6. Don't provide IBM's or another's confidential or other proprietary information.
7. Don't cite or reference clients, partners or suppliers without their approval.
8. Respect your audience. Don't use ethnic slurs, personal insults, obscenity, etc., and show proper consideration for others' privacy and for topics that may be considered objectionable or inflammatory— such as politics and religion.
9. Find out who else is blogging on the topic, and cite them.
10. Don't pick fights, be the first to correct your own mistakes, and don't alter previous posts without indicating that you have done so.
11. Try to add value. Provide worthwhile information and perspective. (IBM, n.d.)

Clearly, IBM expects employee blogs to be both factual and informative, not just collections of rants and opinions. Despite the ruling in *Doe v. Cahill*, it appears that the buttoned-down business blog offers clear evidence that yet another electronic genre has been tamed. At the same time that the court in Delaware expressed its skepticism about the power of blogging, *Fortune* magazine identified the blog as the most important business trend of 2005, and a number of business journalists, following this lead, have urged companies to harness the power of the blog in the service of corporate profit. As the business world explores the latest digital text craze, employers have begun to field company blogs. They see no irony in the fact that, at the same time, they are regulating the personal blogging of their employees, even firing them if they find their blogs inappropriate.

Most employer guidelines require company bloggers to identify themselves, which allows for openness and transparency in corporate communications, but also makes it easier to root out malcontents. That's why the Electronic Frontier Foundation, whose motto is "Defending Freedom in the Digital World," recommends that workplace bloggers hide both their own and their company's identity in order to protect their jobs (EFF 2005). But such masking may vitiate the force of a blogger's complaint and reduce its interest value: how many readers are going to follow an expurgated blog that whines, "My boss at Associated Widgets is a big fat, no good poopyhead"?

Some employers require disclaimers informing readers that posts on employee blogs don't reflect official policy. Managers repeatedly warn bloggers not to divulge corporate secrets and to observe intellectual property rights. Only two employers specifically okay blogging on company time, but all guidelines remind employees not to let blogging interfere with their work. IBM counsels bloggers, "Don't forget your day job" (IBM n.d., 6), though the interpretation of "interfere" is never specified (Wackå n.d.). Plaxo, a software developer, even permits bloggers to disagree with company policy or management, so long as they do so politely. That policy was written by the blogger that Google fired (Pimentel 2005). But Feedster, creator of a popular blog search engine and aggregator, concludes its short list of rules for employees who blog with a warning that even the company whose business is blogging might find it necessary to censor or shut down employee blogs:

> Finally, please be aware that the company may request that you
> temporarily confine your website or weblog commentary to topics
> unrelated to the company (or, in rare cases, that you temporarily suspend
> your website or weblog activity altogether) if it believes this is necessary
> or advisable to ensure compliance with securities regulations or other laws.
> (Feedster 2005)

▪ ▪ ▪ BLOGGING FOR DUMMIES

Students continue to ignore rules against blogging, and not all employees honor the optimistic blogging codes that their employers set forth. But all is not anarchy. Though blogs continue to proliferate with no end in sight, some order is emerging from the blogosphere. It's clear that blogging, like email and instant messaging before it, is already developing sets of conventions as communities of bloggers self-organize, set up formal or informal rules of the road, and exert both subtle and overt pressure to steer novice bloggers along the paths of effective blogging.

Adding to the self-policing activities of blogging communities are the digital how-to-blog guides that are popping up almost as fast as blogs themselves. Soon every college writing text will have a chapter on how to blog, but in the mean time, would-be bloggers who require more detailed instructions than the online sites provide, who need both illustrations and hand-holding, can consult the *Idiot's Guide to Blogs* and *Blogging for Dummies*, books whose existence attests to the fact that conventional printing still plays an essential role in the digital revolution.

One of the earliest of these blogging guides, *The Weblog Handbook* (Blood 2002), devotes an entire chapter to the moral side of blog behavior. Specifically, Rebecca Blood advises bloggers not to offend or attack other people. Apparently few bloggers have read this chapter, since offensive language and public attacks seem staples of the genre, holdovers from the early days when the blog, like email before it, remained largely the property of the unruly digital counterculture. Even as the blog becomes civilized, co-opted by the business world and the mainstream news media, blogs retain a certain edginess as a sign of resistance to the taming forces of mass communication.

Continuing to lay out its own recommended code of conduct, *The Weblog Handbook* also sets forth some rules of etiquette for novice bloggers: acknowledge where you found your links; let readers know your posting schedule; warn readers about offensive material in your links; and answer your email. Again, not many bloggers follow these recommendations. Blood offers a code of blog ethics as well: don't publish lies (the Delaware Supreme Court has found that's in the nature of the genre for bloggers routinely to ignore this stricture); provide links to your sources; don't change weblog entries once they're posted (as if anything on the web is static); disclose conflicts of interest (another instruction more honored in the breach than the observance); let your readers know if any of your sources are untrustworthy or biased (a digital version of the old paradox: *I am a blogger. All bloggers are liars*).

Above all, in the elevated language of Blood's ethic, work hard and you will gain your readers' trust and respect. And it doesn't hurt to "reward the worthy, ignore the ignoble, fight tirelessly for what is right, and speak for those who cannot speak for themselves" (Blood 2002, 125). Finally, Blood counsels bloggers to protect the privacy of others (135) and to protect children from predators by never revealing their identity or location (137–38). This is sound advice for bloggers who combine the virtues of Robin Hood, Mother Teresa, and the average superhero. But most people consulting *The Weblog Handbook* want to learn how to blog, and they will see Blood's moral code as beside the point. Even IBM's injunction to "add value," a gesture in the same positive direction, won't turn bloggers into upstanding citizens any more than it will improve the content of their online posts.

A quick read across a variety of blogs suggests that few bloggers stand ready to receive Blood's commandments: personal data, including names and contact information, abound online, as do photos and other identifying marks. In addition, bloggers, perhaps lulled by a sense that they are lonesome diarists writing unobserved at their laptops, make public all sorts of information that could prove troublesome if read by parents, teachers, present or future employers, law enforcement authorities, or rivals bent on revenge. As Emily Nussbaum puts it in her description of teenage bloggers who both seek and fear readers: "This is their life to read. As long as their parents don't find out" (Nussbaum 2004).

While bloggers may not follow Blood's advice, or even seek it out, her admonitions to be nice reflect an underlying assumption, one that has some basis in fact: that blogs, like email and instant messaging, can be nasty things. Taking a high moral tone, Blood further urges the neophyte blogger to "use your powers for good" (Blood 2002, 123). Such an exhortation suggests that there is a propensity, or at least a temptation, on the part of bloggers to go over to the dark side, to use the genre in ways that are destructive rather than community-building.

It also assumes that the readers of a blog constitute a community, even if they have nothing in common beyond the fact they are reading a particular blog. Community has become an important online goal, perhaps in response to claims by the antitechnology side that devices such as computers disrupt local communities and degrade the quality of modern life by isolating individuals from one another and tying them to machines instead.

The Weblog Handbook is hardly unique in stressing the importance of the blog as a tool for building communities, not vitiating them. Many of the proponents

From the table of contents of *The Weblog Handbook*, by Rebecca Blood (2002). The book provides instructions on how to blog, but in chapter 6, and elsewhere in the text as well, the author focuses on appropriate blogging behavior. Graphic by the author.

of digital writing technologies emphasize their potential to reach out and touch someone, to forge connections between people in ways that are not dependent on physical location. It's certainly true that email and the various genres spawned by the web support the formation of groups of families and friends and those sharing recreational or professional interests that were never possible when alliance depended on face-to-face interaction or the slower pace of conventional mail. Such communities of the like-minded can be a cause for celebration when they connect those who are physically, socially, or intellectually isolated. But the connective powers of the web can also be a cause for worry, as when racists, terrorists, and pedophiles don digital masks to use their powers for something other than good. And the communities created online can be illusions: for example, students with Facebook accounts, and that includes most of the students I know, accumulate collections of "friends"—some number in the hundreds—without necessarily increasing the number of people they can count as actual friends.

▪ ▪ ▪ THE BLOG CAFÉ

Reinforcing the notion that digital space is not all that different from physical space, blogs (and the forums that are evolving from some blogs) have been likened to salons or coffee houses in which groups of readers and writers congregate. But only the most dedicated bloggers manage to keep the salon doors open long enough for a virtual community to coalesce. Like email and instant messaging, blogging is creating opportunities for public writing. As a result, more people than ever become writers in search of readers. But while email and instant messaging have morphed into essential tools for those of us who live at least part of our lives online, those who try their hand at blogging don't necessarily stay with it for very long. The sheer numbers of blogs suggest to some observers that the web log is taking over the web, but the individual blog, like its predecessor the diary, seems basically an occasional and self-limiting enterprise. I can't imagine a day when I don't send an email. The IM'ers I know go into withdrawal when the server is down. And texters may act like they don't know what to do with their thumbs when their phone batteries die. But the typical blog is updated twice a month, two-thirds of blogs are idle for months at a time, and half of all inactive blogs are one-day wonders, blogs never updated after the initial entry. The Perseus survey expresses some surprise at the number of blogs abandoned after being active for a year ("Blogging Iceberg" 2003). But none of these figures is surprising, considering that few of the best-known conventional diarists wrote every day throughout their lives. James Boswell kept journals only sporadically, as did Thoreau. The diary of Samuel Pepys ran for just ten years. And the work of Anne Frank, the one diarist my students seem to have heard of, was not intended for publication and was cut tragically short.

Lifelong diarists are harder to come by. Hester Thrale, the eighteenth-century literary commentator and friend of Samuel Johnson, kept a private diary for twenty-seven years, and her notebooks remained unpublished until the mid-twentieth century. And Anaïs Nin didn't begin the 250,000 handwritten pages of her diary, drafted with an eye toward publication, till her late twenties, but unlike the typical diarist, once she started, she kept on posting.

So far, most bloggers seem to favor the sporadic model over the daily grind. The demands of regular updating can get away from even the best-intentioned writer, and most blogs don't stay active for long. But the short life expectancy of most blogs doesn't stop new bloggers from going online. LiveJournal reports a rate of 405 new blog posts per minute, suggesting that for every blogger who gives up on the effort, new writers stand ready to take their virtual place.

▪ ▪ ▪ MANAGING THE AUTHORS CLUB

With more and more people writing, public concerns about an escalating literacy crisis should be eased. But just the opposite seems to be happening. Instead of welcoming as new members of the authors club those computer adepts who write because they want to, not just because it's assigned, critics slam online content as inferior to analog writing, and they fault keyboards for displacing the human voice as a primary means of human interaction.

Parents find their children's passion for computers isolating. One typical complaint runs, "They do less face-to-face talking, less phone talking, less playing outside than any other generation" (Bahrampour and Aratani 2006). Teenagers are even talking less on their cell phones and texting more. But computers have connected us more than they've isolated us. Surveys of adult computer use in the United States, Japan, and Denmark show that digital communication supports social networks rather than disrupting them (Boase et al. 2006). Email, IM, and web surfing don't replace human interaction, they supplement it, and in many cases they allow people to maintain relationships when face-to-face contact is not possible.

But it's not simply a lack of fresh air and sunshine, it's the quality—more specifically, the perceived lack of quality—of the digital interaction that provokes some critics, who dismiss the time we spend reading and writing on screen as time wasted on the trivia of IM, email, or web surfing. It's time taken away not just from face-to-face interaction, but also from reading and writing what the critics consider more worthwhile texts, or engaging in salon-quality conversations. That position incorrectly assumes that when we're not online we throw ourselves into high-culture mode, reading Tolstoi spelled with an *i* and writing sestinas and villanelles instead of shopping lists, and that every face-to-face encounter is worth a thousand online exchanges. But let's face facts: most f2f conversations are not high-minded, and like blogs and instant messages, much of our conventionally produced reading matter is less than star quality.

As Sherry Turkle (1995) makes clear, there are certainly people who are tempted to withdraw from the face-to-face world and spend their time online instead, but as our increased dependence on email, IM, and blogging to carry out both personal and professional communication indicates, not all life on the screen is pathological. Yes, rather than walk across the hall or talk across the room, many college students IM their roommates, and my daughter no longer shouts for her brother to come downstairs for dinner, she IM's him instead. But most students still leave their rooms for class, work, and recreation, and anyone who's spilled food or drink on a keyboard has learned the hard way to avoid taking meals alone, online.

All writing technologies open up new possibilities for fraud, and digital communication certainly presents users with opportunities for masquerade and deception, opportunities that strike fear in the hearts of parents and school authorities and pique the interest of psychologists. But most people, whether Thoreau would call them quietly desperate or not, lead lives on the screen that reflect their off-screen selves. Those selves may be digitally enhanced, to be sure, but they're really not all that different from the faces we put on when we go out to brave the off-line world.

Instead of replacing social realities with an online fantasy, a never-ending role-playing game, or a scam, most people are simply extending their everyday connections into the digital world, creating a space where they can meet for those times when meeting any other way is just not practical. It is in this activity that we see emerging the latest in the string of new communication genres, the most recent wave of services called by some observers *social media* or *social networking sites*, though I prefer the less-limiting term *space pages*. As we will see in the next chapter, websites like MySpace and Facebook are letting today's digital writers create personal pages for self-presentation, networking, messaging, commercial promotion, and almost every other communication need imaginable.

10

■ ■ ■   A Space of One's Own

The new digital genres rose to prominence as rapidly as they did not because people preferred machines to human contact, but because we couldn't wait to reinforce existing relationships through writing, to develop new writing practices made possible by the new technologies, and to engage new audiences in dialogue. Programmers and hardware engineers may continue to assert their proprietary interest in computers, and it's true that without the continuing innovations of the technology crowd, we'd still be hacking away at typewriters or reading books made from dead animal skins sewn together or, worse yet, sun-baked mud. But from the earliest days of the PC, it was the writers who took over the keyboard and claimed the computer screen as a space of their own. And it is the drive to put our lives online that underlies the popularity of MySpace and Facebook, which offer one-site-fits-all communication portals where writers are busy creating the latest digital genre for doing just that, a subgenre of social media sites that I call the space page.

Almost overnight, Facebook and MySpace have cornered the space page market. Friendster was once an industry phenomenon, too, and it's conceivable that by the time this book is printed, Facebook and MySpace will have become "just so 2008." But right now, they are the sites where users generate multimedia environments for meeting and just, well, being. Who needs to go to the malt shop or the mall when they can hang out on MySpace? Since space pages bring in a lot of cash from investors and advertisers, there's some incentive for competitors to try to get a piece of the action, and at least one, Twitter. com, has had some success offering a no-frills, one sentence updater, a kind of Facebook haiku suitable both for computers and mobile phones, but Facebook and MySpace remain the go-to sites for a full-service meet and greet.

These latest manifestations of the digital communication craze are often referred to as social networking sites because their original goal was to provide yet another place for people to come together online, like the chat room, the email group, or the IM buddy list. But the appeal of Facebook and MySpace goes far beyond social networking. What enabled these sites to soar from creation to widespread use in a mere three years is their capacity to allow users not simply to pose for others, to troll for friends, or to make plans to get together, but also to craft an online persona that complements their analog selves. Anyone with a login can post profiles consisting of text, pictures, and music on these sites, furnishing the internet-enabled public with detailed interest inventories and a whole lot more.

Pageowners, the term I use for people who "do" Facebook or MySpace, post extensive photo albums with pictures ranging from conventional poses to candid snaps of the pageowner at play, sometimes even engaged in risqué or possibly illegal activities. As bandwidth increases, and in response to user demands, more and more pages also feature video essays and music downloads, and for those whose propensities lean more toward videography than typing, there's also YouTube, an increasingly popular site that has been gobbled up by Google for $1.65 billion, where anyone can post short videos. Space pages and other "social media" sites are more than just online diaries, they are entire magazines centered on the pageowner. And unlike email, personal web pages or blogs, which may be commercial free if they use nonprofit hosts such as university servers, the space pages display ads, just like magazines—it's how the hosting sites make their money.

The social media sites are popular with college students, teens, and young adults. And not just some college students, teens, and young adults, but most of them. Facebook, created in 2004 by a Harvard student who quickly dropped out of school to devote himself full-time to his multi-million-dollar innovation, boasted in 2006 that it had signed up more than 85 percent of the college crowd. Facebook sites serve more than 2,100 colleges, 22,000 high schools, and 1,000 companies (facebook.com/press.php), and in a more recent iteration, Facebook opened its pages to pretty much anyone with an email address—a move that, perhaps predictably, angered some of the innovative technology's traditional users, who didn't want their already large private space open to the general public. Awareness of sites such as Facebook and MySpace has moved well beyond the campus. Facebook now boasts 175 million active users, half of them out of college, and claims that its fastest growing demographic consists of adults over the age of thirty-five.

As a result of its popularity, Facebook and its attendant vocabulary have quite literally become household words:

- *To facebook* means to communicate with someone on Facebook.
- From the profile page one can *message* the pageowner, who will be alerted to the message the next time he or she logs on.

- *To friend* someone means adding a person to the list of Facebook friends featured on the user's profile. Friendship comes with privileges: by default, pictures of the pageowner's top friends appear prominently, together with links to their Facebook pages, and only friends can put messages on the pageowner's "wall" (discussed later in this list). Moving someone into or out of the pageowner's list of best friends has real-life ramifications as well. Though critics point to profiles where users seem intent on adding as many friends as possible, to the point where *friending* seems an empty activity, rearranging a friend list can result in heightened self-esteem or hurt feelings.
- Facebookers indicate their relationship status (options include *in a relationship with [name]*, *single*, and *it's complicated*), and friends check regularly to see who's with whom, and who's been dumped.
- Finally, everyone on campus seems to know about "the wall," defined by Facebook as "a forum for your friends to post comments or insights about you." Users have the option of making their wall invisible, deleting messages they don't like, or turning the feature off altogether.

We've seen that digital communications typically face the same issues of credibility and trustworthiness that early writing technologies had to overcome. But authenticity doesn't seem to be a concern for the space pages. Facebook claims that "people on Facebook are who they say they are and behave the way they do in the real world" (facebook.com/press.php). But the attractiveness of these pages that sing of the self suggests that they are not just expressions of narcissism or simple digital representations of the writer's real-world self. Many profiles present a whimsically misleading portrait of the pageowner: one local high schooler claims on his Facebook page to be a university student majoring in aeronautical engineering, while a tone-deaf friend professes a concentration in vocal performance.

Some pages are even more ostentatiously fictional. A Facebook search for celebrities suggests that faux pages form a significant space page subgenre: George W. Bush has Facebook pages at several high schools and colleges that the real George Bush never attended, including NYU and the Boston Latin School. Similarly, while Abbie Hoffman did graduate from Brandeis University in 1959, he cannot be the author of his Brandeis Facebook page, since Hoffman died seven years before Facebook was invented. Joseph Stalin is neither a Washington University graduate student nor a Penn State alum, and while Snoopy and Woodstock share an Emory University Facebook page, they aren't even real people, let alone students at the school. It's clear that many writers view the space page as a blank canvas waiting to express all sorts of creative fictions, and even the authentic space pages are crafted to appeal to the reader as well as the writer. Facebook pages have also become part of the electoral process: the candidates for the 2008 presidential election quickly established a presence on Facebook and MySpace, complete with lists of friends, candid snapshots, and personal videos as they sought voters while at the same time recapturing a bit of their lost youth.

▪ ▪ ▪ SONG OF MYSPACE

Profiles on both MySpace and Facebook are multimedia affairs. MySpace pages often feature music, and Facebook claims to host the internet's favorite photo album (there are also dedicated photo-sharing sites such as Photobucket, "where millions manage their media" [photobucket.com], which went online in 2003). And these sites let people track friendships: as MySpace puts it, "MySpace is an online community that lets you meet your friends' friends" (collect.myspace.com).

On both space page sites, friends may also be sorted into virtual groups, clubs whose members share an interest, anything from students enrolled in a particular class to people with the same first name. One popular Facebook group at my university targets fans of the early educational computer game Oregon Trail and carries the name "I Just Tried to Ford the River and my Fuckin' Oxen Died." When I checked, the group had 4,899 members, about one-seventh of the student body, while another group, "Towns without Wal-Mart," had only fifteen, a reflection of the retailer's massive impact on post–Oregon Trail American geography. Advertising on these sites seems to target the different demographics of each group. The banner ad on the Oregon Trail page offers students summer jobs. Clicking on the ad takes a visitor out of Facebook to the sponsor's job application page. In contrast, the ad on the Wal-Mart club page leads to a site selling gift cards for a down-market, drive-in hamburger chain.

The advertising on personal profile pages—something the pageowner has no control over—seems a little more random. My Facebook profile has boasted an ad for a public interest group and another for Mother's Day gifts (which popped up a week after Mother's Day, a sign that the context-sensitive marketing is not as tightly focused as sponsors might wish). Reloading the page brought a new ad, this time for an upscale hotel chain. And MySpace cluttered my space with flyers for Brazilian tourism and cheap plane tickets, together with animated ads for automobiles and an online dating service.

Account holders on Facebook and MySpace use their pages not just to billboard their friends and interests or flaunt their affiliations, but also to communicate, bypassing more conventional email or messaging programs. In fact, there seems to be a whole new category of space page friends emerging whom we could call pixel pals: like pen pals, they are people one talks to regularly online but never in person (Facebook reports that the average user has 120 "friends"). And there is a new concern that accompanies the popularity of these pages: a digital stranger danger. An early campus nickname for Facebook on campuses was "Stalkerbook," and some of my students refer to the site as "stalker net"—but more on that later.

Until recently, MySpace has been even more popular and profitable than Facebook, though a February 2009 report shows both Facebook and YouTube surpassing MySpace in number of unique visits per month (http://lists.compete.com). MySpace is starting to impact our vocabulary as well: *to myspace someone* means not simply to look someone up, but to leave a message on his or her page. MySpace assumed its present form as a space page site in 2003 and was bought two years later by Rupert Murdoch's News Corporation for more than half a billion dollars. (Murdoch also acquired photobucket.com in 2007, and in the same year Microsoft purchased a $240 million stake in Facebook (*Business Week*, 10-25-07). Much slicker in terms of its production values, and much more commercial than Facebook, in 2006 MySpace became the eighth most popular website in the world, the sixth most highly trafficked English-language site. In comparison, Facebook claims to be the seventh most visited website in the United States. Readers should not worry if they didn't know this. These spaces are heavily used by a dedicated clientele who keep coming back for more. In 2007 Facebook estimated that 60 percent of its account holders signed on daily, and 85 percent of them signed on at least once a week.

It took only a decade for email to rise from near obscurity to a position where, when the server goes down, no work gets done. It took about the same amount of time for cell phones to dominate the telephone market, turning landlines into an endangered species and making pay phones pretty much extinct. Instant messaging, web pages, and the blog have caught on even faster. So vital have they become to the life of America's youth that one student I know actually gave up AOL instant messenger for Lent but, interestingly, not Facebook. The success of IM and blogging was sped in part by the fact that more people were online by the time these genres came into being. However, although they've become essential to the people who use them, the space pages have yet to achieve the centrality of email or cell phone conversation outside the niches where they have established themselves, and it's still pretty common for nonpractitioners to be clueless about the phenomenon or to approach it with fear and distrust.

Facebook and MySpace attract slightly different crowds, but the differences between the two major space page sites are turning out to be superficial. In addition, the sites have enough in common with one another, and with analogous sites such as Twitter, YouTube, and Photobucket, to suggest that a new web-based genre of social media sites is coalescing. The elements of the social media genre are still far from settled, but for hard-core users, Facebook and MySpace are starting to function as their principal digital home, or homes, since many users have accounts on more than one such site. These social network sites may have started out as personal bulletin boards, but they have developed into much more. They combine functions of email and the blog, focused around a kind of personal résumé, and the end result seems in some ways to be more than the sum of the parts. These spaces encourage everyone not just to write, but also to become a diarist, messager, letter writer, web designer, photographer, film-maker, musician, and graffiti artist.

Facebook began its life as a digital version of the ink-and-paper facebook, a book of photos that some schools printed each fall to introduce new students to the local academic community. Its success was instantaneous, spreading from campus to campus and eventually developing a strong presence in the non-college world as well. MySpace continues to draw the lion's share of the high school crowd as well as those not involved in colleges. In contrast to Facebook, MySpace remains strongly associated with the pop music scene and serves as a space for both beginning and established bands to publicize concerts, promote CDs, and provide free samples of their work. Its more commercial focus has led one critic to call it no better than spam (Lapinski 2006).

While MySpace does give advertisers space on millions of American desktops, it's the profiles, not the ads, that make the service so attractive to its users. MySpace profiles are often accompanied by a soundtrack, and users can customize MySpace pages more dramatically than Facebook. Still, MySpace offers similar group and communication utilities—including IM—but on a fairly grand scale: on a visit to the MySpace group homepage in 2006, I counted about 750,000 groups in categories ranging from automotive to fan clubs, perhaps the largest at well over 120,000 groups, to money and investing, with only 4,764 groups. As with Facebook, some groups are large, others very small. The Oregon Trail group on MySpace has only 346 members (a similarly named group has an additional 200), and I can't find a group analogous to Facebook's "Towns without Wal-Mart." On the other hand, the "Make-Out Club" has close to 180,000 MySpace "friends," not all of whom appear to be fully clothed.

Adults Only Beyond This Point

The MySpace Make-Out Club posts a warning that its pages may contain adult material, and visitors must click past that warning link if they really want to enter the space. Clearly this isn't enough to prevent minors from browsing the site, but that's not really what alarms some people about the potential danger that the space pages pose to public morality. It's a fear of pedophiles infiltrating the social networks that sparks schools to forbid students from setting up profiles or visiting Facebook and MySpace. Reports of actual predation—and the publicized arrests of a number of predators who used MySpace to arrange meetings with children, or with police officers posing as children—led one congressman, Michael G. Fitzpatrick (R-Pa.), to sponsor H.R. 5319, the Deleting Online Predators Act of 2006, which sought "to protect minors from commercial social networking websites and chatrooms."

Fitzpatrick's bill sought to amend the Communications Act of 1934 (USC 47, sec. 254), which had already been updated to require schools and libraries to bar from their computers any obscene or pornographic material, or any other visual depiction harmful to children. The new version of the law demonizes space pages and chat rooms, singling them out as sites that children need to be protected from.

The statute would prohibit school access to MySpace, Facebook, and any other sites or chat rooms where minors may access pornography or "be subject to unlawful sexual advances, unlawful requests for sexual favors, or repeated offensive comments of a sexual nature from adults." Libraries could lift the prohibition against space pages only with parental approval. Included in the ban would be any sites that allow users to create profiles providing personal information about themselves, as well as sites offering instant messaging, email, or any other forum for real-time textual communication where messages are "almost immediately visible to all other users or to a designated segment of all other users."

Since minors who use the internet for social networking do so from home, many schools that don't already ban space pages use have counseled students not to disclose addresses or phone numbers on their profiles to insulate them from real or potential threats. Fitzpatrick's revision enshrines that practice in law, directing the Federal Trade Commission to "issue a consumer alert regarding...the potential danger of commercial social networking websites and chat rooms through which personal information about child users of such websites may be accessed by child predators," and with no sense of irony, it orders the Federal Trade Commission (FTC) to establish a website to disseminate information to parents and schools about the dangers of the internet. However, the bill defined social networking sites so vaguely as to cover not just MySpace-style gathering places, but also popular commercial sites such as Amazon, ePinions, cartalk.com, imdb.com, and any of the growing number of web forums where users can create online profiles and share their opinions with others (Read 2006). Ultimately DOPA, as it was called, died in committee the following year.

There's no doubt that the internet offers pornography inappropriate for minors, not to mention most adults—porn is bigger business on the net than just about anything else. And federal law already bans such material in no uncertain terms from school and library computers. But while a vote against the Deleting Online Predators Act would be tantamount to opposing motherhood and apple pie, it's not even clear that school and library computers are places where online predators lurk—if only because those computers tend to be in very public places. Worse still, the Deleting Online Predators Act would not have prevented the salacious emails and instant messages sent by former Representative Mark Foley (R-Fla.) to underage Congressional pages. Foley, who cochaired the House Caucus on Missing and Exploited Children but is not listed as a cosponsor of the DOPA space page ban, resigned his House seat in September 2006 when his own predatory online messages to high school students were reported.

In addition, it's not clear that space pages pose any more danger to children than the nondigital world, where if TV shows such as *Law and Order*, *CSI*, and *Without a Trace* have it right, bad things really do happen to good people, many of them minors, more often than anyone would like. My students, who are not minors, report enough incidents of online stalking or other unwanted virtual contact that many no longer put screen names or cell phone numbers on their space page profiles. But they assume that in most cases, these approaches come from other students rather than from strangers outside the local network. While my students don't report that unwanted Facebook contacts have begun to show up in person at their doors, most play it safe by not disclosing personal data.

The newspapers occasionally run stories about internet stalking as a replacement for more traditional telephone harassment, but these too suggest that when danger comes, it comes more from peers than from strangers, as in the widely publicized story of Megan Meier. Meier, a Missouri middle schooler, killed herself after being harassed on MySpace by a boy named Josh, who friended her but after a series of flirtatious messages began taunting and tormenting her. Josh turned out to be the fictional creation of the mother of a former friend, who lived down the street (Maag 2007).

There's no solid proof that the space pages pose a threat to American youth or that measures like the Deleting Online Predators Act are overreactions to a danger that may be real but is also fairly remote. Schools and libraries are increasingly committed to using the web to communicate not just with staff, but also with students, parents, and the public. In addition, both schools and libraries already control internet access for minors. Adding a specific ban on space pages could actually wind up both limiting the educational potential of the internet and tempting more students to set up forbidden profiles.

Since the number of space page users will probably keep increasing, at least until something better comes along, educating users on how to deploy the technology sensibly and safely will go a lot further than pushing usage underground. In 2006, MySpace.com appointed a security officer to police its profiles, remove offensive material, and alert authorities to threats of violence. One free-speech advocate who follows internet trends and has observed racist, anti-Semitic, and homophobic activities on MySpace, remains convinced that federal regulation of these services would be too extreme a response: "internet actors and market forces are producing a result—a safer and more decent MySpace—that is good for everyone" (Wolfe 2006).

MySpace for Dummies

But internal self-regulation and external policing are only one part of the control picture. As with email and blogging, space page advice is starting to appear on scattered websites. It may not be long before there are multiple versions of the "MySpace for Dummies" books to complement the how-to-blog books I discussed earlier, but right now the advice seems to consist of pleas to behave responsibly online. One such plea, issued by the Cornell University Instructional Technology Policy Office, reads more like a student services pamphlet on alcohol, drugs, and sex.

Cornell's "Thoughts on Facebook" begins with a gee-whiz tone: "Facebook, like much of the internet, is a great innovation!" (Mitrano 2006). But it quickly links space pages with students' career goals: "For the entrepreneurially minded, [Facebook] might be an introduction into business as you think of how to 'market' yourself."

In an example that is probably supposed to appeal to the undergraduate mentality but instead reads like a humorless and slightly off-color fairy tale, the author breathlessly illustrates how quickly a great innovation like the internet can lead to ruin:

A long time ago, well before the advent of Facebook, there was a student at an it-shall-go-unnamed university who used a chat room to post some facts about the size of his penis. What a surprise when he went for his first job interview, all nicely tailored in a new suit and armed with a good

G.P.A. He was rejected. Fortunate for him, there was a friendly alumnus on the search committee who told him the reason. The HR person on the hiring committee had looked him up on the internet and found the boasting posting! Frantically, the student called the university officials asking them to remove it. Alas, they could not help him, because a commercial ISP was the domain of the posted information. In time, the student learned about the labyrinthine procedure in which he had to engage in order to have the posting removed. It never occurred to him that a relatively harmless boast could cause him so much trouble.

Following this anecdote, students are admonished to consider not just their future, but the law and university policy as well when using Facebook:

> Remember, just because it is a new technology does not absolve you of the responsibility to use it in legal and appropriate ways—including taking into account your obligations regarding proper conduct as a citizen of the university.

Students are reassured that Cornell will not monitor their postings—no Net Nannies for these young adults—but in the next breath they're reminded that danger awaits them in unsupervised cyberspace:

> You may be exposing yourself to someone who may not have the same values, assumptions about appropriate behavior or may even have a mental defect or disease which could put you at risk as a victim of criminal behavior.

And as if the potential to attract sickos wasn't bad enough, students are further warned that Facebook not only permits them to hurt other people's feelings, but it also exposes them to lawsuits:

> Think not only about what identity you create for yourself online, but also how you represent others. At the very least, be sure that you take their feelings into account. You would not want to find yourself as a defendant in a tort case that alleged you invaded their privacy.

After suggesting that Facebook can destroy their careers, imperil their personal safety, alienate their real-world friends, and get them hauled into court, students are counseled to enjoy Facebook. But even that advice is tempered by warnings that although Cornell won't be tracking their internet behavior, everyone else will be:

Have fun and make productive use of these new, exciting technologies, but remember that technology does not absolve one of responsibility. Behind every device, behind every new program, behind every technology is a law, a social norm, a business practice that warrants thoughtful consideration. (Mitrano 2006)

Cornell may not monitor student Facebook sites, but many high schools, colleges, parents, and potential employers are starting to do so. Not surprisingly, just as bloggers get upset if the wrong person reads their online diary and loud-talking cell phone users get upset when they realize that bystanders are listening in, students who willingly publicize themselves on Facebook consider such surveillance an invasion of their privacy. In the fall of 2006, Facebook rolled out a new service called "The Feed," consisting of a list of "the latest stories about your friends" together with "news articles that might be of interest to you." While its creators justified the Feed on the grounds that users could get the same information by clicking on their friends' pages anyway, that Facebook was simply "delivering the mail to you instead of forcing you to pick it up on your own," enough Facebookers went ballistic over what they perceived to be this intrusion into their private digital world that Facebook made the service optional.

The space pages are one more example of how digital technologies routinely upset our notions of public and private space in ways that we have yet to come to terms with. When they expose secrets and peccadilloes in open digital arenas that they'd never display either in person or in conventional print, writers are taking the private public. And to complete the reconfiguration of the inside and outside, the public worlds of advertising and anonymous readers of blogs and space pages regularly intrude on the private world of the individual desktop.

It should ease the concerns of the Cornell IT Policy Office that the online universe is both freewheeling and self-regulating. Perhaps one of the most remarkable features of the new digital technologies is the speed at which people have learned both to use them and to develop implicit or in some cases quite explicit user codes. It's likely that as adults become more familiar with the space pages, and as both sites and site users develop mechanisms for self-regulation, some of the concerns about this particular corner of the web's potential for depravity may be relaxed.

The lists of what to do and what to avoid, together with space pages' increasing use as moneymakers—not just in terms of border ads, but also the increasing number of pages whose only goal is to sell a product—also signal a commercialization of the space pages. And the rate at which politicians are establishing a presence on the space pages indicates an increasing depersonalization and professionalizing of the genre. Like email, IM, and blogs, the new genre is moving from radical to conventional at a rapid clip. Even YouTube is losing its attraction for some users as it becomes increasingly bogged down in copyright and trademark battles. At the same time that these sites move more and more toward the cultural mainstream, some of their earliest users have begun wondering where they will find the next countercultural technology.

▪ ▪ ▪ WORKS IN PROGRESS

Most writers think of works in progress as a means to an end: eventually they will finish that novel, poem, history, dictionary, report, email, or memo and move on to something else. But new internet-enabled genres like blogs and space pages are by definition works in progress that end, like diaries, only when the writer dies or loses interest in the project.

Blogs and space pages are advertisements for the self with marginal comments added by others. Typically, one person writes a space page, and one writer, or a small group, keeps a blog, posting individually crafted pieces as short as a sentence or as long as a few paragraphs, or commenting on the posts made by others. In contrast the *wiki*, another new genre to come out of the digital revolution, involves multiple authors creating one text and placing it in cyberspace not just to be read or commented on by others, but also to be rewritten by those readers as well.

The wiki is a user-editable text, a special kind of community space page—something like a digital quilting bee—where people come to work on a common project, typically an article, report, or proposal, not all at once, but serially, one at a time. Some private, work-group wikis may follow a master pattern, with all contributors focusing on a goal they have agreed on in advance. But in the large, public wikis, each writer-editor pursues a different vision of the topic, and each edit produces a different version for the next reader to respond to and, potentially, to rewrite as well.

The basic wiki text is by definition unstable: we read it in its present form, and while we can backtrack to earlier versions, there's no guarantee that when we return to the wiki site we will find the words as we left them, or that they will not have disappeared. While this is true of all web pages, wikis are volatile by definition, not a comforting thought for those who have grown used to treating the written word as stable and authoritative, particularly in comparison to speech or memory.

The term *wiki* is shortened from Wiki Wiki Web, the name of the first wiki, created by Ward Cunningham in 1995 to allow users to correct error-prone hypertext documents or "stacks." It comes from the Hawaiian *wiki wiki*, "very fast," and users soon began to tap the potential of the wiki to create readily editable online databases, repositories where information could easily be added, deleted, or modified.

The wiki is an ideal model for electronic collaboration on group projects where specifically designated users rework a text till they get it right. But the wiki also became the model for an online, user-editable workspace, where the group creating the project could theoretically become as large as the total number of internet users. While the first wikis served small cohorts of writers chosen specifically for the job, today the typical wiki is a public site whose slogan might well be "writers wanted."

With these public wikis, membership in the set of readers and writers is always in flux. What the wiki creates online is a fluid, complex, self-organizing community of writers, a textocracy with citizenship open to all. Each wiki is governed by representatives who review site entries and adjudicate the inevitable conflicts that arise when writers disagree about a topic. But insofar as possible, wiki communities operate by establishing consensus rather than by following rules and regulations. Wiki communities operate in much the same way that off-line communities operate. But the texts that wikis produce have some significant differences from conventional texts.

While some wikis require users to register before they can edit text or contribute new information, registration tends to involve little more than creating a login and password. In effect, wikis let anyone create new articles or modify what they find on the site. The result might seem to critics much like Mark Twain's description of a camel: a horse designed by a committee. But to wiki fans this is writing as it was meant to be, indeterminate, ever changing, never complete, thoroughly postmodern. A wiki is the ultimate work in progress: like the universe, it just goes on forever.

Two of the best-known wiki sites are the Wikipedia (en.wikipedia.org), an online user-generated encyclopedia launched in 2001 with more than 2.7 million English-language entries and almost 5.1 million articles in other languages (as of April 2009), and the Urban Dictionary (urbandictionary. com), a slang dictionary that debuted in 1999 and whose more than 3.8 million entries are furnished by hordes of enthusiastic readers (at best, English only has about six hundred thousand words). Wikipedia now calls itself the largest reference site on the web. It's also ranked as one of the highest-trafficked English-language net sites of any kind. Urban Dictionary is modest in comparison, but as dictionaries go, it's been nothing less than a phenomenon. Urban Dictionary logged about 300,000 new words and expressions in its first four years of operation, and when I checked in on May 30, 2006, it had logged 1,201 new entries for the previous day. By way of comparison, the

2005 print edition of the *Encyclopaedia Britannica* had only 80,000 articles, and it took the compilers of the *Oxford English Dictionary* more than fifty years to define 450,000 words, few of which were slang. Of course both the *EB* and the *OED* have something that these wikis don't: editorial planning and direction, contributors who have been vetted, and professional fact-checkers and proofreaders. Unlike traditional reference works, wikis grow randomly and depend for their correction on the alacrity of readers who may or may not be experts.

Wikipedia's writers have two roles to choose from: they can create articles for posting or they can edit articles that are already online. No experience is necessary, and while there certainly aren't a million writers penning the millions of Wikipedia entries, the total number of contributors to Wikipedia is probably very large indeed. In addition, there's a core of about one thousand regulars, volunteers who provide multiple articles and edits, and who actively discuss Wikipedia policy in its forums. These regulars form an administrative hierarchy that polices the site to delete articles when necessary and protect other articles from vandalism. It's this core who can be counted on to participate in the ongoing life of the Wikipedia collective (Hafner 2006).

According to Wikipedia, volunteer authors "don't have to be experts or scholars, although some certainly are." Since article authors remain anonymous, it's never clear who's a specialist, who's an amateur. In any case, no one checks a writer's credentials, nor does anyone read a submission before it's posted online. Verifying an article's accuracy, correcting it, or even deleting it, are all done after publication, not before.

In the wiki style of communal writing and rewriting, mistakes are anticipated, and it is assumed that they will simply be discovered by subsequent readers and edited out. Editing Wikipedia is even easier than writing articles for it. All a wannabe editor has to do is click the "edit" link at the end of each article, and all changes take effect immediately. The text's authority, like the text itself, is always in flux, and wiki fans are convinced that because of this, every day, in every way, Wikipedia articles are truly getting better and better.

Wikipedia advises readers that the length of time an article has been up is a good indicator of its reliability: old articles will have survived multiple edits to remove misinformation, while newer postings may not have been checked as rigorously for error. Wikipedia further cautions that contributing an article or edit is like giving up one's Fifth Amendment rights. Anything writers say can and will be used against them: "If you don't want your writing to be edited mercilessly or redistributed by others, do not submit it" (en.wikipedia.org).

Wikis can and do contain misinformation, sometimes introduced on purpose by wiki vandals. To control vandalism, sites such as Washington State

University's WSU Wiki limit editing privileges to members of the university community. Even so, there are few real limits placed on wiki contributors. In one highly publicized case, in 2005 John Seigenthaler found a false Wikipedia entry charging him with complicity in the assassinations both of John and Robert Kennedy. Seigenthaler, a retired editor at *USA Today* and a defender of First Amendment press protection, had been at one time an aide to Attorney General Robert Kennedy, but that was the only element in his unauthorized Wikipedia biography that was true.

Although Wikipedia boasts that mistakes are corrected "within minutes" once they are detected by the thousands of volunteer editors who patrol the site, the misinformation about Seigenthaler remained on Wikipedia for 132 days. According to Seigenthaler, only one typo was corrected by a reader-editor during that time. And like all web-based materials, Wikipedia articles may be mirrored by other sites, where they continue to be accessed long after the original has been corrected or deleted from its home site. After getting Wikipedia to take down his biography, it took Seigenthaler a further three weeks to have the false entry removed from answers.com and reference.com, two popular information sites that draw material from Wikipedia. To his dismay, Seigenthaler found that "answers" on answers.com and similar sites are never checked for accuracy or authenticity.

Efforts by Seigenthaler and by Wikipedia itself to uncover who wrote the article came up empty: like all Wikipedia writers, the author may choose to remain both unknown and untraceable (Seigenthaler 2005). An outside investigator did eventually uncover the culprit, a practical joker trying to pull the leg of a coworker, and in response to the controversy Wikipedia began requiring article contributors to register in advance. But Wikipedia's article on the Seigenthaler controversy reports that would-be editors are still trying to place false information on Seigenthaler's new and corrected Wikipedia bio (en.wikipedia.org, "Seigenthaler incident").

In response to continued critiques of Wikipedia accuracy, the encyclopedia decided to suspend editing privileges for certain sensitive entries and to limit editing access to others. Only approved editors can tinker with the articles on Albert Einstein, Christina Aguilera, human rights in China, or elephants, for example. Though I don't understand why anyone would want to tamper with articles on Einstein, the elephant story played itself out on national TV.

Stephen Colbert, host of the comedy show *The Colbert Report*, hoping to demonstrate the contingency of truth, asked viewers to edit the Wikipedia article on elephants to show that the population of African elephants was increasing, not declining. So many fans did so that Wikipedia had to lock that entry and ban Colbert from editing entries. As the Wikipedia editors describe it,

> Colbert…satirize[d] the more general issue of whether the repetition of statements in the media leads people to believe they are true….Colbert suggested that viewers change the elephant page to state that the number of African elephants has tripled in the last six months. The suggestion resulted in numerous incorrect changes to Wikipedia articles related to elephants and Africa. Wikipedia administrators subsequently restricted edits to the pages by anonymous and newly created users. (http:// en.wikipedia.org/wiki/Wikipedia_in_culture)

After such vandalism, even in the interest of humor, Wikipedia imposed a four-day waiting period before volunteer editors could change the articles on the semiprotected list, for example those dealing with George W. Bush, Islam, or Adolph Hitler (Hafner 2006). While this cooling-off period, similar to the one imposed on purchasers of firearms, might discourage heat-of-the-moment wiki vandalism, it won't discourage well-meaning contributors from introducing unintended error, nor will it be an obstacle for those determined to sabotage an entry.

Seigenthaler's experience notwithstanding, undetected error can persist in any text, conventional or digital. One study comparing error rates in Wiki-pedia to those of the *Encyclopaedia Britannica* discovered no significant differences: four mistakes per science article in Wikipedia compared to three per article in the online version of the *Britannica*. Not only that, most of the mistakes in both publications were minor errors of fact rather than serious misrepresentations of the subject (Giles 2005). *EB* contributors tend to be experts in their field, or at least paid *Britannica* staff writers, but a *Nature* survey reported that few scientists either contribute articles to Wikipedia or edit them. Instead, Wikipedians, as they call themselves, tend to be amateurs and enthusiasts. Considering such differences between the two encyclopedias, Wikipedia comes off looking pretty good in the accuracy department.

In addition, wikis, with their open-editing technology, are more quickly corrected than conventional printed texts, or even sites like *Britannica* online or the online *Oxford English Dictionary*. This often-cited example of how a nonexistent word found its way into the second edition of *Webster's New International Dictionary* illustrates both how error can be introduced into a conventionally printed reference text and what it takes to remove it:

> On July 31, 1931, Austin M. Patterson, Webster's chemistry editor, sent in a slip reading "D or d, cont./density." This was intended to add "density" to the existing list of words that the letter "D" can abbreviate. The slip somehow went astray, and the phrase "D or d" was misinterpreted as a single, run-together word: *dord*. (This was a plausible mistake because

headwords on slips were typed with spaces between the letters, making "D or d" look very much like "D o r d".) A new slip was prepared for the printer and a part of speech assigned along with a pronunciation. The word got past proofreaders and appeared on page 771 of the dictionary around 1935.

On February 28, 1939, an editor noticed "Dord" lacked an etymology and investigated. Soon an order was sent to the printer marked "plate change/imperative/urgent." The word "Dord" was excised and the definition of the adjacent entry "Dore furnace" was expanded from "A furnace for refining dore bullion" to "a furnace in which dore bullion is refined" to close up the space (en.wikipedia.org, "dord").

The reasonably accurate Wikipedia article on *dord* cites a classic essay on the subject by Merriam-Webster editor Philip P. Gove and is accompanied by an illustration of the dictionary page containing the *dord* definition. The illustration reproduced here is from my own copy of *Webster's New International Dictionary of the English Language*, second edition, published in 1934. It indicates that *dord* appeared a year earlier than the Wikipedia citation claims, and it shows that the word following *dord* is *doré*, not *Dore furnace*. Noteworthy too, though not mentioned in the Wikipedia entry, is the fact that although the word didn't exist before Webster's accidentally gave it life, an editor at Merriam-Webster was confident enough to assign a pronunciation to *dord* without ever hearing anyone actually say it.

The 1940 printing of *Webster's Second* dropped *dord* and added the correct *D* or *d* as an abbreviation for density. But correcting the problem in a reprint of an unabridged dictionary didn't remove the ghost word *dord* from circulation. People don't buy new dictionaries each time they are reprinted, especially the expensive unabridged kind. Copies of *Webster's Second* containing the spurious *dord* can still be found in libraries and used bookstores today, almost seventy-five years after it appeared. Even so, this oncer had little impact on the course of the English language: *dord* hasn't been used by anyone except lexicographers and curiosity collectors retelling the story of how the word made its way into the dictionary.

The entry in *Webster's Second* (1934) for *dord*. Merriam-Webster; used by permission.

Removing an error on Wikipedia is simpler and is likely to have more immediate impact than correcting a conventionally printed text: all it requires is recognizing the error and clicking the article's edit button. In just a few seconds I amended the date in the Wikipedia article on *dord* from 1935 to 1934 and added the information that lexicographers call words like *dord* ghost words. My changes appeared as soon as I clicked "save page." Though earlier versions of the article may persist on mirror sites, anyone consulting *Wikipedia* itself will see a more accurate version of the *dord* article, unless of course it's been edited again.

Just as it's easy to improve a wiki, it's also easier to introduce error on wikis than in conventional text that is vetted by many editors before it is released to the public. With so many millions of articles in the Wikipedia database, which keeps growing every day, finding and recognizing errors is always going to be a challenge. But apparently Wikipedia-watchers never sleep, and to my surprise I received the following comment on my *dord* revision from one of the site's editorial guardians:

> Hello, and welcome to Wikipedia! We welcome and appreciate your
> contributions, such as those in Dord, but we regretfully cannot accept
> original research. Please be prepared to cite a reliable source for all of your
> information. Thanks for your efforts, and happy editing! K******.sg 19:10,
> 20 June 2006 (UTC)

Three minutes later, K****** revised his comment: "Sorry, I see from Urban Legends that the word indeed first appeared in 1934, and have changed back to your version. Happy editing! K******.sg 19:13, 20 June 2006 (UTC)."

As I noted in my correction, the source for my correction was the copyright page of *Webster's Second* itself, which K****** doesn't seem to trust because it represents original research. Wikipedians evidently put their faith in Urban Legends, a site whose name suggests that it deals in myths, not realities, instead of actual dictionaries, but at least my experience shows that someone is patrolling the wiki, even if the repeated phrase "Happy editing!" makes K****** sound like a member of a cult.

As with each new digital genre, the wiki poses challenges to our notions of accuracy and authenticity. While conventional print tries to eradicate error before publication, wikis take a "soft security" approach of making both intentional and unintentional mistakes easy to undo rather than attempting to prevent them beforehand.

The creators and readers of wikis accept this practice with little hesitation because they are optimistic enough to assume that multiple revisions remove errors in articles and otherwise improve them. As Wikipedia sees it, "most edits make constructive changes, rather than destructive ones," and readers are actively encouraged to leave their mark on the text, revising the substance and polishing the style and appearance of the articles they read. It's more than an invitation to sign the guest book, it's an opportunity to rewrite that book:

> **Don't be afraid to edit**—*anyone* can edit almost any page, and we encourage you to **be bold** (but please don't vandalize)! Find something that can be improved, either in content, grammar or formatting, and fix it. You *can't* break Wikipedia. Anything can be fixed or improved later. So go ahead, edit an article and help make Wikipedia the best information source on the internet!

Wikipedia asks that articles be verifiable as a way of minimizing mistakes, and many Wikipedia articles sport not only footnotes, but also comments left by visitors and links to related sites that permit cross-checking. In spite of this, error is a necessary, built-in feature of the wiki genre, something for the reader to find and correct.

The expectation that error will out may be justified: many of the wiki entries I've looked at seem accurate enough at first glance. But readers may also be lulled by a false sense of security based on the assumption that if there's something wrong with an article, someone else has probably already jumped in to fix it. Wikipedia presents a dazzling array of statistics documenting activity on the site. For example, in February 2006 the encyclopedia was averaging about 1,800 new articles per day, with more than 26,000 Wikipedians contributing more than five edits apiece, and 3,300 making more than 100 edits each. In the previous month, there were 2.9 million edits for the English-language version of the encyclopedia, and over its history Wikipedia has averaged 13.23 edits per page since 2002, an indication that a lot of reading and writing is going on, but hardly proof that the resulting articles are accurate.

Even with figures that suggest every page gets a thorough going-over from reader-editors, Wikipedia cautions readers to test the articles that they read in the encyclopedia the same way they test any text, but despite their obvious pleasure that Wikipedia fared well in error comparisons with the *Encyclopaedia Britannica*, Wikipedia administrators still warn site visitors that wikis may not be as trustworthy as other writing:

> Readers need to apply critical thinking skills to everything they read—everything from Wikipedia and blogs to books and traditional encyclopedias. People need to be aware of how what they read was written and who wrote it, so they identify reliable vs. unreliable sources. In some

cases, it's better to use Wikipedia as the *first* step in the research process, rather than the *last* step.

And Wikipedia founder Jimmy Wales isn't sympathetic to students who complain that they were failed for relying on incorrect Wikipedia information: "For God sake, you're in college; don't cite the encyclopedia" (Technology Blog 2006).

While Wikipedia counsels the anonymous authors and editors of its articles to be neutral and factual, such advice is far from binding and doesn't exactly guarantee accuracy. I have learned some things from Wikipedia about topics that were new to me, but when I search topics that I am familiar with, I find Wikipedia coverage both spotty and not particularly informative. Users won't always find this to be a problem: many readers are happy just to find something on a subject without much effort and don't worry too much about accuracy. And if they don't find what they're looking for on Wikipedia, they'll simply search elsewhere on the web. Certainly my students consider these articles good enough to cite in their papers—for them, "Wikipedia says…" is replacing the commonplace "the dictionary says" as the phrase introducing some alleged fact or other. Wikipedia even has traction with more serious researchers:

> Consider a recent discussion between a reference librarian and a staff member working for an important policy-making arm of the U.S. government. The librarian asked what information sources the staffer relied on most often for her work. Without hesitation, she answered: "Google and Wikipedia." In fact, she seldom used anything else. (McLemee 2006)

Despite this growing complacence, wiki readers would do well to remember that some free information may indeed be worth what they pay for it. Since the wiki process continues serially, with one author at a time modifying, revising, adding, and subtracting text and leaving the result for the next person to deal with, readers should also keep in mind the party game called telephone, which demonstrates that serial revision by a string of independent contributors won't necessarily optimize a text.

▪ ▪ ▪ URBAN LEGEND

The Urban Dictionary home page announces, "If Wikipedia is too dry or too objective for you, Urban Dictionary will give you some cool slang"—at least that was the visitor comment being displayed on the urbandictionary.com home page one day when I first visited the site in 2005. Urban Dictionary may not be a true wiki because users don't actually rewrite one another's texts—but it takes its place alongside Wikipedia and sites like epinions.com, where users post evaluations of products, movies, CDs, and just about everything else, as another element in the emerging genre of group-authored reference works.

On another occasion the visitor quote of the day was "on top of the constant turnover of English slang." There is much on display at Urban Dictionary that is neither dry nor objective. As we might expect with a list of slang expressions, some of the words are both familiar and tame, for example, *cool*, defined as, "The best way to say something is neat-o, awesome, or swell." Readers won't learn much detail about *cool* from Urban Dictionary. Missing, for example, is the information that this particular meaning of *cool* originated with the cool jazz of the 1950s. But at least they will find confirmation that this particular sense of *cool* is still alive. On the raunchy, off-color and off-the-wall end, there are phrases like *I ain't fuck ya*, "To be completely honest with someone," as the UD definer puts it (this is actually fairly tame, too, both in terms of slang in general and the Urban Dictionary's set of words in particular).

But not all slang turns over constantly, and the Urban Dictionary contributor who defined *cool* rightly comments on the word's long shelf life: "The phrase [*sic*] 'cool' is very relaxed, never goes out of style, and people will never laugh at you for using it, very conveniant [*sic*] for people like me who don't care about what's in" (urbandictionary.com). The definition for this word was written by *coolguy*, who is somewhat relaxed about his spelling and who also contributed thirty definitions to this slang wiki between 2003 and 2005, including *neato, i.o.u, Yugo, serb, Seinfeldian, timble*, and *nardofied*. The status of some of these words is vexed, but that seems typical of words found in the Urban Dictionary. Some, like *Yugo*, are proper names. Others may be oncers, or *hapax legomena*—terms that lexicographers use for a word that is found only once. Still others look to be words or phrases that have meaning only to the definer. And many concern sex, drugs, and alcohol, again not surprising with slang.

While conventional slang dictionaries often preface a word list with some general definitions of what slang is (definitions tend to be loose) and how it works, wikis, which depend on the whims of their contributors, don't operate with the same sort of master plan in mind. Entries in the Urban Dictionary reflect not so much the general state of American slang as they do the specific interests of the site's demographic, which UD identifies as 53 percent male and mostly under the age of twenty-five, though the range of readers and contributors is much broader: the site boasts that there are "more than 140,000 daily visitors" to this wiki-dictionary of popular culture "created by hundreds of thousands of people, and read by millions." While each Urban Dictionary page cautions, "Urban Dictionary is not appropriate for all audiences," with such a large readership one might wonder exactly which audience segment is being warned away (urbandictionary.com/ads).

Urban Dictionary has none of the qualms about accuracy that preoccupy professional lexicographers or some of the more thoughtful Wikipedians. Instead, Urban Dictionary tells prospective advertisers that its readers are looking for "witty, honest commentary from everyday people."

Contributors are asked to "document the world" according to three guidelines, none of which have much to do with defining words:

1. Write for a large audience.
2. Don't name your friends.
3. Don't advertise your web site. (add.urbandictionary.com)

As with Wikipedia, contributing requires no expertise. Dictionary "editors" don't revise articles, as they might on Wikipedia. Those who disagree with a definition may vote against it or create an additional entry, not a replacement, for the word. That means that lots of words have multiple entries, and there's no way to consolidate duplication or resolve error.

Like contributors, editors aren't given much in the way of guidelines: publish opinions, the names of celebrities, nonslang words, jokes. Reject sexual violence, nonsense, and ads (the advertising department handles that). Editors are further advised to "publish racial and sexual slurs but reject racist and sexist entries," a direction that seems to invite slurs—admittedly a major slang category—while pretending to protect the site from charges of discrimination or just bad taste. However, reading a random set of definitions on any given day leaves one with the impression that discrimination against others and bad taste in general, while they are occasionally characteristics of slang expressions, are actually qualities that contributors to Urban Dictionary hold dear.

While Wikipedia stresses contributor neutrality, Urban Dictionary encourages opinions, and the opinions expressed are often extreme. Furthermore, while Wikipedia hopes that its articles will be accurate, or at least that they will become accurate over time, Urban Dictionary editors are told outright, "Don't reject an entry because you think it's inaccurate." The final recommendation, "publish if it looks plausible," gives contributors free rein to do what they like. While readers are asked vote on words once they are posted, many words appear in the dictionary despite hugely negative votes from site visitors.

Conventional dictionaries typically verify words and illustrative quotations to make sure that somebody actually said or wrote them. And typically, words don't enter the dictionary until they've been used frequently enough, or they've gained enough prominence, to suggest that they deserve some ink. Urban Dictionary requires none of that, and one suspects that many of the words and definitions on the site are either made up or not very accurate. For example, an entry defines *da Vinci* as "The act of telling the truth through fiction" and gives this explanatory but undocumented citation: "Steven Colbert pulled a Da Vinci at the white house press dinner" (urbandictionary.com). The term in question comes from *The Da Vinci Code*, a best-selling novel that was about to be released as a movie at the time the word was posted, and the citation, which seems made up by the definer for the purposes of illustration, refers to a speech given by Colbert at the annual White House Press Corps dinner in 2005, during which the comedian satirized the president and other high-ranking attendees.

Neither the *Da Vinci Code* nor Colbert's speech really involved telling truth through fiction. Nevertheless, Urban Dictionary readers approved the definition two to one. In contrast, one particularly unobjectionable definition for *pad*, "apartment," a meaning the word has had since the early 1900s, apparently didn't meet with approval from UD visitors, who voiced their disapproval two to one.

Despite its flaws, like Wikipedia, Urban Dictionary has become the go-to site for the latest info, the 4-1-1, or whatever the newest slang term for information happens to be. And although readers cite Wikipedia in their research despite its obvious unreliability, they seem to treat Urban Dictionary more as an entertainment site than a source of wisdom. It's a place to go to have fun or to check out a recently heard expression. That said, Urban Dictionary can also be a place to track emerging language trends, a place where both general readers and professional lexicographers can go to see how words are being used.

Here's an illustration of what I mean by that. In early 2006 I received a letter from someone claiming he had coined a new word, *yola*, which he defined as "a greeting, combining the Spanish 'hola' and the slang term 'yo.' Hence, 'yola,'" adding, "Being recognized for a word I've created has always been a goal of mine."

Unfortunately, my correspondent wasn't the first to happen on *yola*. According to Urban Dictionary, *yola* already had two slang meanings: in Northern California, it was a synonym for cocaine. And in entries dated between 2003 and 2006, several different contributors separately defined *yola* exactly the way my correspondent did, as a greeting that blends *yo* and *hola*, and one of them further indicates that it's used on the East Coast. While readers of Urban Dictionary vote favorably on *yola*, "cocaine," they disliked *yola*, "yo" plus "hola." This isn't the kind of evidence that a lexicographer can take to the bank, but it's certainly an indication that the greeting *yola* warrants further study. It also suggests that my correspondent, who sent his letter from the Midwest, may indeed have coined *yola* independently, but he clearly wasn't the first to put it into play.

Wikipedia and Urban Dictionary demonstrate that not all wikis produce reliable reference works. As Wikipedia itself warns, "users are bound to add incorrect information to the wiki page." But wikis are having an impact on the digital world that cannot be ignored. The very existence of multiple, ongoing authorship—the essence of the wiki text—forces us to rethink the roles of reader and writer. Instead of asking us to read and make notes in the margin, the wiki asks us to charge right in and rewrite the center of the page. It also asks us to rethink the nature of reading. Never in itself a passive activity, reading becomes even more active in the context of wikis. Readers consult wikis to find information—just as they consult more traditional texts. But they are invited, in fact encouraged, to become authors as well, to leave a trace behind them, reshaping what they find for the next reader. We have come to think of reading as an isolating activity in the modern world, one that we do quietly, alone, and for ourselves. But the wiki returns reading to a communal space, inviting us to recognize the reader-writers who came before us as well as those who will follow.

Democratized text is one thing, but a democratically constructed reference work is something else again. When a Wikipedia editor pointed out similarities between the Wikipedia article on Georgia and Sen. John McCain's speech about Russia's invasion of that country, some political commentators criticized McCain for constructing foreign policy from so unreliable a source (Goddard 2008; on the other hand, others pointed out that at least the presidential candidate, who had confessed serious ignorance about all things digital, was finally using the internet). Many teachers, concerned about the unreliability built into Wikipedia's structure, refuse to allow their students to use it as a source. But even in its present, imperfect state, Wikipedia has proved so quick and easy to use that most of its readers, including teachers and presidential candidates, are willing to accept what they find as good enough for their purposes.

11

■ ■ ■ The Dark Side of the Web

Wikipedia and sites like it hope to achieve accuracy by depending on the kindness of strangers willing to locate and correct error. In this they are very much like free speech advocates who argue that the best way to counter lies and propaganda is not to suppress them, but to expose them to the light, test them, and, if necessary, argue strongly against them. Unfortunately, not all lies manage to get corrected, and not all the bad things on the web fade when they're exposed to the light: in some cases, the web's dark side seems still to be getting darker.

The digital world is full of information, commerce, art, intellectual inquiry, and a seemingly endless amount of blathering. If the computer is an extension of the mind, much as the pencil has been characterized by its fans as an extension of the hand, then the world of cyberspace offers a new place to exist as well as new ways for existing. Web surfers flock to digital role-playing games, poker tournaments, or the many other online gathering places where everybody knows his or her name (Turkle 1995), or at least, since the web can be both intensely personal and totally anonymous, where everybody knows his or her screen name.

Once online, people can either be themselves or they can reinvent themselves, and sites like the increasingly popular Second Life promise web surfers a chance to replay their own, digitally enhanced version of the analog world they live in. Unfortunately, just as the web allows us to interact with others, or at least with avatars representing others, just as it allows us to express who we are, or who we think we might like to be, it also gives those people who hate and exploit new ways to express that hatred and new targets to exploit. These are the people who write the dark side of the web.

The dark side of the moon is hidden from Earth, but the web's darkness is visible to all. It's a space where pedophiles, misogynists, racists, anti-Semites, white supremacists, skinheads, holocaust deniers, Ku Klux Klan members, survivalists, violent opponents of abortion, and antigovernment militias gather to promote their particular brands of evil. For a number of years, two organizations that log acts of discrimination, the Anti-Defamation League (ADL) and the Southern Poverty Law Center (SPLC), have tracked hate groups and their increasingly visible online activities. The SPLC reports a 33 percent increase in hate groups between 2000 and 2005 and names as one factor enabling that growth "the internet, which has helped the radical right get its ideology out to the broader public" (SPLC 2006).

The ADL fights both anti-Semitism and discrimination in general, and it too notes with concern the presence of hate on the web. As early as 1985, the ADL warned of an online white supremacist bulletin board that was being maintained with little more than a modem and a single PC. A decade later, a Ku Klux Klan veteran, who had learned his computer skills in prison, set up Stormfront.org, a site that holds the dubious honor of being the first white supremacist web page. In 2001, Stormfront.org was logging five thousand visits a day (McKelvey 2001). In 1996 the ADL reported the existence of three holocaust denier websites. By 1997 half the hate groups being watched by the ADL had established a significant presence in cyberspace, and a year later the number had exploded, with "hundreds and hundreds" of additional hate sites. In 2001 the Simon Wiesenthal Center reported 2,500 hate sites on the web, forty-four of them with links specifically aimed at children (McKelvey 2001).

The ADL has noted that while email and listservs allowed like-minded hate mongers to band together in virtual communities when they couldn't meet face to face, extremists have made the World Wide Web "their forum of choice." A web page not only facilitates fund-raising and recruiting new members to these groups, it allows them greater control over their message than other electronic media. In addition, the availability of inexpensive web design tools enables hate sites to present a professional appearance and consequently "more easily portray themselves as legitimate voices of authority" (ADL 2001).

The ADL concludes that the growth of online bigotry simply mirrors the growth of the web as the latest and perhaps the most addictive of the mass media. Many observers agree that the digital revolution has facilitated hate groups mainly by letting them transcend time and space the way all internet users do. But in addition, the web increases the opportunities for extremists to hide behind a cloak of anonymity more effective than the traditional white-sheeted KKK uniform, as they publicize their agenda, forming and reforming communities that center on their common focus.

But it's not just the anonymity, the speed of communication, or the ability to reach a huge audience that attracts bigots to the net. The World Wide Web

TEACHING TOLERANCE
A PROJECT OF THE SOUTHERN POVERTY LAW CENTER

| FOR TEACHERS | FOR PARENTS | FOR TEENS | FOR KIDS | Home | About Us | Site Guide | | Search |

HATE ON THE INTERNET

The wonder of the Internet has been tarnished by hundreds of Web sites that spew hate. Using the Net, hatemongers can now reach into the room of any child who has a home computer. Their sites are often deceptive. Many attempt to disguise their message under a veneer of respectability. They use manipulation and lies to make their ideas sound almost reasonable.

Below, you may "tour" a hate site, and learn the truth about it.

Don't worry. The tour will only take you to a reproduced page of the hate site -- not to the site itself. But be prepared. Hate is ugly, and some people may be offended by the language and images revealed here.

Stormfront
Started and run by Don Black, a former member of the Ku Klux Klan, stormfront.org has become a kind of portal to hate on the Internet.
Go

The National Alliance
America's premiere neo-Nazi group may have provided the inspiration for the Oklahoma City bombing. Go

The 11th Hour Remnant Messenger
Created by Silicon Valley millionaires Carl Story and Vincent Bertolini, the 11th Hour Remnant Messenger despises blacks, homosexuals, abortionists, and a host of others, but reserves its true hatred for Jews, who it sees as enemies of God." Go

American Knights of the Ku Klux Klan
Associated with the racist South of a distant past, 100 Klan groups exist in the U.S. today. The modern-day Klan has gone to great lengths to clean up its image with such revisionist tactics as replacing the phrase "white supremacy" with "white separatism." Go

Do Something
▶ Respond to bigoted comments
▶ 10 Ways to Fight Hate
▶ 10 Ways to Fight Hate on Campus
▶ 101 Tools for Tolerance
▶ Respond to hate at school
▶ Mix it up at lunch
▶ Make every victim count
▶ Find a social justice group
▶ Order our materials
▶ Get our newsletter

Dig Deeper
▶ Explore your hidden biases
▶ Deconstruct biased language
▶ Explore hidden history
▶ Visit the Civil Rights Memorial

Bookmark equity and diversity Web sites on your home computer.
101 Tools for Tolerance

Screen shot of the home page of tolerance.org, a project of the Southern Poverty Law Center, which tracks internet hate sites, showing neo-Nazi, anti-Semitic, and Klan hate sites. Southern Poverty Law Center, www.tolerance.org/hate_internet/index.jsp; used by permission.

offers a public space that functions as a digital version of the analog world's Main Street (Turkle 1995). For many of us, meeting in cyberspace represents a convenient way to gather regardless of the weather or the constraints of geography. But it is also a place where those who can't carry on their activities in the light of day, in real-world public spaces like the town square, the mall, or the public access cable channel, can operate without fear of face-to-face confrontation, attack, or even arrest.

The internet gives hate groups the ability to hide in plain site, to operate in the open in ways that they could not do before—another troubling inversion of public and private space. And as if that weren't enough, hate groups, taking advantage of the commercial popularity of the web, set up virtual gift shops to market hate merchandise, not at all the sort thing one finds at the typical mall. There is a "classified ads" link on stormfront.org where on the day I checked, a seller with the screen name "civil liberties" offered white pride bracelets in adult and youth sizes ($2 plus shipping), and another peddled "no aliens" bumper stickers ($5.00). Klanstore.com featured Confederate-flag bathing suits (one and two-piece) and comforters (king, queen, and twin size), as well as an array of racist t-shirts, jewelry, and money clips, and a CD of Klan music that sported a burning cross on the cover. Sites like these reject governmental authority and so probably do not collect sales tax on purchases, but I don't actually intend to find this out.

There are remedies against internet fraud, assuming its perpetrators can be identified. Congress has already enacted legislation to protect minors from the sexual dangers of the internet. And international police sweeps regularly remind us that while the net is full of adult websites, child pornography, digital or not, is illegal. But the problem of what to do about hate sites comes up against much clearer First Amendment concerns. As a result, groups such as the Southern Poverty Law Center and the Anti-Defamation League argue that the best way to counter hate speech, whether on the web or on Main Street, is not through government controls or censorship, but through a combination of exposure and rational argument, on the one hand, and refusal to listen to the message on the other. Pressuring internet service providers (ISPs) to remove offensive sites hasn't been particularly effective. Human rights groups occasionally sue or petition ISPs to block hate sites, and in 2005 Stormfront complained that AOL was preventing customers from visiting the site. But hate groups are always able to find less-scrupulous hosts for their pages, and so the ADL developed a filter that users can install on individual computers to block hate sites on their local machines: let the Neo-Nazis march on skokie.com's virtual Main Street, just divert their links directly to the trash folder.

The use of the web to further fraud, sexual predation, and hate may strain free speech protections in the United States, and it provides an uncomfortable but necessary reminder that new communication technologies always bring with them new ways to do bad things. But there is yet another dark side to the web. While most governments try to maintain a balance whereby communication is controlled only when its harm can be clearly demonstrated, and when that harm far outweighs any redeeming social value the communication may have, in many parts of the world limiting access to the web in order to pursue a specific government agenda is a normal practice. American technology companies helping the rest of the world get online sometimes come up against the uncomfortable reality that they're being asked to help governments suppress political opposition, and a number of these companies have gotten some bad press for putting the dollar above the presumed right to free and unfettered access to the digitized word. China is one place where American technology firms have to weigh ethics against the bottom line.

▪ ▪ ▪ GOOGLE IN CHINA

According to Nielsen/NetRatings, there were roughly 220 million internet users in the United States in 2008, a number quickly approaching the saturation point (www.internetworldstats.com/am/us.htm). In contrast, with 298 million Chinese online that same year (www.internetworldstats.com/stats3.htm), representing 23 percent of China's population, that country not only has more net users than the United States, it is adding new users at the rate of 30 million a year (Zeller 2006; Watts 2006; Reporters 2005).

In the United States, internet access is relatively unrestricted, and this lack of control over a space that can sometimes seem too available to pornographers, stalkers, con artists, and hate mongers concerns parents, school authorities, employers, and some government officials. While American critics gingerly explore ways to monitor and regulate digital text in ways that balance long-established principles of privacy and unfettered self-expression against equally important parental concerns about child safety, the need for maintaining school discipline, keeping a lid on hate crime, and preserving public order, other governments don't hesitate to control the internet when it gets in the way, which it seems to do with some regularity.

Chinese internet censorship is more extensive than that of most countries. A list of fifteen top enemies of the internet issued in 2005 by the organization Reporters sans frontières (RSF, or Reporters without Borders) includes such highly restrictive regimes as Cuba, Myanmar, Saudi Arabia, and North Korea. Cuba's constitution guarantees that all media be used in the service of the Cuban people. In practice, this means that all print and digital media are strictly censored by the government, which permits very limited use of email or the web. RSF reports that a Cuban journalist whose email was suspended in the winter of 2006 because he was posting unauthorized news stories conducted a hunger strike that garnered some international publicity but had no impact on the Cuban regime's strict policy of internet control.

But according to Reporters sans frontières, China has met the challenges of the new and increasingly popular writing technologies head-on with a clear policy of net control that features severe punishment for writers who don't conform to guidelines or otherwise fail to meet expectations. China holds the dubious honor of being the nation most successful at cleaning up its digital networks, purging critical information from Chinese computer screens through a combination of technology filters, overt repression at home, and energetic dollar diplomacy abroad.

The Chinese government, with a long tradition of keeping a tight rein on its writers and readers as a way of managing dissent, has had no trouble demonstrating that the internet is not the unbounded and ungovernable final frontier that Americans perceive it to be, but a digital arena where information can be filtered and massaged, or simply disappeared, to further the government's political agenda. To this end, China is reputed to employ as many as thirty thousand web police who regulate that nation's growing virtual space in much the same way that the country's more traditional police manage China's vast geography and population.

China is right to fear that the web can be an effective revolutionary tool. Zapatista rebels in Mexico gained international attention when they publicized their cause on the internet, and despite government regulation, some one hundred thousand bloggers manage to publish their ideas in Iran's restrictive cyberspace. Egyptian bloggers have even been successful organizing small demonstrations against government policies (Levinson 2005). But China has also proved that the web can be an agent of government repression and control. Dissident websites just can't exist on Chinese servers, and digital dissidents meet the same fate as their more conventional peers. China leads the world in throwing its cybercritics into prison.

Net censorship seeks both to control a population's behavior inside its borders and to limit access to the world outside. When the Yale University Press announced the publication of a new biography of the Thai king, Thailand's government, without seeing the book but anticipating that it might contain negative material, blocked Yale's website, based on a server in New Haven, from that nation's computers (Jaschik 2006). Thais clicking on the site received the message, "This web site has been blocked by Cyber Inspector, the Ministry of Information and Communications Technology" (Monaghan and Overland 2006). But Thailand's move was hardly extreme compared to what neighboring countries do. Nepal actually shut down its internet connection to the rest of the world for a week during a coup in 2005, and Myanmar unplugged its internet for several days in 2007 after bloggers broadcast pictures of soldiers attacking Buddhist monks who were demonstrating against the repressive government (Gibbard 2007).

China's regulation of information from abroad is both ongoing and even more extensive. What has come to be known as the "Great Firewall of China" blocks Chinese net users from accessing all sites foreign and domestic that refer to a group of taboo subjects called the three Ts and the two Cs: Taiwan, Tibet, and Tiananmen Square, plus cults such as Falun Gong and criticism of the Communist Party. In 2004 China used its ability to control the internet to limit information about the SARS, or bird flu, outbreak that was sweeping Asia. More recently, at the start of the 2008 Beijing Olympics, journalists complained that the Chinese had gone back on their promise to permit free and unfettered web access for reporters. In response, Chinese authorities loosened some controls, a move that benefited both reporters and Beijing residents in general. However, according to the international web access monitor Open Net Initiative (2008), "the majority of advocacy sites and politically 'sensitive' organizations remain[ed] blocked." Furthermore, because China's net censors use robust keyword filters, simply unblocking a site didn't guarantee that all of a site's content could be accessed. In one test of the system, Open Net noted that while Wikipedia's Chinese site was open, videos of free-Tibet protests remained blocked, as did some Chinese human rights sites and sites critical of the controversial Three Gorges hydroelectric project.

China may be the biggest net censor in the world, but it also represents the largest potential internet market, which is certainly why American companies such as Cisco Systems helped set up the country's firewall (Harmsen 2006). To increase its own presence in China, where the Chinese search engine Baidu has a lock on the market, the American web giant Google eagerly agreed to Chinese government demands to block objectionable content on its Chinese server, google.cn (Sabbagh 2006). Critics were quick to see this as a violation of the sixth of Google's ten commandments for doing business ethically, "You can make money without doing evil" (google.com/corporate/tenthings.html).

Screen shot of google.cn. The two characters below the Google logo read "China." The radio buttons allow users to select all websites, all-Chinese sites, simplified Chinese sites, or the official China website. From google.com; used by permission.

After all, in order to preserve its image as a company that protects user privacy, Google had just refused to kowtow to American government requests for data on a week's worth of internet searches by its U.S. users to aid in a child pornography investigation. In that case, Google's attorney argued that "acceding to the Justice Department's request would suggest that [Google] is willing to reveal information about who uses its services. This is not a perception that Google can accept" (Liptak 2006).

But Google seemed willing to live with the perception that it was making money in China while restricting what users could pull up on their China-based computer screens because the company claimed that, in order to do business in China or any other foreign country, Google must conform "to local law, regulation or policy." To comply with German law, for example, Google's German search engine blocks access to sites that deny the Holocaust. French law forbids the dissemination of racial hatred, and French human rights groups want American hate sites off their internet. Google.fr actively complies with French web restrictions, including those limiting the use of the English language on the internet. And despite Google's posturing as guardian of our keystrokes, Google and its competitors regularly and quietly comply with subpoenas from U.S. courts requesting patron usage records because the law says that they must. Those subpoenas come regularly: AOL reports nearly a thousand a month, and many internet service providers maintain subpoena compliance departments to handle the traffic (Hansell 2006). Soon after Google announced its China business plan, MSN fell into step, explaining that when in China, it too would do as Chinese internet law allowed.

Google's insistence that providing some information to Chinese computer users is better than providing none at all didn't shield the company from complaints that its sixth commandment had been amended to read, "You can make money without doing evil, except in China." Agreeing to censor google.cn also appears to violate Google's eighth commandment, "The need for information crosses all borders." That generally accepted internet principle contradicts the Chinese insistence that borders exist to keep out information, as if information were just one more form of contraband.

The fact that Google will go the extra mile and precensor google.cn searches, blocking those that are not simply on a government hit list, but ones that the company feels are likely to anger Chinese authorities, angers those at home who feel that search engines should not steer readers toward some sites and away from others. At a Congressional hearing looking into the business practices of American companies entering the Chinese market, one critic called Google "a megaphone for communist propaganda" (Blakely 2006). More recently, the Global Online Freedom Act introduced in the House of Representatives calls for the establishment of a State Department

Office of Global Internet Freedom and would prohibit American companies from complying with foreign laws involving the abridgment or denial of commonly accepted American free speech protections: "The control, suppression, or punishment of peaceful expression of political or religious opinion, which is protected by Article 19 of the International Covenant on Civil and Political Rights, does not constitute a legitimate foreign law enforcement purpose" (H.R. 275, 2007; the bill never came to a vote).

The negative response at home may have led Google to have second thoughts. Its cofounder, Sergey Brin, admitted that the company "had adopted 'a set of rules that we weren't comfortable with'" (Blakely 2006). But just before that, google.cn rebranded itself as Gu Ge, which can mean "harvesting song" in Chinese, and Google chief executive Eric Schmidt announced, "We believe that the decision that we made to follow the law in China was absolutely the right one" (Blakely 2006).

Steering readers is exactly what search engines are supposed to do. It's just that most searches aim to give users what they want, not hide it from them. Google's Chinese adventure creates a search engine that couldn't. Users who tried to access forbidden sites were greeted with this message: "Because of legal restrictions, your search cannot be completed." And that, in turn, would appear to violate two more Google commandments, the fourth, which says, "Democracy on the web works," and the first and foremost of the company's business principles, "Focus on the user and all else will follow."

Even after Brin questioned his company's involvement in China's program of internet control, a search of the term *falun gong* on the google.cn site returned only articles critical of the religious group. The thumbnail for one of these pages proclaimed, "The Tragedy of Falun Gong Practitioners...Falun Gong Followers Repent of Tian'anmen Suicide Attempt · Falungong Accused of Intercepting Satellite Signal · Falun Gong Practitioners Jailed for Libeling Gov't..." (mingjing.org.cn/e-falun/index.htm; and another, from the English-language version of the online *People's Daily*, reads, "Fifteen Falun Gong cult followers were sentenced to prison terms ranging from 4 to 20 years by the Intermediate People's Court...Taiwan-based followers of the Falun Gong cult hijacked mainland satellite signals twice in the past week..." (english.people .com.cn/zhuanti/Zhuanti). These sites can be accessed only by through the Google search engine (google.cn), by pasting the address in the search box. These specific articles may no longer be available, however.

To be fair, a search for Tibet on google.cn returned sites for the Tibetan government in exile and a Wikipedia article on the political status of Tibet, neither of which follow the Chinese party line on the subject of Tibet, but a search for Tiananmen Square returned descriptions of the square's architecture, not its troubled history as the place where Chinese troops massacred

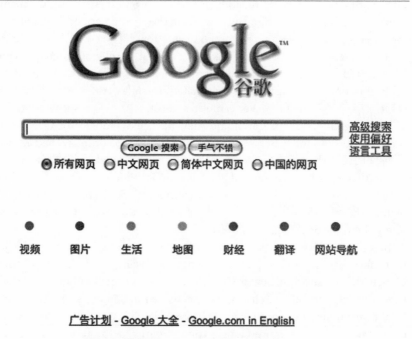

A screen shot of google.cn, rebranded in the characters below the Google logo as Gu Ge, "harvesting song," to show Google's commitment to doing business the Chinese government's way in China. The interpretation "harvesting song," however, is a stretch in Chinese, though this sort of phonetic branding is common both in China and Taiwan. From google.com; used by permission.

unarmed protestors. My search was done on a computer outside China, and I could only read the English-language sites, not the ones in Chinese, so that undoubtedly skewed the results. Nonetheless, there's no reason to doubt that China web policy still influences the operation of google.cn.

▪ ▪ ▪ THE GOOD, THE BAD, AND THE UGLY

The fact that the issues of online predation, depredation, and control of the flow of information have been surfacing again and again in the news reminds us that new communication technologies offer both real and perceived benefits and dangers. Certainly people use their web spaces to advance knowledge, but they also use them to promote misinformation, disinformation, and hate. The space pages enable us to reestablish community in a fragmented and disaffected world. But the attractiveness of the web as a public gathering space for hate sites challenges both our support of the right to assemble freely and our deep conviction that the best way to fight evil is to let everyone see it for what it is.

Touring the dark side of the web challenges as well our assumption that community is always positive and desirable. Even the proliferation of more benign do-it-yourself web spaces drives the online community into ever-smaller and more narrowly focused interest groups, demonstrating that the web has a fragmenting effect as well as an integrating one, and critics of the World Wide Web find more to complain about and legislate against than the obvious proliferation of pornography, hate, fraud, disinformation, and the odd bit of political insurgency. Spam has become a legislative concern, and as we will see in the next chapter, so has the ability of webmasters to track our keystrokes.

Critics object as well that there's too much to read in cyberspace, because too many people are filling our screens with too much text. Even if the web can't or shouldn't be censored, they argue, someone needs to sort and catalog it so that users can more easily visit the places they want to and avoid the ones they don't.

▪ ▪ ▪ TOO MUCH INFORMATION

Now that everyone's an author, not just copying text, but also creating it, the text that we are all writing piles up. One result of this is TMI (too much information), or more commonly in this context, the information glut. Before the digital revolution, everyone had trouble keeping up with print materials. Now, in addition, unread emails fill our inbox. We don't follow the scores of links that clamor for our attention every time we open a web page. Or we follow those links, getting lost down the rabbit hole and never finding our way back to our original search. Or we read partway down a file, then don't bother to scroll down or click to the next page. With all the text around us, who has time?

There's no argument that computers are responsible for the latest textual explosion. But textual explosions, and how we deal with them, aren't new. Anyone who has belonged to a monthly book club, subscribed to a magazine, or vowed to keep up with assigned reading for work or school knows that no matter what format it takes, text always has a way of outstripping our ability to keep up with it. No one read all the books in Shakespeare's day. No one went through all of the scrolls and codices of the great library at Alexandria. Probably no single person read all the hieroglyphs of Egypt or the Mesopotamian clay tablets. Today there are more readers and writers than ever, and each one of us can deal with only a very small subset of what's out there.

Everyone knows that the glass can be either half full or half empty, a reflection of the observer's purported optimism or pessimism. But the comedian George Carlin proposed another, more pragmatic option: the glass is actually twice as big as it needs to be. Carlin might rewrite Geoffrey Nunberg's assessment that there has always been too much to read (1996) this way: there's always more to read than necessary.

The trick to dealing with too much information is filtering out what to ignore. To do that, we invent ways to organize reading matter, index it, and search it. Google may have juggled questions of money and ethics in formulating policy for its China site, policy that continues to evolve, but no search for information is ever neutral. Whether it's the conventional library search or the digital engine that we use online, we navigate storehouses of information using algorithms that always include some data while excluding the rest. A Google search that returns thousands of hits, or hundreds of thousands, may daunt us, because even without government censorship, the search engine still fails to filter irrelevant information. In contrast, we can enter the Library of Congress, with its twenty-nine million volumes and ninety million other items, and not feel totally overwhelmed. Reassured by the existence of catalogs and librarians, reviews and indexes, we know that we don't have to read everything in the building in order to find what we're looking for.

Without some plan for selecting and retrieving information, navigating a library would present the kind of existential challenge that Jean-Paul Sartre describes in his 1938 novel, *Nausea*. At one point the book's narrator meets a character who seven years earlier had entered a public library and, faced with the collection of *la science humaine*—all of human knowledge—arranged in alphabetical order, took the first book from the first shelf on the far right, opened it to the first page, and "with a feeling of respect and fear, made an irrevocable decision." After seven years he had reached L. K after J; L after K. Sartre's narrator concludes, "and the day will come when he will say, in closing the last volume from the last shelf on the far left, 'And now?' "

Web searches, whose algorithms are closely guarded secrets, work in a similarly exhaustive way, scanning page after page looking for keywords. They just do it at a dizzying pace, much faster than Sartre could have imagined, and while it's never entirely clear to the user how Google arranges the sites it returns in response to a search, we accept those results and sift through them until we too either find what we want, get to the end of the list, or simply run out of steam.

Even the encyclopedic reading excursion described by Sartre, first A, then B, and so on until Z, constitutes a search algorithm, and while the alphabet itself is old, the practice of storing and retrieving information alphabetically is not. In 1604, when Robert Cawdrey published his *Table Alphabeticall*, the first English dictionary, he thought it necessary to warn his readers that in order to use the book efficiently, they'd better memorize the alphabet:

> If thou be desirous (gentle Reader) rightly and readily to vnderstand, and to profit by this Table, and such like, then thou must learne the Alphabet, to wit, the order of the Letters as they stand, perfectly without booke, and where euery Letter standeth: as (b) neere the beginning, (n) about the middest, and (t) toward the end. Nowe if the word, which thou art desirous to finde, begin with (a) then looke in the beginning of this Table, but if with (v) looke towards the end. Againe, if thy word beginne with (ca) looke in the beginning of the letter (c) but if with (cu) then looke toward the end of that letter. (Cawdrey 1604, "To the reader")

Alphabetical order—which seems to us to be one of our most basic organizing systems—was itself a technology that had to be invented before it could be used for data sorting. Cawdrey acknowledges this when he advises his readers to learn the alphabet, "the order of the letters as they stand," by heart, or as he puts it, "without booke," assuming that many of his readers would not have mastered a skill that we now take for granted.

The first libraries didn't store their collections from A to Z—that's only one of many systems that came into play as the number of documents increased beyond anything that could be handled by memory alone. Libraries with large enough collections were forced to create sorting measures so their collections could be used. The Dewey Decimal and the Library of Congress systems familiar to users of American libraries are only two of the many other ways of cataloging *la science humaine* found around the world today. The seventeenth-century bibliophile Robert Cotton shelved his books in cases, each of which was topped by a bust of a Roman emperor, and he classified his books first by emperor, then by shelf, and finally by position on the shelf. Thus the lone copy of the *Beowulf* manuscript came to be designated Cotton Vitellius A.xv—the fifteenth volume from the left on the first shelf—the A shelf (the alphabet did have some importance, after all)—under the likeness of Emperor Vitellius. The equally well-known book manuscript in which we find the text of "Gawain and the Green Knight" was Cotton Nero A.x. Cotton's library became the nucleus of the present-day British Library, whose collection required many more shelves than Rome had emperors, so new methods were needed to sort its vast contents. The library began sorting its books by subject rather than by royal, but following Cotton's lead, each book still winds up with a unique identifying number marking its location on a shelf.

But even when they could be located on a shelf, the first books themselves did not divulge their secrets by means of tables of contents or indexes, two information retrieval systems that we rely on heavily in the twenty-first century. Without a way to find stored information, written data remains locked from view. The earliest municipal archives, in ancient Athens, had no such system. Once a record was placed for safekeeping in one of many look-alike stone jars, there were only two ways to locate it again: remember where it had been put, or search jar by jar until it was found (Thomas 1989). Frustration, together with the belated recognition that stored items would actually be needed at some future date, eventually led to the development of classification systems, precursors to the ways that modern libraries guide readers through the stacks.

Like the first libraries and archives, the first sites on the World Wide Web could be reached only if one already knew the correct address, and like the first books, there was little to indicate what a particular site might contain when you reached it. The earliest computer search engines—Archie and Gopher, followed by Excite, Infoseek, and, eventually, Yahoo—weren't capable of much refinement. Type in a word and they'd return thousands of hits, with little in the way of thumbnails to indicate a site's actual contents. Most users checked out the first few sites listed on their screen and either contented themselves with what they found there or gave up the search. No one, even those given to Sartrean ennui, had the stamina to click through page after page of the sites returned—it was too frustrating, and the payback was minimal.

Internet search engines are getting better. They're very good at pattern matching, locating a string of symbols by searching millions of sites in seconds, and reporting back thousands, sometimes millions of hits. But just as computers haven't mastered the art of face or voice recognition well enough to rival humans, they also remain less sophisticated in many ways than conventional library tools, where material is assessed and sorted by humans, not machines. But while the lure of looking up information online has become stronger than the lure of visiting the bricks and mortar library, computer users, who remain reluctant to scroll and are willing to click only up to a point, frequently limit the depth of their search to whatever is returned by the webcrawler on the first screen or two. True, thanks to the digital revolution, more people than ever are searching the web. But skeptics wonder if our growing dependence on the millions of pattern-matches that machines are programmed to find for us means that in exchange for ease of searching and undeniably awesome speed we're actually settling for less, not more, when we let Google, Yahoo, and company navigate the web's information glut for us.

■ ■ ■ THE END OF CIVILIZATION AS WE KNOW IT?

As Ted Kaczynski demonstrated in explosive detail, reliable information retrieval is not all that critics of our growing dependence on digital information are worrying about. Even if computers lead us to do more reading and writing, their detractors remain convinced that the latest word machines are diluting our literacy, not enhancing it. In their view, virtual texts aren't worth much in comparison with conventional ones because they take too much or too little effort to compose and read, depending on who's complaining. Many critics, like Theodore Roszak and the members of the Lead Pencil Club, insist that computer writing is a step backward in the history of literacy. It's true that no writing technology, from the earliest Mediterranean carved stones to the Linotype or the IBM Selectric, came without drawbacks, but whatever the downsides to digital literacy practices may be, considering how prevalent computers have become in the United States, and how quickly they are gaining ground across the globe, like it or not, most people seem to have embraced the virtual word as a great leap forward.

Nonetheless, detractors complain that writing on-screen is actually too fast and too furious. The raw speed that computers provide means that writers don't stop to think about their words, as they might were they using clunkier composition methods such as the ink pen, goose quill, or stylus. Because of this, the argument continues, digital writers pay less attention to the niceties of language, and they're prone to spout ideas that are only half-baked, indiscreet, or too charged with venom.

Keyboarding is not only too speedy for those who prefer the virtually extinct typewriter or the lined legal pad for their scribbling; it's also too professional looking. There's no messy crossing out or writing between the lines on computers, because there's no need to, and that makes the writing look both effortless and finished, even when it isn't. Add to this the print-quality typefaces, spelling and grammar checks to give language a clean veneer, and preformatted paragraphs that make each page look professionally designed, and writers may be lulled into thinking that just because it already looks like a printed book or magazine, contract or office document, their creation doesn't need revision, doesn't need the careful going-over that most printed text receives from authors, editors, proofreaders, and fact-checkers before it is released for general consumption. In short, if a page on the screen looks like it's already been printed, say critics of digital communication, then writers won't bother with the corrections and polishing that all but the most casual writing always needs.

It's undeniable that the temptation to go public with a document before it's ready for prime time results in some virtual publications that are truly half-baked. But it's also true that there will always be some writers too lazy to revise, regardless of the technology they're using. As I mentioned earlier, the first print shops didn't throw out pages with typos. They corrected new pages when they found errors but bound the old ones into books anyway, mistakes and all, because paper was too expensive to waste (Johns 1998).

Surely when the pace of life got too hectic, even Shakespeare must have protested to himself, "This is good enough for blank verse. Besides, I can't face sharpening up another quill just to change one inauspicious word that these bumbling actors will flub *abhominably* anyway, and as for the groundlings, well methinks 'tis already too good for them."

And speaking of half-baked, how many Sumerians really agonized over the mistakes immortalized in clay that they noticed only after the hot Mesopotamian sun had worked its magic on the tablets? There's only so much a scribe can be expected to do when the next tablet's waiting to be filled with lists of sheep and goats that are going to wind up on some royal person's dinner plate long before those tablets crumble into shards.

Perhaps these scenarios seem far-fetched. Even Homer nods, as they say, but more to the point is the fact that not everything we write on paper or on-screen needs to be letter perfect: many emails, instant messages, and blogs are informal enough to tolerate a sloppiness that would never work in other sorts of writing. Plus, as an editor of mine once told me ruefully, even printed books are never error free: there's always some infelicity of style, misstated fact, or typo that has escaped the eagle eye of editor and proofer, and even with the more formal writing tasks that all of us undertake, perfection really lies in taking whatever steps are needed to get the job done rather than in matching our words to an imaginary ideal that no one could ever hope to realize.

Perhaps the doomsayers and even the mild complainers are right that the computer lulls writers into a false sense of accomplishment, but it's also the case that many people who prefer writing on the computer, as I do, are actually encouraged to concentrate more on what the text says, not less, because digital text is so easy to hone or overhaul. Typos, when caught, vanish with a few keystrokes. There are no messy erasures, no literal cuts and pastes, no spilled or lumpy Wite-Out. New ideas are easy to insert, and poorly expressed thoughts easy to delete, since paragraphs reformat automatically and the hole left by a deletion closes up without a trace. Entire sections of text can also be moved seamlessly from one part of a document to another. And the ability to exert artistic as well as editorial control of the text, choosing fonts, colors, margins, the whole organization of our words on the page, focuses writers more than ever on the visual impact that our ideas will have on readers.

But that doesn't stop the critics from trying to spoil the fun. If writing on the computer is too easy, they warn, then publishing that writing is easier still. After all, hate sites and money scams spread filth and misinformation unchecked. The accuracy of Wikipedia and its ilk depends too heavily on people who may not know what they're talking about. And like a gun with a hair trigger, email and IM in particular let writers inflict damage that cannot be undone by a simple reedit.

These are telling points. I know people who admit to being scammed online. And many of us will have had the embarrassing experience of sending an email in haste, only to repent at leisure. At least an ill-considered phone call might get a busy signal or no answer at all, reminding an angry caller to take a little time to cool off.

But the problems of rogue and deceptive texts didn't start with computers. We've been buying snake oil almost as long as there have been snakes, and being too quick to press "send" was recognized as a problem long before email. As early as 14 BCE, Horace warned nondigital writers bent on premature publication, *nescit uox missa reuerti*, "the word, once sent, doesn't know how to return" (Horace, *Ars Poetica*, 390). In the good old paper and pencil days of no crossing out, it was common enough for students to fail tests for writing down the wrong answer just as the right one rose to consciousness. A standard old-time movie gag revolved around trying to retrieve a prematurely sent letter from a mailbox. And long before caller ID became widespread, some phone calls, like the one in Alfred Hitchcock's *Dial M for Murder*, might better have gone unanswered.

What may be a significant difference for the digital word over previous ill-conceived utterances, and those simply not ready for prime time, is a combination of its staying power and the ability of even the most private expressions to persist in public space. After all, we are still dealing with echoes of *dord*, revived in cyberspace while it silently crumbles inside yellowing copies of a 1930s dictionary.

But while we continue to think of digital files as easily lost—a computer crash tends to be more dire than a broken pencil point, and, as many observers have pointed out, paper remains a more stable medium than magnetic recording on silicon chips—it turns out that such things as email are less evanescent than we think. Even if we erase them from our own hard drives, copies of emails that we send are backed up on many of the computer servers through which they pass on their way from sender to recipient. This isn't typically a concern: embarrassing emails don't spontaneously resurface on their own to bite us from behind. But while government investigators can't open our mail or tap our phones without a warrant (in most cases), email is not considered private communication and doesn't enjoy that kind of legal protection. Employers can access employee email, and investigators can demand copies and produce them in court, which means that anything we write on email can and will be used against us.

Students blogging or Facebooking become upset when parents or school administrators read their posts because they don't believe they're writing for a general audience, or any audience at all beyond their small circle of friends and conspirators (Bartlett 2005). But despite constant reminders that email, with its risks of exposing us to ridicule or legal action, is anything but private, the rest of us treat our electronic communications—even business-related email—as intensely personal, private correspondence, to the point where we are frequently annoyed or embarrassed when a recipient forwards one of our emails to a third party or posts it to a public list without first getting our permission.

Turning everyone into writers increases the tendency to merge our public and private worlds, but while we relish the ability to reach out to the World Wide Web and bring that public world of words, sounds, and pictures back to the privacy of an individual computer screen, we tend to forget that whether through user error, outright theft, or court order, our words may be only a keystroke away from public display. The information superhighway is a two-way street, one capable of displaying everything we write just the way we want it, or outing those words without permission.

To the frequently asked question, "Is the web a benefit or a curse?" the answer appears to be a frustrating and ambiguous, "Yes." Entrepreneurs use digital technologies to sell useful goods and services or to commit fraud. Governments use them to enlighten or to suppress the world's peoples. In effect, today's communication technologies, just like those of the past, enable their users to delight and instruct a willing audience or to exploit or control an unsuspecting one. Most people use technological innovation to create new modes of connectivity and to promote the betterment of the planet. But not all technology users are high-minded, or simply out to make an honest buck. And just as they used the pencil and paper technologies that preceded the digital revolution (as I mentioned before, the Nigeria money scam so common on the internet actually operated by snail mail well before the computer revolution), those whose goals are not so pure deploy the latest communication breakthroughs to foment hatred and sow the seeds of destruction.

There's often a halo effect with new communication technology—its fans may be less critical because it seems to offer so much, but as the newness wears off they begin to see that problems are not so easy to ignore. And critics who may start out with a reverse-halo effect, hating everything about the technology, grudgingly begin to see some of its advantages and eventually acknowledge its importance (Roszak wrote his critique of computers on a computer, using WordPerfect, which he names as his favorite word processor). This happened with predigital technologies, and it's happening again.

In addition to worrying over the impact of technology on how we do things with words, we pay a lot of attention to the money aspects of the digital revolution. The promise of gold in Silicon Valley is powerful. It took Bill Gates a while to build up the Microsoft empire, but the tantalizing vision of overnight dot-com fortune leads more and more entrepreneurs to launch what they hope will be the next big thing, or to invest in it.

As with everything new, sometimes those ventures pay off, sometimes not. Twelve-year-old Google—by now a household word—has turned founder Sergey Brin into the sixteenth-richest man in the world, according to Forbes. In the second quarter of 2006, Google was bringing in over $1 million an hour (in comparison, the federal minimum wage at the time was $5.15 per hour), and although Google stock showed a fifty-two-week high of $747 per share—while in the same 2007–8 period earnings for Google's competitors were down—Google stock was back in the mid-$400 range with the 2008 market slowdown. Investors aren't likely to forget that the technology bubble burst in 2001: NASDAQ lost 59.3 percent of its value between March 2000 and March 2001, leading to massive financial losses for many investors and producing a small army of unemployed programmers (Motley 2001).

It wasn't quite the same in the old days. I don't know whether fortunes were made and lost in volatile pencil and paper markets—though certainly the War of 1812, which abruptly cut off supplies of British graphite to America, boosted the value of John Thoreau's New Hampshire graphite mine and the pencil business that he built using its ore. And while Gutenberg's press catapulted him to fame, that fame was mostly posthumous. Gutenberg may have made a decent living from his print shop, but that shop wasn't among the fifteenth-century's Fortune 500. That is not to say that the written word is not connected to wealth: the printing press lies behind the fortunes of William Randolph Hearst and Rupert Murdoch; of Malcolm Forbes and his avocation of listing everybody else with money; even of writer J. K. Rowling, who's got more money than the Queen of England. Their wealth came quickly, perhaps, though not overnight as the result of a public stock offering.

Impressive as the rapid technological and economic changes associated with the digital word are, what seems to differentiate pixels from pencils most is the speed of digitized communication, their reconfiguration of the public and private spheres, and the ways that the new technologies have dramatically increased both who gets to write, and how much they write.

12

■ ■ ■ From Pencils to Pixels

In 2002 Google began a project to scan millions of printed books in libraries around the world. The goal was to make these fully searchable texts available online at no cost to readers, a kind of *livres sans frontières*, or——with apologies to one large American bookstore chain——books without borders. Two years later, five major libraries—those at Harvard, Oxford, Stanford, and the University of Michigan, together with the New York Public Library—agreed to let Google digitize their collections, and the world's most massive scanning enterprise began in earnest, with much of the scanning outsourced to China and India. Along with the libraries, which see the project as a way of making their collections more generally available, a number of major book publishers signed on as well, hoping that Google Book Search would keep some of the marginal titles on their backlists in circulation. Some of these same publishers have since gone to court to stop the project for infringing on their copyright. Pending a resolution to the suit, Google has restricted online access to the books that have been scanned to snippets (a few lines) or limited views (several pages). Books are presented in full only if they are out of copyright or if the publisher agrees.

Regardless of the merits of the publishers' lawsuit, the prospect of upgrading all the world's books from print to digital format excites some observers and terrifies others: they see in it both the future of the book and its death. As one might expect, a computer fan such as *Wired* magazine's Kevin Kelly can't wait until everything ever written, composed, photographed, filmed, and played on instruments will be available in searchable, universally accessible form on the web, on our iPods, or better yet, wired directly into our brains (Kelly 2006). Kelly envisions a truly democratic cyberlibrary consisting of one infinite book along the lines of a mega-Wikipedia. Users will be able to excerpt text or tag it with comments, corrections, and analyses, then pass it on to others who will do the same. It will be the best and the worst of times, as readers create playlists of their favorite passages ("Call me Ishmael…"; "I would prefer not to…"), something they now do with their iTunes, producing a thoroughly postmodern literary remix never before possible with text.

In contrast to Kelly's unbridled optimism, the novelist John Updike feared that digitizing projects such as Google's would doom us to a world where no one will write because writers will no longer be paid for their words (Updike 2006). Some of Updike's own work is available online at Questia.com, a fee-based service that claims about 66,000 works in its database so far. Questia reimburses publishers each time a subscriber clicks to view one of their books, and the publishers in turn—one presumes—pass some of those pay-per-click fees along to authors like Updike.

Of course Updike was right that although Google positions its book project as a way to extend the reach of the library, unlike libraries, Google is a business out to make a profit. At the same time that Google promotes its book project as a public good and pays no royalties to publishers when books are "checked out" on-screen, the folks at Google charge booksellers such as Amazon and Barnes and Noble a fee for placing links to their websites on its book search pages, so that readers can buy the books they find at books.google.com. Google argues that this will ultimately lead to profits not just for Google, but also for publishers and authors, so everybody benefits: readers, writers, and a lot of middlemen.

But *Wired*'s Kelly claims not to care about profits: he happily looks forward to a new economic model of publishing where writers aren't paid for what they do. That, in his view, will get more people involved in the writing game, not fewer, and since their eye won't be on the almighty dollar, perhaps their motives, and their writing, will be purer. Of course, like every professional writer from Updike back to the days of the first scribes, Kevin Kelly gets paid for what he writes. Presumably Kelly didn't write his defense of Google Book Search in the *New York Times Magazine* without first securing a promise of payment, and it's likely that his day job as "senior maverick" for *Wired* is not a volunteer position either. To Updike, disconnecting writing from remuneration would cause professional writers like Kelly himself to change professions, since they do have to eat. And removing the monetary incentive could dissuade many potential processors of words from becoming writers in the first place.

Despite the posturing by Kelly and Updike, we're a long way from turning everything written into a searchable database or radically changing the economic foundation of publishing. As Anthony Grafton (2007) observes, while that may be Kelly's goal, Google and the other digitizers have more modest aims, for example scanning much of what's in print but out of copyright in the United States and maybe Britain—the writing of the rest of the world can wait a bit. Grafton further points out that scanning is no replacement for the actual physical print object, not only because scanners occasionally omit pages or copy them out of order, but also because the print artifacts themselves tell the reader more than what the words on the page may about the conditions of manufacture, ownership history, and ultimate significance of the work.

Grafton is confident that books and documents will retain their importance alongside new internet-enabled genres like the blog and email, and he prefers to see the internet as the latest tool for text storage and retrieval rather than a replacement for conventional print and writing:

> The rush to digitize the written record is one of a number of critical moments in the long saga of our drive to accumulate, store, and retrieve information efficiently. It will result not in the infotopia that the prophets conjure up but in one in a long series of new information ecologies, all of them challenging, in which readers, writers, and producers of text have learned to survive. (Grafton 2007, 51)

In their enthusiasm for a brave new digital world, or their fear of it, both the visionaries and the critics tend to miss what the computer is actually doing to the processes of writing and reading. To recap some themes that I have touched on in this book: because of computers, more people are writing more; they are creating new genres of writing; and they have more control over what they write and how it is distributed.

As with the other technologies that facilitated textual production, the computer is giving both writers and readers the opportunity to produce and consume massive amounts of text. Though schools are looking to computers as a way to increase literacy, we have no hard proof that the digital revolution has increased reading. What is certain, however, is that more people are writing, and they are writing more than ever.

In addition, as other writing technologies did before it, the computer is allowing writers to develop new genres and encouraging readers to read in new ways. Moreover, unlike the printing press or the typewriter, the computer gives writers greater and more direct control over what they write. In the office, as writers switched to computers, they began to bypass the typing pool, composing, revising, and printing final drafts of letters, reports, and other business documents on their own rather than relying on secretarial help. In school, computer-generated text is becoming the norm. Children are taking control of the design of their school writing even as they learn to write, and handwriting, which often posed an insurmountable aesthetic stumbling block for some young writers, has been replaced in many curricula by keyboarding.

Computers enable both everyday writers and professionals to exert greater creative control over their text. More and more writers consider fonts, graphics, even sound and video to be integral parts of the composition process. Computers also give writers new options for controlling the distribution of their work. Increasingly, writers find themselves bypassing traditional editorial supervision of publication, and the self-publication of blogs, web sites, and space pages often finds a niche audience. While much of that publication involves putting the writer's ego onstage in a way that we traditionally associate with the vanity press, enough of the digital text manages to escape the stigma that accompanies vanity publishing to make us acknowledge it as a powerful, unstoppable force.

It's not just professional writers who've seen their working conditions change because of computers, not just those who write occasionally on the job or students who've adjusted to the new ways of doing things with words. In addition, computers have significantly impacted life outside of work and school: email, instant messaging, blogs, and space pages are more and more a part of leisure-time activities, and it's in this nonprofessional realm that the authors club has undergone a massive increase in membership. Half of today's bloggers have never put their work on display before they began blogging, and our everyday writing has become so invested in new digital genres that there are already a couple of email novels, at least one consisting of instant message exchanges, and a couple of teen-oriented novels structured around text messaging. As for more mainstream literature, if Helen Fielding had written *Bridget Jones's Diary* (1997) just five years later, she might have called it *Bridget Jones's Blog.*

▪ ▪ ▪

Computers are changing how, what, and when we write. They are also changing how, and what, we read. Kelly and Updike are right that publishing is still trying to adapt to the computerization of our literacy. But we're in the very early stages of that process and it's too soon to predict how it will ultimately change the economics of the book world. On one hand, bookstores are bursting with shoppers and sales of print materials remain strong. On the other hand, the store's inventory isn't always enough to keep customers' attention, and many bookstore visitors are sitting not in the aisles but in the café, using their laptops to connect wirelessly to a world of text beyond the shelves. Computers bring more words to us, faster, than any previous technology. While they don't actually speed up our reading, they allow us to find things to read more quickly. And while we aren't necessarily reading more because of computers, just as the computer expands possibilities for writers, it's giving readers greater control over the text that they read.

But the reading revolution facilitated by digital technology has been subtler than the writing revolution. Today when people read books, they still read conventional printed books, not the relatively small number of electronic books that are available either on their computer screens or on portable ebook readers. The ebook audience won't grow until that technology evolves to a point where digital text is as easy to access and as inexpensive as an MP3 player or a paperback. But we don't read only books, and the many people who use computers are routinely shifting their nonbook reading from page to screen: mail, newspapers, magazines, encyclopedia articles, weather reports, store catalogs, diaries, airline schedules, hotel brochures, government reports. In fact just about everything that is not book length is being read digitally by someone, and many texts skip the print stage and exist only in virtual format. Most of my students still prefer printing out their online class readings, but these same students do much of their recreational reading online; and most of the people I know have shifted their work-related reading from print to screen as well.

Despite this migration toward digital text, which is occurring at the expense of newspapers, journals, and magazines, the conventional book continues to thrive. And despite predictions that the book of the future will be an infinitely malleable text file that readers will appropriate, modify, and recast to suit their needs and moods, shuffling its content or revising its plot to the point where each copy will be the unique product not just of the original author (and any editors who have massaged the text), but of every reader who added a note or took an idea in a new direction—despite all these dreams of a great literary breakthrough, or nightmares about the death of the author—the book of today and of the foreseeable future remains a relatively stable entity.

That said, the digital revolution is changing how we read not just by shifting more and more reading to the screen, but also by changing how and where we find what we read. The typical wired reader now has access to more materials online than off, and even for those nontypical readers who might be working with the massive print and manuscript collections of the Library of Congress or the Bodleian or the New York Public Library, the computer still offers faster searching and faster access to words.

Searching for a word or phrase in a digital text now takes seconds, even microseconds, and readers who are looking for specific information can't be faulted for preferring that kind of speed and accuracy to the conventional method of paging through a series of index entries at the back of a book, jumping back and forth from index to text until they find what they're after, or skimming large sections of print looking for a few words that they might well wind up missing after all. Conventional searching is a tedious and frustrating business. I have spent days in libraries looking in vain through dusty volumes for an elusive bit of information that never did reveal itself, and I revel in the computer's ability to find one item out of billions in the time it takes to click a few keys.

As with all technological innovation, however, searching text on a computer involves a trade-off. Skimming printed books and articles may be tedious, but it can produce unexpected results, turning up something by accident that proves to be significant, taking us in an unanticipated but nonetheless productive direction. In contrast, the instant, focused digital search we have come to depend on causes us to miss such serendipitous information that we might or might not have found the old way. In addition, because the secret, proprietary algorithms used by computer search engines such as Google and Yahoo match patterns instead of intuiting, as a human searcher might, what we're really trying to find, we may wind up with a huge amount of irrelevant data. But many readers seem content to sacrifice serendipity and risk irrelevance for the certainty of an immediate response that tells us, "Results 1–10 of about 25,300 for 'gender-neutral pronoun' (0.20 seconds)," as the search that I did to illustrate this point just told me. Even if the search reports, "0 items found," it does so just as quickly, and I can either change my search terms or give up and move on to something else.

True, the precision with which we can now direct our info-mining typically means that less is more: less effort produces greater results. But even when a search returns appropriate material, as it often does, readers may also become so complacent with the tunnel-vision snippets they find that they ignore the big picture. Instead of the whole texts we used to wade through to locate a single fact, a keyword search can lead us to the ultimate form of reader's digest, a highlight surrounded by a couple of sentences of context. Yes, all searches involve a continual narrowing of the subject matter, but keyword searching can really put the blinders on. Eliminating distraction in this way may backfire, obscuring rather than illuminating the subject of our search. When that happens, less may actually prove to be less. However, such worries don't seem to be stopping us from an increasing reliance on the computer to find things: for more and more of us, if it's not online, it's invisible. John Updike's resistance to electronic authorship notwithstanding, the message for those who want what they write to be read is clear: digitize your ideas or they will be ignored.

■ ■ ■

The computerized text also feeds the visionary's notion of readers as rewriters, but that's not as revolutionary as it may initially seem. Reading is in itself an act of rewriting. As our minds process the words we read, we create meanings that a writer may never have intended or even imagined possible. In addition, from the days when words first began to be inscribed, readers have always been able to physically annotate what they've read, and this too is a kind of textual revision. Manuscripts and books frequently contain marginalia, corrections, questions, or comments penned by readers who came before us. Although most of the people I grew up with were admonished, "Don't write in books," the invention of the highlighter in the 1970s encouraged readers to take up annotation big time, despite the fact that critics of that new technology griped that highlighting was quite different from marginal comments that actually dialogued with the author.

Readers are so accustomed to scribbling on their reading that they chafed at not being able to highlight or annotate on-screen documents, but digital writing eventually caught up with more conventional methods in this regard, permitting us both to highlight and to add notes in the margin, though it's still hard to *write* between the lines of computer text. But advances in digitizing text do more than just reproduce the old ways of doing things. Not only can readers now mark up a document for their own use, they can also actually remake what they read, seamlessly revising it, transforming it into something completely different, even unrecognizable, even doing so without leaving visible tracks. That's what Kevin Kelly means when he predicts that readers will eventually deal with all digital text the same way that they approach Wikipedia, not just as consumers or even repackagers, but as authors and editors ready to get down to business.

While imagining the future the way Kelly and Updike do is a popular activity of both the critics and the fans of our emerging digital literacy, it's also risky business, because things always have a way of defying the fortunetellers and turning out differently. More to the point, though, both sides prefer to speculate about the future instead of taking a good, close look at the present. Not only is online technology turning readers into writers at an ever-increasing pace, it's also upsetting the balance between public and private communication by spying on us as we type and turning the information it gathers from our keystrokes into cash.

▪ ▪ ▪ THESE RECOMMENDATIONS ARE BASED ON ITEMS YOU OWN AND MORE

As if the new interchangeability of reader and writer weren't interactive enough, computers complicate the mix by recording our online behavior and making that information available to third parties. Government spy-catchers and snooping employers checking up on worker productivity may be eager to learn what we're reading and where on the web we're finding it, but this data's most immediate value is to marketers who are desperate to track our behavior in order to influence our buying habits. We've all seen how advertisers tempt us with products that link to what we've been doing online. Anyone who's shopped more than once on Amazon.com will be greeted upon returning to the website with a message similar to the one in the header to this section, together with a list of recommended things to buy based on their record of earlier purchases. In that message, "the items you own" is a clickable link. The last time I clicked, Amazon showed me each of the fifty-three items I had bought from the site over the years (many were actually purchased not by me, but by family members using the same computer, or the same log-in), and in an attempt to convince me that I had been assigned a personal shopper, the company offered this explanation of the recommendation process:

> We determine your interests by examining the items you've purchased, items you've told us you own, and items you've rated. We then compare your activity on our site with that of other customers. Using this comparison, we are able to recommend other items that may interest you.

I've never told Amazon what I already own, nor have I ever rated an item, but I learned that I could do both if I wished, so that Amazon could fine-tune their calibration of my literary taste—that's not Amazon's personal shopper doing the fine-tuning, it's Amazon's software. The company's recommendations for what I should buy next are also influenced by my browsing record, displayed in a section called "The Page You Made." This is actually a page that their software made for me, without my knowledge, under the guise of further personalizing my shopping experience:

> The Page You Made is meant to help you keep track of some of the items you've recently viewed, searches you've recently made, and product categories you've recently visited, and help you find related items that might be of interest. As you browse through the store, we will bring to your attention items similar to those you are looking at. The Page You Made continually updates as you browse. We try to offer purchase suggestions that are most relevant to your recent shopping sessions.

Building on a desire to keep up with the Joneses, or simply to eye what's in other people's shopping carts when I'm checking out at the grocery store, the company offers even more suggestions each time I click on an item: "Customers who bought this item also bought…" followed by even more titles, CD's, or DVD's that they would like to move off their shelves.

Google and other digital marketers also troll for online custom by placing what Google.ads calls "keyword-targeted advertisements" on websites. Some of those ads seem appropriate to the site's message, while others show that a reliance on keywords can leave out too much context. For example, a *New York Times* article on cultural repression in Turkey (Van Gelder 2006) was accompanied by three Google.ad links: one taking surfers to a website showing Turkish art, presumably art that has survived the government censorship process, and another linking to a Turkey travel guide, useful perhaps for those who want to see the cultural repression up close. The first and least appropriate of the links takes those who click on it to a site selling cookbooks, presumably ones that include some turkey recipes. The problem is obvious: keywords don't provide enough context.

Even so, search engine developers are optimistic that if they collect enough keystrokes, they will be able to predict not just individual behavior but the direction of entire markets (Leonhardt 2006). Microsoft used to advertise its Windows operating system with the slogan, "Where would you like to go today?" Google Trends is one new product that promises to improve on Microsoft's question by letting marketers know where it is that web-surfing consumers will want to go tomorrow. To bring about this crystal-ball insight, Google harvests what we write when we search online in order to produce what they call a "database of our intentions," one which should eventually be able to track the popularity of search terms over time and in particular locations. The company will sell information about which terms are hot and which are not to subscribers, who in turn can use that knowledge for everything from refining online ad placement to decisions about what inventory to stock.

Another thing that our keystrokes tell Google is exactly where we are. In its next generation of "geotargeting" ads, Google will actually locate users with the company's earth satellite technology, then fill their screens with ads for nearby dealers offering merchandise that lines up with their search behavior (Elliott 2006; no doubt Google maps [maps.google.com] will provide a street-level snapshot of the stores, to enhance your shopping experience). So far there's no indication that Google will go door-to-door to fully personalize its marketing strategy. That's probably a bit too Fuller-brush for the digitally enhanced twenty-first century, where consumers respond more readily to pop-up ads than knock and announce tactics, so for now Google will probably rest content with perfecting its ability to shadow us online instead of confronting us face-to-face.

The company's seventh principle among the "ten things Google has found to be true" is, "There's always more information out there." Some of that information consists of knowing where we are, and Google's interpretation of its first principle, "Focus on the user and all else will follow," apparently involves finding that user and selling anything you can find out about him or her, including keystroke patterns, ZIP code, and IP address, to the highest bidder.

▪ ▪ ▪ TMI AGAIN, BUT THIS TIME IN THE PERSONAL SENSE

Although it's common to refer to the present as the Age of Information, humans have been processing information since they started noticing, and altering, their environment. Considering the glut of digitized data that comes at us every day, to the point where it's starting to become easier to ignore the analog, a better term for today might be the Age of *Computer* Information. For example, the library at the University of Illinois is one of the largest in the country, a vast storehouse with more than ten million volumes and twenty-two million items and materials in all formats (so far, none of them being scanned by Google Books). But the university's Chief Information Officer manages not the books and journals of this massive library, but the school's computers and networks. Other colleges and businesses have found that they, too, can't operate without a CIO, because computers, not books, have become central to their mission.

An early fear voiced by computer critics was that computers—electronic brains, as they were called in the 1960s—would replace humans, or at least control them the way the computer HAL did in *2001: A Space Odyssey*. But instead of assimilating us, it's people who are assimilating computers. It's too early to tell how useful Google Trend data will be for marketers, who seem eager to pay for any information they can get about the behavior of potential customers, even if Google's massive banks of computers can't tell the difference between Turkey, the country, and turkey, the bird. But the enterprise symbolizes how closely we align our computer activities with the rest of our behavior: as Google might put it if they were cooking up a new slogan in its ongoing rivalry with Microsoft and Yahoo, we are what we type.

▪ ▪ ▪ DID YOU MEAN . . . ?

But sometimes what we type is wrong, and Microsoft, Yahoo, and Google are not only interested in guessing what we want to buy before we ourselves know what it is, they also want to predict what we're trying to write even if we have yet to figure it out.

In the analog office, professional typists had to demonstrate their touch typing skills before they were hired, but today many computer users have no formal keyboard training at all, and now that even instant messaging programs come with spell-checkers, most users don't worry about getting the keystrokes right the first time. On the other hand, search engines don't have spell-checks, and so to accommodate people like me who are prone to typos, Google has been programmed to compare what we type in the search window with a stored database of words, and when it can't find a match, it offers a suggestion: "Did you mean to search for: [search term]?" in much the same way that a spell-checker, finding an error, offers a set of correctly spelled alternatives.

My typing is far from perfect, and Google's effort to push me in the right direction is useful, but when what I'm looking for is spelled correctly but not in the database, Google unapologetically hints that the problem might be mine, not theirs:

Your search—[search term repeated here]—did not match any documents.
Suggestions:

- Make sure all words are spelled correctly.
- Try different keywords.
- Try more general keywords.

Techies are quick to blame the user, not the technology. But it's not only our typing and our spelling that they fault. Computers follow directions literally because that's what they've been built to do, and this literalness can be maddening when we mistype instructions and the computer responds by resolutely carrying them out: trashing a file when we inadvertently hit delete instead of another key, or sending a message prematurely while we were just trying to switch to another window on the screen. To help prevent the disasters that users inadvertently precipitate, but that the technology has enabled in the first place, some programs warn us when we are about to do something that might be ill-advised, like closing a file without saving it first. For example, before emptying the trash in Apple Mail, the program asks,

Are you sure you want to permanently erase the deleted messages in "On My Mac?"
This cannot be undone.

Users must respond to the warning by clicking either "cancel" or "OK" before they can proceed.

Warnings that anticipate where we're likely to go wrong when using the technology may aid users, but they may also encourage programmers to do even more in the way of predicting our behavior, not just to guard against data loss or to make a sale, but also to be used in evidence against us in a court of law. The spring of 2006 saw news reports that the National Security Agency (NSA) was secretly collecting the telephone, email, and internet records of ordinary citizens in its attempt to track terrorists on the net and predict their behavior. That sort of data mining might succeed if terrorists were concerned enough about our welfare to type their secret messages in plain English instead of code or, worse yet, some foreign language that the spymasters haven't mastered. But it might be wiser from a public relations perspective for the surveillance wallahs to subcontract such information gathering out to Google, Yahoo, and Microsoft. Americans were scandalized at the hint that the government might be spying on its own citizens, but when respected Fortune 500 companies do it, most web surfers embrace the practice as free-market capitalism at its best.

Not only that, but the likes of Google and Amazon seem further along than the NSA in predicting from keystrokes what people are likely to do next, and, unlike the federal government, they have also demonstrated some ability to function in more than one language. But catching bad guys may prove even trickier than mounting a sales campaign. Those of us who remember the Edsel and New Coke, not to mention the eight-track tape and the minidisc, are inclined to believe that consumers, like technology users and terrorists, may not be all that easy to predict. Writers don't necessarily behave like the characters in their books—even when those books are autobiographical. Similarly, bloggers and Facebookers depict themselves in ways that may not correspond to their off-line selves. Fortunately, humans are still a whole lot more than a collection of their genes or their keystrokes.

Perhaps I'm just too skeptical about the usefulness, and the appropriateness, of all this data collection. While my spell-checker occasionally recommends the correct version of a word I've misspelled, I can recognize the mistake and know how to correct it without consulting the list of options. Google has yet to read my mind. And I haven't bought anything on Amazon's recommended list. Like the now-defunct Psychic Network, which was unable to predict its own bankruptcy, internet companies don't seem able to predict their own direction any more than they can predict where the rest of us are going to go tomorrow—hence IBM's inability to capitalize on its own best-selling PC, not to mention the technology stock crash of 2002.

Worse still, it's ironic if not disconcerting that in a culture where librarians are willing to go to jail rather than tell the FBI what their patrons are reading, online booksellers freely invade my privacy by collecting and sharing data on what they presume to be my reading habits. This may be the most telling illustration of how digital literacies reconfigure private and public space and enable both freedom and control. The outside world comes to my screen while at the same time my surfing, my email, and my instant messages all have become private acts that double as public ones insofar as they are tracked in one database or another. No one's looking over my shoulder as I write in my study or at the coffee shop. But somewhere out there, backup copies of my digital life online are being stored, or worse, analyzed to see where I might go wrong next.

Because more computer users are becoming concerned with this sort of intrusion, a coalition of consumer protection groups and privacy advocates have called for a federal "Do-Not-Track List" similar to the "Do-Not-Call" lists that protect users from unwanted marketing phone calls, and the Federal Trade Commission indicated that it might ask marketers to offer computer users a way to opt out of the commercial data mining that supports the new online "behavioral advertising" (Story 2007; FTC 2007).

As readers and writers we are free both to create text and roam the internet in ever-expanding arcs, but as we do that, the new options that we open, and the ones that open up before us, give governments and entrepreneurs both a motive and a means to limit, or at least to influence, our behavior. Does that mean I'm going back to pencils? Not a chance.

▪ ▪ ▪ THE PRICE OF FREEDOM OF INFORMATION

Whether or not we find ourselves one day simultaneously inhabiting our own bodies while also maintaining an online existence, our literacy is moving inexorably away from pencils and toward pixels. Sometimes the steps in that direction are small, sometimes they are dramatic leaps. But in a world where both literacy and electricity are far from universal, access to the older technologies of pencils and typewriters remains vital, and despite the hype and the undeniable effects of the digital revolution, there are still major limits to where computers can take most people.

The most fanatical of techno-forecasters predict that the world's libraries will disappear once engineers shrink their collections down to microdots. But although our words may be infinitely compressible, the machinery needed to store and transfer them isn't. It may be years before pocket-sized textPods carry not just the best, but also the worst that e'er was thought or writ, on nano-thin wisps of silicon. But for now those words are being stored not just in traditional brick and mortar libraries and the secret police headquarters of the world's far too numerous dictatorships, but also more and more in giant "server farms," high-tech steel and concrete warehouses the size of multiple football fields containing banks and banks of computers that house the data that Google, Yahoo, and Microsoft feed us, and collect from us, every day.

As they grow our information exponentially, these server farms use electricity—lots of it—both to run and to cool their machinery. In 2001, U.S. Dataport drew complaints from environmentalists because it planned a billion-dollar server farm—the largest at the time, ten buildings on 174 acres in San José, in the silicon heart of energy-starved California. To keep its computers online and humidity-free at a comfortable 68° Fahrenheit, the facility would consume enough electricity to run a city the size of Honolulu (Konrad 2001).

Google is building its own new server farm on the Columbia River in Oregon in order to be close to cheaper electricity, and both Microsoft and Yahoo are developing server farms in Washington state areas where power is also inexpensive and reliable. They will need all the power they can get. When Google started storing data back in 2001, it ran some 8,000 of its own computers, all actively responding to user requests for information. By 2003, that number had jumped to over 100,000, and current estimates show Google with upwards of 450,000 computer servers chained together in twenty-five more or less secret locations around the world, handling billions of information requests each day. At the same time, Microsoft expects to jump from 200,000 to 800,000 of its own servers in the coming years in an attempt to catch up to Google's lead, and Yahoo is growing at a similar rate (Markoff and Hansell 2006).

Books can be written and read so long as there's a supply of paper and a light source—the sun will do in a pinch. But computers, whether on our desks or laps, or in racks in server farms, only work when the power is on. There's some debate over how much of our energy resources are being tied up by computers, but it's clear that server farms are a significant drain on local supplies. Power outages are common-enough occurrences in much of the world, and power shortages, brownouts, and rolling blackouts, as well as outright failures, have even become part of the summer scene across America, from California to Chicago, St. Louis, and the Northeast. Many people can function on little or no power, but computers can't. The energy dependence of digital technologies is a critical worry as we port more and more of our literacy from paper to machine.

There's another aspect to server farms besides energy consumption that makes them seem like black holes sucking up our energy reserves, and that brings us back to the public/private dichotomy. Server farms, our new information storehouses, resemble top-secret military complexes more than they do libraries: they are outfitted with bullet-proof glass, security cameras, walls lined with Kevlar, earthquake resistant floors, and state-of-the-art access codes. Google and friends may be in the business of publishing information for all to read, but it takes more than a library card to get access to their information storehouse. Google's website sports two testimonials from users who got in touch with long-lost loved ones through Google's search engine ("Google Users Say" 2006). But these people could never have been reunited inside a Google server farm, because they wouldn't have the right level of security clearance.

Although as I said before, one of Google's ten guiding principles proudly announces that "the need for information crosses all borders," the manner in which today's new information providers actually provide information either across or within borders seems more like the military's "Don't ask, don't tell." At Google, provider of information to the world (and in China, insofar as local law permits), information is as closely guarded as an undercover CIA operation.

It's no surprise that corporations have proprietary secrets. Nor should it come as news that all technologies of the word control access, or attempt to do so: the full force of the law will come down on anyone who tries to sneak a peak at the latest Harry Potter before its release date or to print a story in the *New York Times* disclosing a covert government program to collect information about Americans' phone calls. Violate a copyright and lawyers will be contacting you. But what's different about digital technologies is that information is not just one commodity to buy and sell, it's become *the* commodity, and anyone who tweaks the technology to bring information to users a nanosecond faster stands to gain a lot of market share.

So in yet another irony of the technologically motivated inversion of public and private, the business of making information public, of publishing it to our computers, involves ever-greater degrees of secrecy. That in turn brings with it the prospect that the all-digital library of the future could be the most open storehouse of words ever, but also the most inaccessible.

▪ ▪ ▪ A LAST STORY ABOUT WRITING MACHINES

That said, it's time for our last story, one that should help put our current thinking about computer communications into one final historical perspective. Between 1929 and 1932, Ben Wood, a professor at Columbia University, and Frank Freeman, a professor at the University of Chicago, conducted a large-scale experiment to demonstrate the educational impact of the typewriter. With funds obtained from the four major typewriter manufacturers, they placed several thousand portable typewriters in kindergarten through sixth-grade classrooms in a variety of public and private schools scattered across the United States. The typewriter was already the word processor of choice in the American workplace, a standard tool both in business and in the lives of professional writers. Those high school students enrolled in a commercial track took typing to prepare them for workplace success, though in typing class they learned, like the future ruler of the Queen's navy, to copy documents, not create them. For all their other classes, students in schools still worked with the older technology of pencil and paper.

Wood and Freemen suspected that the typewriter could improve more than a child's chances for an office job. They knew that many college students were using typewriters for their postsecondary academic work, everything from writing term papers to typing up study notes, and the researchers wanted to see if typing might improve not just the writing of grade school students, but also their spelling, arithmetic, geography, and history. In short the researchers hoped to prove that typing would increase learning in all the subjects covered in the elementary curriculum.

A class of third graders typing their work during a quiet study period. Even kindergartners used typewriters as learning tools in this large-scale, two-year-long study of the impact of the latest writing technology on the educational process. According to the researchers, the noise from the typewriters did not distract other students who were reading or engaged in other tasks. From Wood and Freeman 1932, plate 4.

Although the typewriter makers kept their distance while the project they were financing unfolded, to no one's surprise Wood and Freeman found what they were looking for. Students doing schoolwork on typewriters scored higher on a battery of standardized tests than a control group working with pencil and paper. In some cases the typists improved as much as 7 percent compared to the nontypists. The researchers concluded that educational advantages for typists in earlier grades were small but important and that, furthermore, in later grades those students who typed outperformed their nontyping peers in subjects as diverse as reading, arithmetic, and geography. To calm any fears of the champions of penmanship, the researchers also found that none of this academic progress occurred at the expense of handwriting skills (Wood and Freeman 1932, 181–82). In addition, a subjective assessment of the students by their teachers showed that typing facilitated self-expression, increased the amount of independent writing that the children did, and taught the children correct writing form and good use of language.

Perhaps most striking, in light of the common assumption at the time that typewriters made writing both mechanical and impersonal, is the teachers' conclusion that typing created the most direct path from mind to page:

> The typewriter reduces distraction of writing. In typewriting, the teachers
> say, the child's mind is more on *what* he is writing than on the task of
> transmitting it to the paper in legible form. There is less interference
> with thinking when writing with the machine than with pen, pencil, or
> crayon, particularly in the lower grades. This judgment…should reassure
> those who may fear the "mechanizing" influence of the typewriter, for
> in [the teachers'] opinion the machine tends to reduce and simplify the
> mechanics of writing, and tends to free the mind of the writer for more
> effective thinking and composing. (Wood and Freeman 1932, 122–23)

Despite positive findings on both objective and subjective measurement scales, Wood and Freeman's noble experiment didn't wind up putting portable typewriters in classrooms. For one thing, even though children with typewriters in hand may have been ready to write back in 1932, their teachers were not. Ninety percent of the teachers involved in the elementary school typing study had never before used a typewriter. They had to be taught the machine's basics, for example, how to insert the paper, change the ribbon, and clear a type bar jam, before they could begin learning how to type themselves, or how to teach typing to their first graders. In addition, the Depression was in full swing, and schools had no money to replace the inexpensive and perfectly serviceable pencils and dip pens they had been relying on with high-tech writing tools that needed constant mechanical attention, required secure storage space in classrooms, and made a lot of noise to boot. So typewriters stayed where they were, in administrative offices, not on students' desks—as well as in the school's typewriter classroom, where typing, along with stenography, filing, and bookkeeping, the modern equivalents of copying the letters in a big round hand, continued to be taught to students in the secretarial course.

Fifty years after education officials greeted with a big yawn the news that typewriters apparently helped small groups of children to learn, and despite the fact that there is no data to demonstrate that computers actually improve writing, specifically, or learning more generally, schools are rushing to get their students involved in digital learning—though they remain hesitant to let children surf the internet unsupervised. But unless they're just coming out of college, many teachers are still strangers to the writing technologies of the postpencil age. And those teachers who are comfortable with computers aren't sure how to fit them into their teaching. Some of these teachers wind up using computers more at home than in the classroom, while others simply try to replicate conventional schoolwork on the screen. In addition, many schools aren't sure how to set up the machines, exactly what to use them for, or how to keep students from using them inappropriately. Nor do teachers receive sufficient technical support when things go wrong, as frequently happens both with individual machines as well as networks. Consequently, many school computers languish in labs, disconnected from the day-to-day work of the classroom, and while some students get to use a classroom computer for writing and learning, many of them are given computer time on the one or two machines in the back of the room to play games or surf the web as a reward for good behavior or for finishing their paper-and-pencil assignments early (Cuban 2001).

▪ ▪ ▪

Until recently, handwriting was a required subject in school (in many schools it remains a focus, alongside or instead of keyboarding). Typing, when it came on the scene, was required, at least for some students. Even those writers whose handwriting was poor or who never took formal typing instruction eventually used pencils, pens, and Remingtons to create as well as copy text. But computers never came with the baggage that can accompany required subjects such as penmanship and typing class. Many students still learn to use computers for writing and reading not in school, but at home, and they do so voluntarily, not because they're made to.

Although the current generation of computers is easier to navigate than the clunky systems I learned on, learning to word process may still be more complex, technically, than previous writing technologies. But my students are probably not atypical in thinking of their computer ability as something that was easy to acquire, just about painless compared with the ancient technologies their parents and teachers had to deal with, and they're horrified at the thought that once, long ago, people who chose to write were forced to do so on clay or papyrus. For these students, email and IM and Facebook are second nature. They have few problems with word processors. And they're undaunted by the keyboard, whether it's on a computer or on their cell phone. The fact that people may be using computers more because they want to than because they have to in itself may account for part of the computer's popularity among writers today—that, and the fact that digital technologies can boldly go where paper, pencils, and portable typewriters could not. A child with a pencil in hand may be ready to write, but a writer with a laptop doesn't have to wait to be told what to do.

The digital revolution changes what we do with words in much the same way that previous revolutions in writing technologies have done: enabling more people to communicate in more ways. Each new word technology built on what came before. Each had to become user friendly and affordable. Each had to establish trust both in the technology and in the communications that it produced, a trust often achieved through replicating the familiar before experimenting with the new. The technologies enabled the development of

Despite the optimism produced by "scientific" studies of the impact of typewriters on learning, we still lack proof that technology in and of itself can improve either writing or education in general. Nonetheless, unlike the typewriter, in only twenty years computers have become a regular feature of schools both in the United States and in other parts of the world, as we see in this image from a high school computer classroom. Courtesy of University of Illinois Laboratory High School; photograph by the author.

new genres that moved along a path from radical to conventional. And each technology, whether graphite marks, stone tablets, pigment on paper, optical pulses, magnetic charges, or text messages bounced off cell towers and satellites, introduced both new ways to promote the flow of information and new challenges for managing that flow. These technologies included and excluded communicators in new ways as well, reconfiguring the divide between the haves and have-nots, sometimes increasing it, rarely erasing it. The effects of the technologies have typically been positive, with some negatives inevitably mixed in—the plusses and minuses owing as much to the vagaries of human nature as to the advantages or disadvantages of the technology itself.

In this cycle of development from pencils to pixels, there are some differences that make the digital communications revolution stand out: it happened faster; it opened writing up to increasing numbers of text copiers but also to text creators; and it encouraged writers to combine the written word with sounds and images to the point where not only is everyone potentially an author publishing directly to an online audience of readers, but also more and more people are producing and publishing their video outlook on the world as well. The digital word has radically redefined public and private space, and it significantly upped the amount of raw and processed information available to us. But maybe the most significant thing that we can learn from putting today's digital reading and writing in the context of five thousand years of literacy history, using past results to predict future performance, is that the digitized text permeating our lives today is the next stage, not the last stage, in the saga of human communication, and that it's impossible to tell from what we're doing now exactly where it is that we will be going with our words tomorrow.

▪ ▪ ▪ Works Cited

Allen, Andrea. 2005. "The Dual-Career Divorce." *Chronicle of Higher Education*, Aug. 1. chronicle.com.

Anti-Defamation League. 2001. "Poisoning the Web: Hatred Online." adl.org.

Bahrampour, Tara, and Lori Aratani. 2006. "Teens' Bold Blogs Alarm Area Schools." *Washington Post*, Jan. 17, p. A1. washingtonpost.com.

Baldinger, Alexander. 2006. "Candidate Profiles Pop Up on Facebook." *Washington Post*, June 19, p. B1.

Barboza, David, and Tom Zeller, Jr. 2006. "Microsoft Shuts Blog's Site after Complaints by Beijing." *New York Times*, Jan. 6. nytimes.com.

Bartlett, Thomas. 2005. "Inside the Student Mind." *Chronicle of Higher Education*, June 17, p. A26. chronicle.com.

Barwick, Daniel. 2006. "The Blog That Ate a Presidency." *Inside Higher Education*, Aug. 1. insidehighered.com.

Belson, Ken. 2004. "No, You Can't Walk and Talk at the Same Time." *New York Times*, Aug. 29. nytimes.com.

Bickham, George. 1743. *The Universal Penman*. London.

Biever, Celeste. 2005. "Instant Messaging Falls Prey to Worms." *New Scientist*, May 14, p. 26.

Blakely, Rhys. 2006. "Google Admits Being Compromised over China." *London Times*, June 7. business.timesonline.co.uk.

"Blog Reader Survey." 2004. blogads.com.

"The Blogging Geyser." 2005. perseus.com; the report is no longer online. A summary can be found at www.webmarketingassociation.org/wma_newsletter05_05_iceberg.htm.

"The Blogging Iceberg." 2003. perseus.com; no longer available. A summary can be found at: dijest.com/bc/2003_10_03_bc.html#1065214361053333320.

Blood, Rebecca. 2002. *The Weblog Handbook*. Cambridge, MA: Perseus.

Boase, Jeffrey, John B. Horrigan, Barry Wellman, and Lee Rainey. 2006. "The Strength of Internet Ties." Washington, DC: Pew Internet and American Life Project.

Borgerson, B. R., M. L. Hanson, and P. A. Hartley. 1977. "The Evolution of the Sperry UNIVAC 1100 Series: A History, Analysis and Projection." *Communications of the ACM* 21.1 (1978): 25–43.

Bull, Lucy C. 1895. "Being a Typewriter." *The Atlantic Monthly* 76 (December): 822–31.

"Businesses Turn to Texting." 2002. BBC News, Dec. 9. news.bbc.co.uk.

Casson, Lionel. 2001. *Libraries in the Ancient World*. New Haven, CT: Yale University Press.

Cawdrey, Robert. 1604. *A table alphabeticall, conteyning and teaching the true writing, and vnderstanding of hard vsuall English wordes, borrowed from the Hebrew, Greeke, Latine, or French. &c*. London: Edmund Weauer.

CBS News. 2004a. "CBS Stands by Bush Guard Memos." Sept. 10. cbsnews.com.

———. 2004b. "CBS Statement on Bush Memos." Sept. 20. cbsnews.com.

Clanchy, Michael. 1993. *From Memory to Written Record: England 1066–1307*. 2nd ed. Oxford: Blackwell.

———. 2007. "Parchment and Paper: Manuscript Culture 1000–1500." In *The History of the Book*, ed. Simon Eliot and Jonathan Rose, pp. 194–206. Oxford: Blackwell.

Cressy, David. 1980. *Literacy and the Social Order: Reading and Writing in Tudor and Stuart England*. Cambridge: Cambridge University Press.

CTIA—The Wireless Association. 2007. ctia.org.

Cuban, Larry. 2001. *Oversold and Underused: Computers in the Classroom*. Cambridge, MA: Harvard University Press.

Doe v. Cahill. 2005. 266 2005, Delaware Supreme Court. courts.delaware.gov/opinions/ (qjhoyn45ctchliamauw5oz55)/download.aspx?ID=67130.

Doyle, Arthur Conan. 1912/1995. *The Lost World*. Oxford: Oxford University Press.

Durland, Stu. 2004. "E-mail on Steroids." *National Underwriter*, Aug. 9.

Eden, Dawn. 2005. "Don't, Sez N.J. School." *Morris County (NJ) Daily News*, Oct. 30, p. 36.

Edison, Thomas Alva. 1877. Letter to T. B. A. David. August 15. russell.whitworth .com/quotes.htm.

Eisenstein, Elizabeth. 1980. *The Printing Press as an Agent of Change*. Cambridge: Cambridge University Press.

Electronic Frontier Foundation (EFF). 2005. "How to Blog Safely (About Work or Anything Else)." eff.org.

———. n.d. "Bloggers FAQ: Student Blogging." www.eff.org/bloggers/lg/faq-students .php.

Eliot, Simon, and Jonathan Rose, eds. 2007. *The History of the Book*. Oxford: Blackwell.

Elliott, Stuart. 2006. "Marketing on Google: It's Not Just Text Anymore." *New York Times*, Sept. 22. nytimes.com.

Epstein, David. 2006. "The Many Faces of Facebook." *Inside Higher Education*, June 15. insidehighered.com.

"Experts Seek Clues in a Bioterrorist's Penmanship." 2001. *USA Today*, Oct. 21. usatoday.com.

Federal Trade Commission (FTC). 2007. "FTC Town Hall Will Examine Privacy Issues and Behavioral Advertising." ftc.gov/opa/2007/10/thma.shtm.

Feedster. 2005. "Corporate Blogging Policy." feedster.blogs.com/corporate/2005/03/corporate_blogg.html.

Fischer, Claude S. 1992. *America Calling: A Social History of the Telephone to 1940.* Berkeley: University of California Press.

Foster, B. F. 1832. *Practical Penmanship, being a development of the Carstairian system.* Albany: O. Steele. Plate 3.

Frean, Alexandra. 2006. "Y txtng cn b v gd 4 improving linguistic ability of children." *The London Times*, Sept. 9, p. 9.

Friedrich, Otto. 1983. "The Computer." *Time*, Jan. 4. time.com.

Gand, Gail. 2004. "Butter It Up." *Sweet Dreams*, Mar. 17. foodnetwork.com.

Gesner, Konrad. 1565. *De omni rerum fossilium genere, gemmis, lapidibus, metallis, et hujusmodi, libri aliquote, plerique nunc primum editi.* Tiguri: Jacobus Gesnerus, 104r–104v.

Gibbard, Steve. 2007. "Myanmar Internet Shutdown." CircleID, Oct. 4. circleid.com/posts/710413_myanmar_internet_shutdown/.

Gibbs, Nancy. 1996. "Tracking Down the Unabomber." *Time*, April 15. time.com.

Giles, Jim. 2005. "Internet Encyclopedias Go Head to Head." *Nature*, Dec. 14 (updated online, Dec. 22, 2005, and March 28, 2006). nature.com.

Gillis, Charlie. 2006. "You Have Hate Mail." *Maclean's*, Jan. 9, p. 35.

Goddard, Taegan. 2008. "Did McCain Plagiarize His Speech on the Georgia Crisis?" *Political Insider*, Aug. 11. blogs.cqpolitics.com/politicalinsider/2008/08/did-mccain-plagarize-his-speec.html.

Goodwin, Bill. 2004. "Messaging Threat Affects Firms of All Sizes." *Computer Weekly*, Nov. 19.

"Google se plie à la censure de Pékin pour percer sur le marché de l'Internet chinois." 2006. *Le Monde*, Jan. 26. lemonde.fr.

"Google users say…" 2006. July 12. google.com.

Grafton, Anthony. 2007. "Future Reading: Digitization and Its Discontents." *New Yorker*, Nov. 5, pp. 50–54. newyorker.com.

Hafner, Katie. 1998. "Tracking the Evolution of Email Etiquette." *New York Times*, Dec. 10. nytimes.com.

———. 2006. "Growing Wikipedia revises its 'Anyone can edit' policy." *New York Times*. June 17. nytimes.com.

Hale, Constance. 1996. *Wired Style: Principles of English Usage in the Digital Age.* San Francisco: Hardwired.

Hansell, Saul. 2006. "Increasingly, Internet's Data Trail Leads to Court." *New York Times*, Feb. 4. nytimes.com.

Harmsen, Peter. 2006. "Google Joins 'Race to the Bottom' in China, Say Critics." *Agence France Presse*, Jan. 26.

Harris, William V. 1989. *Ancient Literacy.* Cambridge, MA: Harvard University Press.

Henderson, Bill. 1994. "No E-Mail from Walden." *New York Times*, March 16, p. A15.

———. 1997. *Minutes of the Lead Pencil Club.* New York: Pushcart Press.

Henig, Robin Marantz. 2004. "Driving? Maybe You Shouldn't Be Reading This." *New York Times*, July 13, p. D5.

Henkin, David M. 1998. *City Reading: Written Words and Public Spaces in Antebellum New York*. New York: Columbia University Press.

Hitlin, Paul, and Lee Rainie. 2005. "Teens, Technology, and School." Washington, DC: Pew Internet and American Life Project.

Horace. 1912. *Ars poetica*. Leipzig: Teubner. thelatinlibrary.com/horace/arspoet.shtml.

H.R. 275. 2007. Global Online Freedom Act. Thomas.loc.gov/home/gpoxmlc110/ h275_ih.xml. All Congressional bills can be found at Thomas, the Library of Congress search site.

IBM. n.d. "Guidelines for IBM Bloggers." www.edbrill.com/storage.nsf/00d4669dcd9 456a386256f9a0056e956/0647e7a30060773e86257003000bab08/$FILE/IBM_ Blogging_Policy_and_Guidelines.pdf.

Ihejirika, Maudlyne. 2005. "Blogs Get Three Students in Trouble." *Chicago Sun-Times*, Dec. 8, p. 3.

Jaschik, Scott. 2006. "The King and Yale University Press." *Inside Higher Education*, Feb. 3. insidehighered.com.

Johns, Adrian. 1998. *The Nature of the Book: Print and Knowledge in the Making*. Chicago: University of Chicago Press.

Kaczynski, Theodore. 1995. *Industrial Society and Its Future. Washington Post*, Sept. 19, 1995, special supplement.

Kasim, Sharifah. 2003. "Computers and Cursive Writing," letter to ed. *New Straits Times*, June 12.

Kelly, Kevin. 1995. "Interview with the Luddite." *Wired Magazine*. June.

——. 2006. "Scan This Book!" *New York Times Magazine*, May 14. nytimes.com.

"Kids Learn Lesson about Online Threats the Hard Way." *Chicago Sun-Times*, editorial, Dec. 12, p. 41.

Koloff, Abbott. 2005. "Student at Pope John XXIII High School and His Father Are Speaking Out." *Daily Record*, Bergen, NJ, Oct. 28.

Konrad, Rachel. 2001. "Server Farms on Hotseat amid Power Woes." *CNET News*, May 14. cnetnews.com.

Krampitz, Edwin, Jr. 2003. "Why Teach Cursive Writing?" letter to ed. *Richmond Times Dispatch*, June 26, p. A-14.

Lapinski, Trent. 2006. "MySpace: The Business of Spam 2.0." Sept. 11. valleywag.com.

Lemelson—MIT Program. 2004. "2004 Invention Index." web.mit.edu/invent/ n-pressreleases.

Lenhart, Amanda, and Susannah Fox. 2006. "Bloggers: A Portrait of the Internet's New Storytellers." Washington, DC: Pew Internet and American Life Project.

Lenhart, Amanda, John Horrigan, and Deborah Fallows. 2004. "Content Creation Online." Washington, DC: Pew Internet and American Life Project.

Lenhart, Amanda, Oliver Lewis, and Lee Rainie. 2001. "Teenage Life Online." Washington, DC: Pew Internet and American Life Project.

Lenhart, Amanda, and Mary Madden. 2005. "Teen Content Creators and Consumers." Washington, DC: Pew Internet and American Life Project.

Leonhardt, David. 2006. "The Internet Knows What You'll Do Next." *New York Times*, July 5. nytimes.com.

Levinson, Charles. 2005. "Egypt's Growing Blogger Community Pushes Limit of Dissent." *Christian Science Monitor*, Aug. 24. csmonitor.com.

Levinson, Paul. 2004. *Cellphone: The Story of the World's Most Mobile Medium and How It Has Transformed Everything!* New York: Palgrave/Macmillan.

Liptak, Adam. 2006. "In Case about Google's Secrets, Yours Are Safe." *New York Times*, Jan. 26. nytimes.com.

Longley, Robert. 2005. "No Postage Increase until 2006, USPS Promises." usgovinfo .about.com/od/consumerawareness/a/noposthike.htm.

Maag, Christopher. 2007. "A Hoax Turned Fatal Draws Anger but No Charges." *New York Times*. Nov. 28. nytimes.com.

MacFarquhar, Neil. 2006. "In Tiny Arab State, Web Takes On Ruling Elite." *New York Times*, Jan. 15. nytimes.com.

Maloney, Liz. 2004. Letter. *Computer Weekly*, Nov. 2.

Markoff, John, and Saul Hansell. 2006. "Hiding in Plain Sight: Google Seeks Expansion of Power." *New York Times*, June 14, p. A1. nytimes.com.

Marvin, Carolyn. 1988. *When Old Technologies Were New: Thinking about Electric Communication in the Late Nineteenth Century*. New York: Oxford University Press.

McKelvey, Tara. 2001. "Father and Son Team on Hate Site." *USA Today*, July 16. usatoday.com.

McLemee, Scott. 2006. "A Wiki Situation." *Inside Higher Education*. insidehighered .com.

Mitchell, William J. 1994. "When Is Seeing Believing?" *Scientific American*, February, pp. 68–73.

Mitrano, Tracy. 2006. "Thoughts on Facebook" cit.cornell.edu/policy/memos/facebook .html.

Monaghan, Peter, and Martha Ann Overland. 2006. "Thailand Blocks Yale U. Press's Web Site in Anger over Forthcoming Royal Biography." *Chronicle of Higher Education*, Feb. 8.

mosnews. 2005. "Russian Student Expelled for Blogging." May 24. www.mosnews .com/news/2005/05/24/bloggersentdown.shtml. No longer available.

Motley Fool News Staff. 2001. "Nasdaq 2000: Lessons Learned." March 12. fool.com.

Napoli, Lisa. 1997. "Penmanship in the Digital Age." *New York Times*, Oct. 8. nytimes .com.

National Commission on Writing for America's Families, Schools, and Colleges. 2005. "Writing: A Powerful Message from State Government." College Board. www .writingcommission.org/prod_downloads/writingcom/powerful-message-from-state.pdf.

National Highway Traffic Safety Administration (NHTSA). 2002. "National Survey of Distracted and Drowsy Driving Attitudes and Behaviors: 2002—DOT HS-809–566 .nhtsa.dot.gov.

Newman, Heather. 1996. "Online Etiquette Makes Good Citizens." *Saratogan*, Nov. 1, p. 5B.

Nunberg, Geoffrey. 1996. "Farewell to the information age." In *The Future of the Book*, ed. Geoffrey Nunberg, pp. 103–38. Berkeley: University of California Press.

Nussbaum, Emily. 2004. "My So-Called Blog." *New York Times*, Jan. 11. nytimes.com.

Oates, John. 2006. "India Rejects One Laptop per Child." *The Register*, July 26. the register.co.uk.

Obejas, Achy. 1999. "Point, Counterpoint." *Chicago Tribune*, May 26.

"Of Lead Pencils." 1938. *New York Times*, Aug. 22, p. 12.

Open Net Initiative. 2008 "ONI Analysis of Internet Filtering during Beijing Olympic Games: Week 1." Aug. 19. opennet.net/blog/2008/08/oni-analysis-internet-filtering-during-beijing-olympic-games-week-1.

Parsley, Abbott. 2005. "Suspended for Blogging." Oct. 25. teenpeople.com.

Paulson, Amanda. 2006. "Schools Grapple with Policing Students' Online Journals." *Christian Science Monitor*, Feb. 2. csmonitor.com.

Perrone, Jane. 2005. "Crime Pays." July 27. *Guardian* newsblog. guardian.co.uk.

Petroski, Henry. 1990. *The Pencil: A History of Design and Circumstance*. New York: Alfred A. Knopf.

Pierson, Ashley. 2003. "Addicted to Instant Messenger? Join the Club." *Iowa State Daily*, Dec. 11.

Pimentel, Benjamin. 2005. "Writing the Codes on Blogs: Companies Figure Out What's OK and What's Not in Online Realm." *San Francisco Chronicle*, June 13. sfgate.com.

Plato. 1925. *Plato in Twelve Volumes*. Vol. 9, trans. Harold N. Fowler. Cambridge, MA: Harvard University Press.

Plunkett, John. 2005. "French Bloggers Held after Paris Riots." *Guardian*, Nov. 9. guardian.co.uk.

Read, Brock. 2006. "Lawmakers Search, Vaguely, for Online Predators." *Chronicle of Higher Education*, Jul 28. chronicle.com.

Remington. 1875. Advertisement for Remington Type-Writers. *The Nation*, Dec. 16, p. xviii.

Remington, Frank. 1957. "The Formidable Lead Pencil." *Think* 23, Nov. 1957, pp. 24–26.

Reporters sans frontières. 2005. "Reporters san frontières rend publique sa liste de 15 ennemis d'Internet." Nov. 16. rsf.org.

Robinson, Andrew. 1995. *The Story of Writing: Alphabets, Hieroglyphs and Pictograms*. London: Thames and Hudson.

Robson, Eleanor. 2007. "The Clay Tablet Book in Sumer, Assyria, and Babylonia." In *The History of the Book*, ed. Simon Eliot and Jonathan Rose, pp. 67–83. Oxford: Blackwell.

Roduta, Charlie. 2005. "Schools Keep Wary Eye on Student Blogs: Public Accessibility to Private Thoughts Sometimes Creates Hurt Feelings, Fights." *Columbus (Ohio) Dispatch*, Jan. 21.

Roemer, Cornelia. 2007. "The Papyrus Roll in Egypt, Greece, and Rome." In *The History of the Book*, ed. Simon Eliot and Jonathan Rose, pp. 84–94. Oxford: Blackwell.

Roszak, Theodore. 1999. "Shakespeare Never Lost a Manuscript to a Computer Crash." *New York Times*, March 11. nytimes.com.

Sabbagh, Dan. 2006. "No Tibet or Tiananmen on Google's New Chinese Site." *The London Times*, Jan. 25. business.timesonline.co.uk.

Sale, Kirkpatrick. 1995. "Unabomber's Secret Treatise: Is There Method in His Madness?" eff.org/Censorship/Terrorism_militias/sale_unabomber.analysis.

Salon. 2002. "Fancy Dialer." salon.com/people/col/reit/2002/08/29/npthurs/.

Schaarsmith, Amy McConnell, and Sally Kalson. 2005. "As if Teens Don't Talk Enough, Now There Are Blogs." *Pittsburgh Post-Gazette*, March 27.

Schiesel, Seth. 2004. "Finding Glamour in the Gadget." *New York Times*, April 15, G1.

Schmandt-Besserat, Denise. 1996. *How Writing Came About*. Austin: University of Texas Press.

Seigenthaler, John. 2005. "A False Wikipedia 'Biography.'" *USA Today*, Nov. 29. usatoday.com.

Shiu, Eulynn, and Amanda Lenhart. 2004. "How Americans Use Instant Messaging." Washington, DC: Pew Internet and American Life Project.

"Singapore Eases Threat against Student Blogger." 2005. Associated Press. May 10. ctv.ca.

"Six Rules for IM-ing at Work." 2004. Dec. 3. cnn.com.

Southern Poverty Law Center (SPLC). 2006. "Hate Group Numbers Top 800." *SPLC Report*, March. splcenter.org.

Spohn, Meg. 2005. "Dooced" (blog posting). Dec. 16. megspohn.com/?m=20051216.

Story, Louise. 2007. "F.T.C. Chief Vows Tighter Control of Online Ads." *New York Times*, Nov. 1. nytimes.com.

"Student's Blog Gets Him Banned from Class." 2005. Associated Press, April 29.

Technology Blog. 2006. "Wikipedia Founder Discourages Academic Use of His Creation." *Chronicle of Higher Education*, June 12. chronicle.com.

Thomas, Rosalind. 1989. *Oral Tradition and Written Record in Classical Athens*. Cambridge: Cambridge University Press.

Thoreau, Henry David. 1849. "Economy." In *Walden*. xroads.virginia.edu/~HYPER/WALDEN/walden.html.

Thornton, Tamara Plakins. 1996. *Handwriting in America: A Cultural History*. New Haven, CT: Yale University Press.

Turkle, Sherry. 1995. *Life on the Screen: Identity in the Age of the Internet*. New York: Simon and Schuster.

Twohey, Megan. 2005. "Marquette Suspends Dental Student for Blog Comments." *Milwaukee Journal Sentinel*, Dec. 5. jsonline.com.

Updike, John. 2006. "The End of Authorship." *New York Times Book Review*, June 25. nytimes.com.

Van Gelder, Lawrence. 2006. "Chomsky Publisher Charged in Turkey." *New York Times*, July 5. nytimes.com/2006/07/05/books/05chomsky.html.

Wackå, Fredrik. n.d. "Corporate Blogging Compared." corporateblogging.info/2005/06/policies-compared-todays-corporate.

Warren, Ellen. 1997. "What Next? Now You Can Write Poison Pen Letters in Murderers' Script." *Chicago Tribune*, March 14.

Washington, Robin. 2004. "Roads Scholar; Distracted Driving—There Ought to Be a Law." *Boston Herald*, Feb. 2, p. 18.

Watts, Jonathan. 2006. "Backlash as Google Shores Up Great Firewall of CHINA." *The Guardian*, Jan. 25. technology.guardian.co.uk.

Weik, Martin. 1961. "The ENIAC Story." http://ftp.arl.mil/~mike/comphist/eniacstory.html.

West, Anthony James. 2001. *The Shakespeare First Folio: The History of the Book*, Volume I. Oxford: Oxford University Press.

Westhoff, Ben. 2004. "Attack of the Blog." *St. Louis Riverfront Times*, Dec. 22. riverfronttimes.com.

Wolfe, Chris. 2006. "MySpace: Protecting Kids Online." April 25. forbes.com.

Wong, Edward. 2005. "American Journalist Shot to Death in Iraq." *New York Times*, Aug. 3. nytimes.com.

Wood, Ben D., and Frank N. Freeman. 1932. *An Experimental Study of the Educational Influences of the Typewriter in the Elementary School Classroom*. New York: Macmillan.

"Young Prefer Texting to Calls." 2003. BBC News, June 13. news.bbc.co.uk.

Zeller, Tom. 2006. "China, Still Winning against the Web." *New York Times*, Jan. 15.

Zerzan, John. 1994. "The Mass Psychology of Misery," from "Future Primitive and Other Essays." www.spunk.org/library/writers/zerzan/sp001182.txt.

▪ ▪ ▪ Index